Prefigurative Democracy

Series Editors: Alex Thomson, Benjamin Arditi, Andrew Schaap
International Advisory Editors: Michael Dillon, Michael J. Shapiro, Jeremy Valentine

Offering new perspectives on contemporary Political Theory, books in this series 'take on' the political in accordance with the ambivalent colloquial sense of the phrase – as both an acceptance and a challenge. They interrogate received accounts of the relationship between political thought and political practice, criticise and engage with the contemporary political imagination, and reflect on the ongoing transformations of politics. Concise and polemical, the texts are oriented towards critique, developments in Continental thought, and the crossing of disciplinary borders.

Titles in the *Taking on the Political* series include:

Polemicization: The Contingency of the Commonplace
Benjamin Arditi and Jeremy Valentine

Cinematic Political Thought
Michael Shapiro

Untimely Politics
Samuel A. Chambers

Speaking Against Number: Heidegger, Language and the Politics of Calculation
Stuart Elden

Post-Marxism versus Cultural Studies
Paul Bowman

Post-Foundational Political Thought: Political Difference in Nancy, Lefort, Badiou and Laclau
Oliver Marchart

Democratic Piety: Complexity, Conflict and Violence
Adrian Little

Gillian Rose: A Good Enough Justice
Kate Schick

Ethics and Politics after Poststructuralism: Levinas, Derrida and Nancy
Madeleine Fagan

Space, Politics and Aesthetics
Mustafa Dikeç

History and Event: From Marxism to Contemporary French Theory
Nathan Coombs

Immanence and Micropolitics: Sartre, Merleau-Ponty, Foucault and Deleuze
Christian Gilliam

Shame: A Genealogy of Queer Practices in the 19th Century
Bogdan Popa

Visions of Council Democracy: Castoriadis, Arendt, Lefort
Benjamin Ask Popp-Madsen

Laughter as Politics: Critical Theory in an Age of Hilarity
Patrick T. Giamario

Political Agency and the Medicalisation of Negative Emotions
Dan Degerman

Prefigurative Democracy: Protest, Social Movements and the Political Institution of Society
Mathijs van de Sande

https://edinburghuniversitypress.com/series-taking-on-the-political.html

Prefigurative Democracy

Protest, Social Movements and the
Political Institution of Society

Mathijs van de Sande

EDINBURGH
University Press

Edinburgh University Press is one of the leading university presses in the UK. We publish academic books and journals in our selected subject areas across the humanities and social sciences, combining cutting-edge scholarship with high editorial and production values to produce academic works of lasting importance. For more information visit our website: edinburghuniversitypress.com

Edinburgh University Press Ltd
The Tun – Holyrood Road
12(2f) Jackson's Entry
Edinburgh EH8 8PJ

First published in hardback by Edinburgh University Press 2023

Typeset in 11/13 Sabon
by Manila Typesetting Company

A CIP record for this book is available from the British Library

ISBN 978 1 4744 5185 7 (hardback)
ISBN 978 1 4744 5186 4 (paperback)
ISBN 978 1 4744 5187 1 (webready PDF)
ISBN 978 1 4744 5188 8 (epub)

Contents

Acknowledgements

Although we are increasingly encouraged to perceive ourselves (and each other) as competing entrepreneurs rather than colleagues with a common purpose, at the end of the day all academic work is a collective effort. Of course, this book is no exception to this. Although I alone am responsible for the content of this book, many people have contributed to it in a variety of ways. The list of colleagues, but also friends, comrades and family members, who have made it possible for me to write this book is so long that it would be impossible to mention everyone.

I initially started to write on prefigurative politics as a philosophy student at Radboud University in the immediate wake of the Egyptian revolution of 2011, and continued to explore this concept and its political relevance as a visiting researcher at the Centre for Applied Philosophy, Politics, and Ethics (CAPPE) at the University of Brighton (2011–12). I would like to thank my friends and colleagues at CAPPE, and Bob Brecher, Mark Devenney and Andy Knott in particular, for the many engaging discussions we have had over the past years and for their valuable feedback to my work. In the following years, I continued to explore the meaning and relevance of prefiguration as a PhD student at the Institute of Philosophy at KU Leuven (2012–17). I am much indebted to my supervisor Tim Heysse for his wise advice and his good-spirited support and encouragement. Tim has given me all the freedom to pursue my own research interests and always kept believing in it. I have very fond memories of our many discussions on Hannah Arendt, Claude Lefort, Walter Benjamin and other political theorists who have come to (re)shape my philosophical views in the course of these years. As well as Tim and my co-supervisor Evert van der Zweerde, I want to thank the members of my examination committee – Antoon Braeckman, Robin Celikates and Dimitris Gakis – for their valuable feedback and for encouraging me to further pursue my research on prefigurative democracy. I am also very grateful to all my colleagues and friends at RIPPLE (Research in Political Philosophy Leuven) for creating such an intellectually stimulating environment in which my ideas on prefigurative democracy could come to fruition. They are too numerous to mention everyone, but there is one person to whom I owe a word of thanks in particular: it was Anya Topolski who convinced me to study Hannah Arendt's work in light of my project on prefigurative politics. Anya has continued to be an inspiring friend and supportive colleague for many years now, and she has given valuable input for, and feedback to, various parts of this book. As part of my PhD project, I had the pleasure of being a Fulbright scholar at the New School for Social Research in New York in 2015. I am particularly grateful to my host Andreas Kalyvas, and to Simon Critchley, Banu Bargu and the Theory Collective for the many engaging discussions and inspiring seminars.

In 2016 I returned to my alma mater Radboud University to teach political philosophy. I am very thankful for the support that I have received from the Faculty of Philosophy, Theology and Religious Studies and from my colleagues at the department of Ethics and Political Philosophy and the Radboud Centre for Philosophy and Society. I especially want to express my gratitude to Evert van der Zweerde, who has been my mentor since I was a student and served as a co-supervisor during my PhD. Not only has Evert always been a great example to me, in many respects, but he has also planted the seeds of several ideas and insights that I have sought to develop in this book. Last but not least, I would like to thank my students at Radboud University, who have never tired of challenging my ideas and with whom I have had countless inspiring discussions on democracy, anarchism, protest and social movements, and many other interesting topics.

This book could not have been written without the help and advice of the editors of this wonderful book series: Alex Thomson, Benjamin Arditi and Andrew Schaap. Their suggestions have been of great help in both shaping the structure of this book and in articulating its central argument. I especially want to thank Andrew for his detailed feedback and insightful comments to an earlier version of the manuscript. I also want to thank Jen Daly, Ersev Ersoy and Sarah Foyle of Edinburgh University Press for their invaluable support at various stages of the writing and editing process. Parts of this book and various of its chapters have been presented at a number of conferences, workshops and seminars. I would like to mention a few friends and colleagues who have contributed to my understanding of prefigurative democracy, who provided a space (both inside and outside of academia) in which I could share and develop my ideas on this topic, or with whom I have collaborated during the past years. Among them are Robin Celikates, Brecht de Smet, Lisa Disch, Matthias Flatscher, Sara Gebh, Femke Kaulingfreks, Sonja Lavaert, Johny Lenaerts, Daniel Loick, Fred Louckx, Oliver Marchart, Vivienne Matthies-Boon, Paul Raekstad, Enzo Rossi, Guido Ruivenkamp, Peter-Ben Smit, Peter Snowdon, Dan Swain, Thomas Swann, Nadia Urbinati, Mariecke van den Berg, Dominique Willaert, and many others. With Gaard Kets, Laura Roth, Ramón Feenstra, Carolien van Ham and Evert van der Zweerde I have recently embarked on a new and related project on communalism as a democratic repertoire (which was generously funded by the Gerda Henkel Stiftung).

I have also received so much help, support and inspiration from many people outside of academia. I would like to thank my political comrades, especially the members of Doorbraak and my friends and former housemates at De Grote Broek, from whom I have learned more about politics and prefiguration than any academic study could possibly teach me. Although they often took interest in my attempts to understand the world, they also kept reminding me that the point still is to change it. Kladderadatsch taught me that if you can't dance there is no point in having a revolution. No less meaningful and significant was the unconditional support of my parents Dimphy and Jos van de Sande, my sisters Merlijn and Celine and their partners, and the Geerlings family. Finally, the person most deserving of my gratitude is my partner and best friend Jolien Geerlings. Words cannot express how thankful I am to share my life with such a brilliant, powerful, politically and intellectually inspiring person. It simply would have been impossible to write this book without her loving care, continuous encouragement and critical advice. Our children Lex and Polle are not only the main reason why it took much longer than anticipated to finish the book, but also the best one I could possibly imagine. Much like the activists whose experiences I have tried to grasp in the following pages, I wish that our precious time together will last forever.

*

Chapter 5 has appeared in a different version as 'They Don't Represent Us? Synecdochal Representation and the Politics of Occupy Movements', in *Constellations* (Van de Sande 2020). I thank the editors and reviewers of *Constellations* for their valuable feedback to earlier versions of this piece.

Introduction
'It's prefigurative, so to speak'

Tahrir Square lies in the heart of London's financial district. Or, at least, this is what a faux street sign, attached to one of the office buildings next to the imposing St Paul's Cathedral, seemed to suggest. It was October 2011, nine months after the people of Egypt had ended Hosni Mubarak's thirty-year dictatorship, and Occupy London Stock Exhange (Occupy LSX) had set up camp on the steps of St Paul's. For more than four months the occupiers defied the winter cold, only to be evicted by the end of February. In the meantime, their movement would give rise to a lively public debate on austerity politics, democracy, the accessibility of higher education and the private ownership of public space. The London occupiers obviously did not seek to topple a military dictatorship, and no one died defending the encampment. But they nevertheless felt that they had something essential in common with the Egyptian revolutionaries. Arguably, they shared a rudimentary understanding of what it means to seek change and to act democratically.

These London protesters surely were not the only ones who gave expression to this sense of commonality. As a matter of fact, in 2011 and the ensuing years the world witnessed a wave of similar 'occupy movements'.[1] It is impossible to pinpoint how, where and when exactly this global wave of protest movements has commenced, but clearly the occupied Tahrir Square and the miniature society that emerged on it was one of its most prominent icons (Douzinas 2013: 8; Gerbaudo 2012: 76: 108–9; Harvey 2012: 161–2). The Egyptian revolution, in turn, was but one instance of what was often referred to as an 'Arab Spring', which started in December 2010 and stretched well into 2011. Mass mobilisations against autocratic regimes emerged in Tunisia, Algeria, Jordan, Oman, Egypt, Yemen, Sudan, Iraq, Bahrain, Libya, Kuwait, Morocco, Lebanon, Syria, and several other countries in the Middle Eastern and North African region.

Later that spring, similar occupy movements would emerge in various European cities. The 15-M movement or *Indignados* campaigned against the ongoing austerity measures of the Spanish government. Protesters took possession of the Puerta del Sol in Madrid and the Plaça de Catalunya in Barcelona. In Athens, a protest camp was erected on Syntagma Square, right in front of the Greek parliament. Israel also had a short-lived, but strikingly diverse, 'tent movement' in the summer of 2011. On 17 September, an action group called Occupy Wall Street (OWS) set up camp in Zuccotti Park, a privately owned public space just around the corner from the New York Stock Exchange. In the following months, more than 950 local Occupy groups around the world – from Oakland, Boston, and Washington DC to London and Amsterdam, and from Frankfurt to Hong Kong – would follow their example. As Paul Mason (2012) euphorically stated, for at least a while it appeared to be 'kicking off everywhere'.

A decade has passed since 2011 and much of the euphoria seems to have ebbed away. Most revolutions in the Middle Eastern and North African region did not lead to regime change – and if they did (as for instance in Egypt), the established change was short-lived. In some cases (such as Syria, Libya and Yemen), attempts to topple autocratic regimes led to destructive civil wars. In Europe and North America, the political outcomes of this 'revolutionary year' were less dramatic, but they evidently did not lead to any systemic or radical political change either.

Nevertheless, the movements of 2011 seem to have had a lasting impact on the repertoire and practices of contemporary social movements. In the decade that followed, similar occupation movements would continue to emerge in many different parts of the world: the Gezi Park protests in Istanbul of 2013; the French Nuit Debout movement of 2016; the Sudanese revolution of 2018; the occupation of another Tahrir Square in 2019–20, this time in Iraq's capital, Baghdad; and the Capitol Hill Autonomous Zone (CHAZ) of Seattle that was established in the wake of Black Lives Matter protests in 2020 – to name a few prominent examples.

The present study departs from the hypothesis that these various movements – some of which may be described as 'protest movements', whereas others had a more explicitly revolutionary aspiration – are the most recent and prominent exponents of a particular, radical form and understanding of democratic politics. They are underpinned by a formal idea of radical change and how to reach it, but in practice they also (implicitly or explicitly) evince a more substantive concept of democracy. In order to reconstruct this understanding of democracy and contribute to its further articulation, this book will engage with the histories of various democratic movements and traditions of radical thought. But first, let me try to pinpoint what exactly it is that these occupy movements had in common.

The Prefigurative Politics of Occupy Movements

Surely, there are many significant political, demographic, economic, discursive and cultural differences between the various occupy movements listed above. They also intervened in rather diverse contexts, and often faced very different challenges. There is also no particular reason to regard these movements as the exponents of a single, 'global' movement or uprising, as is sometimes suggested (Hardt and Negri 2012; Mason 2012). Nevertheless, these movements did often refer to each other as important sources of inspiration (Graeber 2013: 237). They also do seem to have had several distinctive features in common – which, notwithstanding the obvious and innumerable differences between them, warrant their comparison in a number of respects.

The first, and most obvious, shared feature is that these movements all revolved around the (semi-)permanent occupation and recomposition of public space (Harvey 2012: 161–2). Arguably, this occupied public space was not merely a strategic means or instrument, but also at the same time an end or demand in itself (Brown 2015: 220; Butler 2015: 126). Second, these movements had a strikingly diverse composition: on Tahrir Square Muslim Brothers joined sides with the *shabab-al-Facebook* or 'Facebook Youth' (Gerbaudo 2012: 48; see also Mensahawy 2020: 130), whereas the Occupy movement in the United States attracted a similarly diverse crowd that included 'radicals (anarchists, socialists, anticapitalists), left-leaning Democrats, moderates, and even a sometimes vocal group of libertarian Ron Paul supporters' (Juris 2012: 265; see also Kotsev 2013). Third, none of these movements was initially spearheaded by established political parties or politicians (Tormey 2015). This often fed the assumption that they dismissed either representative democracy in its current state – or, even more fundamentally, political representation *tout court* (Sitrin and Azzelini 2014). However, as I will argue later on in this book, this widespread idea may be based on a limited understanding of political representation and its relation to (radical) democratic politics. This is closely related, finally, to a fourth feature that was shared by many of these movements. The often-parroted claim that these movements had no clear demands is not entirely founded (Frank 2013; Mirowski 2013: 327): many of them did, in fact, make demands. But they often did lack a comprehensive agenda, and in most cases refused to engage with the state and its institutions. It appears that their primary aim was not to implement a pre-set agenda, but rather to try something new. As Judith Butler (2011a: 193) argued when she addressed the protesters of OWS in Zuccotti Park:

> [I]t is true that there are no demands that you can submit to arbitration here because we are not just demanding economic justice and social equality. We are assembling in public, we are coming together as bodies in alliance, in the street and in the square. We're standing here together making democracy, enacting the phrase 'We the People!'

These characteristics – the occupation of public space, the lack of involvement from the political establishment, the diversity of these movements' composition, and the lack of a comprehensive agenda – all point to a more fundamental point of commonality. Within the confined space of an occupied square, they all sought to embody an idea of what a different society might look like. They often experimented with new forms or procedures of decision-making (Bray 2013; Cornell 2012; Graeber 2013), and alternative organisational structures (Gerbaudo 2012; Swann 2018). They developed new networks of communication (Castells 2015) and established redistributive and educational infrastructures (Flesher Fominaya 2020; Howard and Pratt-Broyden 2011; Khalil 2011: 245–50). In short, it could be argued that in their activist tent camps these protesters established a miniature society-in-development (Hardt and Negri 2017: 68). These protest camps did not merely serve as an instrument or as a strategic means of pressure, but also played a distinctive *experimental* and *experiential* role. The occupied square was shaped into a political laboratory (Flesher Fominaya 2020: 314). It also had an important symbolic, aesthetic and performative function, in that 'a numerical minority of individuals physically gathered in a public space' and claimed to speak for, or embody, the shared grievances and interests of a much larger 'people' (Frank 2021: 70).

How, then, can this particular understanding of political action or change that was implied in many of these recent movements' practices be pinpointed? A significant answer to this question was given by the late David Graeber, a prominent radical anthropologist and one of OWS's co-founders. In an interview with Ezra Klein for the *Washington Post*, Graeber explained his movement's modus operandi and its categorical refusal to engage with the powers that be as follows: 'It's pre-figurative, so to speak. You're creating a vision of the sort of society you want to have in miniature' (quoted in Klein 2011). Within its own practices and forms of organisation OWS tried to present a model or 'vision' of the radically democratic and egalitarian society that it sought to bring about on a grander scale. Graeber employed a specific term to describe the rationale behind this form of activism: this movement was 'prefigurative'. As Graeber has explained elsewhere, this term tends to be closely associated with the history of anarchism. It refers to an understanding of societal change and activist practice that has arguably underpinned this tradition from its inception in the nineteenth century, and that has been described in various ways:

> The original inspiration for Occupy Wall street was the tradition not just of direct democracy, but of direct action. From an anarchist perspective, direct democracy and direct action are – or ought to be – two aspects of the same thing: the idea that the form of our action should itself offer a model, or at the very least a glimpse of how free people might organize themselves, and therefore what a free society could be like. In the early twentieth century it was called 'building the new society in the shell of the old,' in the 1980s and 1990s it came to be known as 'prefigurative politics.' But when Greek anarchists declare 'we are a message from the future,' or American ones claim to be creating an 'insurgent civilization,' these are really just ways of saying the same thing. (Graeber 2013: 232–3)

Notwithstanding the many differences between the various occupy movements that have emerged throughout the past decade, what they arguably had in common was precisely this 'prefigurative' element – even though the term 'prefiguration' was not explicitly used (or even known, for that matter) in all of these contexts. In consequence, the term 'prefiguration' or 'prefigurative politics' has received increasing attention in the course of the past decade – especially in academic studies of said occupy movements (De Smet 2016; Douzinas 2013; Flesher Fominaya 2020; Gerbaudo 2017; Graeber 2013; Hammond 2013; Juris 2012; Pickerill and Krinsky 2012; Sitrin and Azzellini 2014; Smucker 2017; Van de Sande 2013). However, with its growing prominence, 'prefiguration' has also acquired a much broader application. It is no longer merely employed in the context of anarchism or other tendencies of the revolutionary left, but has come to describe the democratic practices of different – and, in many cases, politically more diverse – contemporary social movements. This renders visible a radical aspect that inheres in many forms of protest and contentious politics. It suggests that protesters and social movements have something valuable to teach us about democracy and radical political change.

The prefigurative practices of recent occupy movements challenged us to radically rethink democracy in a number of ways. These movements sought to change society by altering its political and institutional form. They experimented with new forms of participatory decision-making and political representation – such as the public assembly and council democracy. At the same time, they gave expression to a radically open-ended and non-instrumental understanding of democracy. Rather than a mere instrument or a means to a particular end, democracy also entails an immediate experience of freedom for those engaged in it. At the backdrop of these movements and their prefigurative forms and practices, the aim of this book thus is to develop a theory of 'prefigurative democracy'. It both derives from and breaks with the original, anarchist conception of prefiguration in a number of ways, and reconceptualises prefigurative politics from a radical-democratic perspective. But before laying out the general structure of this book, let me first briefly discuss the genealogy of the term 'prefiguration' or 'prefigurative politics'.

'Prefiguration:' The Uses of a Term

The history of the term 'prefiguration' is messy, complex and diverse. Several attempts have been made to trace its origin (Gordon 2018; Raekstad and Gradin 2020; Yates 2020), or to disentangle its various uses and meanings in practice (Cornell 2016: 284; Wilson 2014: 174–5; Yates 2015). One of the main challenges of this endeavour is that the term 'prefiguration', which is relatively new in this context, refers to an understanding of politics that long predates the term itself. Today, however, it tends to be employed in various fields of study. It is also used in rather different – sometimes complementary, at other times contradictory – ways.

Although the term 'prefiguration' is often associated with anarchism, it originally stems from the tradition of biblical exegesis (Gordon 2018: 524–5). According to the eminent philologist Erich Auerbach (1984: 11), it is an adaptation of the classical notion of *figura*, which translates as 'plastic form'. Tertullian, one of the earlier Latin Christian theologians, first used it to describe how persons or events in the Old Testament prophetically foreshadowed the story of Christ in the New Testament. From the fourth until the eighteenth century, it was common among biblical exegesists to collect examples of such 'foreshadowings' in biblical sources. For instance, Passover was a prefiguration of Christ 'through the likeness of the saving blood and of the flock of Christ' (Tertullian, quoted in Auerbach 1984: 29), the sacrifice of Isaac prefigured that of Jesus (Auerbach 1946: 64), and Noah's Ark was considered a *praefiguratio ecclesiae* ('a prefiguration of the Church', St Augustine quoted in Auerbach 1984: 38). It must be stressed that such 'prefigurations' were not merely understood as symbolic similarities between historical events. Instead, there is a *real* interconnection between them: 'in the former the latter is as it were announced and promised, and the latter "fulfils" . . . the former' (Auerbach 1946: 64). In its original use, the term 'prefiguration' thus is underpinned by a typically premodern *kairotic* or non-chronological conception of time, which allows us to understand various historical moments, events or places as being 'simultaneous-along-time' (Anderson 2006: 24).

It is not quite clear how the term 'prefiguration' has re-emerged in radical political thought in the twentieth and twenty-first century. Luke Yates rightly stresses that it was 'already part of conversations about Left strategy' well before it was coined as a distinctive strategic concept (Yates 2020: 4). French anarchist and (heterodox) Marxist theorists loosely used it in the 1960s. André Gorz has been mentioned as one of the first sources to invoke it (Gordon 2018: 527; Gorz 1968), but an earlier reference can be found in the work of Daniel Guérin, who described Italian workers' councils of the 1910s and 1920s as 'a prefiguration of the socialist society' (1965: 129).[2] However, probably the first theorist to establish it as a distinctive conception was Carl Boggs, who in 1977 published a number of articles on what he called the 'prefigurative tradition' (1977a: 100; see also Gordon 2018; Hammond 2015). This tradition comprised various anarchist, syndicalist and council communist workers' movements of the nineteenth and twentieth century, as well as 'New Left' movements of the 1960s and 1970s, which all seem to have shared a similar critique of (orthodox) Marxism. Marx and many of his followers had generally failed to offer a comprehensive theory of what a socialist order might look like, 'with the result that the *means*, in effect, [had] become the institutionalized ends' (Boggs 1977b: 366). Arguably the best illustration of this is Lenin's Bolshevist regime – which, informed by a 'mechanistic' conception of socialist organisation (Luxemburg 1961a: 90), ended up reproducing significant aspects of the very bourgeois state bureaucracy that it sought to replace. In order to fill this hiatus and avoid the pitfalls of instrumentalism, anarchists, syndicalists and council communists instead aspired to be an 'embodiment, within the ongoing political practice of [their] movement, of those forms of social relations, decision-making, culture and human experience' that they eventually aimed to bring about (Boggs 1977a: 100). By 'creating local, collective small-scale organs of socialist democracy' (Boggs 1977b: 363) they prefigured a radically different society within their own practices. This is what anarchists and syndicalists of the nineteenth and early twentieth century often described as 'building a new society in the shell of the old' (Graeber 2013: 233; Schmidt and Van der Walt 2009: 21).

A few years after Boggs coined the term 'prefiguration', it was taken up by scholars of the 'New Left'. The socialist feminist Sheila Rowbotham used it in her analysis of women's self-help groups and consciousness-raising within the broader Left movement. She claimed that these initiatives had often been 'the main organizational form through which the idea of prefigurative politics has begun to influence the contemporary left' (1979: 140). Through prefiguration, the feminist idea that 'the personal is political' had gradually sedimented into the discourses and practices of New Left movements. Social movement theorist Wini Breines (1980: 1989) famously used the term in her studies of New Left students' movements such as Students for a Democratic Society (SDS). Young activists in 1960s and 1970s felt that, in the pursuit of political power, traditional workers' movements had done too little to establish social and political change in the 'here and now'. This new generation of leftists insisted that radical change requires a more radical and immediate remodelling – not only of the political regime, but also of one's own movement and everyday life. They experimented with alternative forms of decision-making and organisation, but also sought to establish a radically different power dynamics within their own social environment, sexual or gender relations, and communicative discourses (Epstein 1991: 83; Kauffman 2017: 58). Employing the term 'prefiguration' in this context, Breines thus emphasised the aspect of 'personal and cultural transformation' that was central to the practices of New Left movements. 'The crux of prefigurative politics,' she argued, 'imposed substantial tasks, the central one being to create and sustain within the live practice of the movement, relationships and political forms that "prefigured" and embodied the desired society' (Breines 1989: 6).

Breines's work on prefigurative politics has significantly contributed to its prominence in the field of social movement studies. In the past decades, the term has increasingly been invoked in the context of New Left and civil rights movements of the 1960s and 1970s (Cornell 2011; Epstein 1991; Kauffman 2017; Maeckelbergh 2011b; Polletta 2002), alter-globalisation movements of the 1990s and early 2000s (Graeber 2002: 2009; Juris 2008; Maeckelbergh 2009), and autonomous movements in Latin America (Dinerstein 2015; Sitrin 2012). It is from this body of literature that more recent studies of prefigurative politics in the context of movements such as OWS or 15-M seem to have derived the term.

However, as we have seen, the term 'prefiguration' has also come to be associated with one radical political tradition in particular: anarchism. Since the early 2000s, anarchist academics such as Benjamin Franks (2003: 2006), David Graeber (2002) and Uri Gordon (2008) have further established the idea of prefiguration as a distinctive or even essential feature of the anarchist tradition. Anarchists, it is claimed, have always insisted that the means of revolutionary change be consistent with its eventual ends – even though these ends may have been envisioned in quite different ways (Kinna 2016b: 199). As opposed to Marx and many of his followers, they dismissed the appropriation and employment of state power as a revolutionary instrument. As argued, although the term 'prefiguration' has only been in use since the second half of the twentieth century, it refers to a principle whose origins lie in the political thought of 'classical' anarchist theorists such as Mikhail Bakunin (Graham 2015; Van de Sande 2015), Peter Kropotkin (Kinna 2016a: 39–43), Gustav Landauer (Newman 2020: 438) and Emma Goldman (Gordon 2008: 37–8).

Towards a Radical-Democratic Theory of Prefiguration

In short, the genealogy of 'prefiguration' as a political term is messy and diverse. Its history is riddled with various meanings and uses, and there seem to be a number of differences and tensions between the various ways in which it has been invoked since the late 1970s. What most, if not all, definitions so far seem to have in common is that prefiguration is often described as an attempt to act in accordance with one's ultimate ends. A prefigurative politics or practice typically pursues an exceptionally high measure of consistency between such means and ends.

However, such a means/ends equivalence can be pursued at a variety of levels: within the organisational structures and political practices of a political movement, or at the level of one's everyday life and social environment. And this is precisely where significant tensions emerge between different accounts of prefiguration. Boggs, as well as a number of anarchist and syndicalist theorists, presents prefiguration as a distinctively revolutionary strategy that should eventually lead to systemic or structural societal change. In contrast, others, who focus on its more 'everyday' or personal aspects, instead define prefiguration as an a-strategic (Epstein 1991: 18) or even an anti-organisational principle (Breines 1989: 6). Seen from the latter perspective, prefiguration implies the prioritisation of immediate liberation within one's own everyday life – and not the realisation of a radically different social or political order in the long term. But this a-strategic interpretation has, in turn, been contested by social movement theorists who either claim that strategic and prefigurative approaches are compatible (Polletta 2002), or emphasise the strategic merits of liberation itself. 'If the goal is to create a world in which people are empowered to collectively set their own agendas and pursue their own aims,' anthropologist Marianne Maeckelbergh (2011a: 13) argues, it follows that 'the process of creating political structures that make that possible is a necessary step in achieving the goal.' Strategic and 'everyday' conceptions of prefiguration may thus complement or even presuppose each other.

Another important question is whether prefiguration must be perceived as a purely formal term, or whether it is also underpinned by a more substantive idea of democracy or social justice (Gordon 2018: 527; Raekstad and Gradin 2020: 36). The advantage of a purely formal conception of prefiguration is that it can be employed or recognised in a variety of contexts. If it is merely understood as an insistency to act consistently with one's ultimate ends, or an attempt to anticipate or foreshadow a distant future within one's own practices or organisational structure, then prefiguration can also be seen to play a role in neoliberal governance (Cooper 2017), in the politics of conservative Christians (Cooper 2019: 41), and even in white supremacist movements (Futrell and Simi 2004). In most accounts, however, the idea of prefiguration tends to be associated with a more limited range of political tendencies or traditions. It then is assumed that there must be an interconnection between the strategic form of prefigurative politics on the one hand, and its substantive aims or aspirations on the other. In its narrowest sense, prefiguration tends to be most closely associated with anarchism (Franks 2018: 40; Newman 2016: 64). As we will see in the next chapter, from its emergence as a distinctive political tradition anarchism has always favoured a strong consistency between its revolutionary means and the ultimate end of a classless and stateless society. But in a similar fashion the term 'prefiguration' is also invoked in the context of various, and often heterodox, Marxist or socialist movements (De Smet 2016; Holloway 2010a, 2010b; Raekstad 2018; Rowbotham 1979).

This book seeks to develop a theory of prefiguration from a radical-democratic perspective. To this end, it engages with the work of political theorists from the 'post-Marxist' tradition, such as Ernesto Laclau and Claude Lefort – and with Hannah Arendt, who has significantly influenced this tradition. These theorists are, or can be interpreted as being, radical democrats in the sense that they understand the political as an autonomous sphere. Seen from their perspective, the social does not precede the political but instead is politically instituted. There is no 'pure' or authentic society underlying the established political institutions (as for instance classical anarchists seem to suggest), nor is the political part of a 'superstructure' that lies on top of a material or economic base (as some Marxists claim). Instead, our understanding of 'society' is shaped precisely by its political and institutional form. This also implies that the political institution of society must always continue to be open to contestation and subject of debate. Social division and conflict have an important constitutive role. What is prefigured in the politics of contemporary social movements, then, is not so much a 'model' of a future society that is based on voluntary association and devoid of political conflict. Prefigurative democracy instead gives rise to new institutions and forms of organisation that render such conflicts and antagonism more visible, and that make democratic politics more accessible to everyone.

There are a number of reasons why, compared with classical anarchist theory, such a radical-democratic perspective may help to better appreciate the democratic potential and relevance of prefigurative politics and protest movements today. First, as argued above, recent occupy movements often had a strikingly diverse composition. Although some of them (such as OWS and 15-M) had a strong contingent of activists with previous experience in anarchist or alter-globalisation movements (Bray 2013; Graeber 2011; Hammond 2013), they were often more politically diverse (Juris 2012; Kotsev 2013; Mensahawy 2020: 130). Contemporary radical-democratic theory accommodates a more diverse or pluralistic understanding of social movements than, for instance, anarchist theory, as it accounts for the productive role and democratic potential of disagreement or even agonism – both outside and within a social movement. Moreover, although a host of traditional revolutionary theories (such as anarchism and heterodox Marxism) have been employed in order to analyse these movements, it appears that many of their participants were not necessarily dismissive of representative democracy per se. They instead sought to 'actively reclaim democracy and its institutions for the citizens' (Flesher Fominaya 2020: 80) and often proposed a more participatory, decentralised or 'bottom-up' form of representative democracy than what is afforded by electoral-representative democracy in its current state (Gerbaudo 2017: 84).

Another reason to propose a radical-democratic reading of prefiguration, in light of recent developments, is that it makes apparent the close interconnection between its form and content. As Cornelius Castoriadis (1997: 11) argues, democracy cannot be reduced to a mere set of formal procedures or principles. It is a 'regime of explicit and lucid self-institution' (Castoriadis 1997: 4). Democracy nourishes substantive rights and liberties and must continuously create the conditions in which citizens are able to question its own meaning and revise its institutional form. This implies the establishment of a public sphere in which *paideia* (παιδεία) – the education of autonomous and critical citizens, and the exercise and development of their political skills – is encouraged and facilitated (Castoriadis 1997: 11). Form and content, procedure and substantive ideals or values, thus presuppose each other. This may explain why so many recent occupy movements not only demanded 'real' democracy instead of neoliberal governance or dictatorship, but also sought to bring it into practice within their occupied public spaces (Flesher Fominaya 2020: 23).

The third advantage of a radical-democratic approach to prefigurative politics, compared with, for instance, its anarchist interpretations, is that the former may allow us to appreciate the democratic relevance and impact of recent occupy movements and their prefigurative repertoire. It is evident that most of these movements did not lead to any systemic or radical change in the long term. But does this, from a retrospective point of view, render them meaningless or unsuccessful? Traditional theories of prefiguration suggest that, even if a prefigurative practice turns out unsuccessful, there may be important lessons to be learnt from it. As we have seen, some anarchist or New Left sources also hold it to be a valuable and worthwhile way to improve one's own quality of life in the 'here and now'. But when it comes to the broader political impact of prefiguration, these theoretical perspectives often seem to fall short. How may prefigurative movements or practices be understood to contribute to political or institutional change in the present?

From Arendt to Laclau: A Theoretical Framework

In short, this book seeks to develop a radical-democratic theory of prefiguration – or, alternatively, a theory of what I will call 'prefigurative democracy'. Its broader theoretical framework will largely be derived from the work of two important radical-democratic philosophers: Hannah Arendt and Ernesto Laclau – and, to a lesser extent, from some of their main interlocutors such as Rosa Luxemburg, Judith Butler, Chantal Mouffe and Claude Lefort. There clearly are significant differences between these authors, and this range of sources may strike the reader as eclectic or even incompatible. Arendt's work, on the one hand, has been used and endorsed across the range of the political spectrum (Arendt 2018b: 470–1). However, I side with those commentators who read her as an advocate of participatory council democracy (Kalyvas 2008; Marchart 2005; Muldoon 2011; Popp-Madsen 2021). For the 'neo-Gramscian' populist Laclau, on the other hand, democratic politics instead revolves around the articulation of majoritarian, representative claims and the struggle for discursive hegemony. Why, then, engage with these two very different political thinkers? One consideration is of a theoretical nature, the other is more empirical.

A first reason to warrant the involvement of theoretical sources as diverse as Laclau and Arendt is that both their views are underpinned by a radically pluralist and constructivist or 'post-foundational' ontology (Marchart 2007). By this I mean that they understand society to be politically instituted: it has no natural, social, economic or otherwise 'given' foundation on which it rests. How society must organise and understand itself is, ultimately, always a political question. Both Arendt and Laclau thus promote an agonistic idea of democracy that nourishes and caters to difference and disagreement. What they have in common, Linda Zerilli argues, is the fundamental insight that there is 'nothing that we all share by virtue of being human or of living in a particular community that guarantees a common view of the world' (Zerilli 2004: 93). And this not only means that it is impossible to even imagine a world without politics – as there is no common understanding or interest that we naturally share by virtue of being human – but also that there always inheres a radical potential in political action. After all, it is arguably through politics that we are able to imagine our world differently.

At a more practical level, moreover, the Arendtian and the Laclauian perspectives on politics each address different aspects that are elementary to our understanding of prefigurative democracy and social movement politics today. Whereas the former draws attention to its participatory character, the latter caters to its more representative dimension. What is more, in practice social movements are hardly ever informed by a single and consistent theoretical framework or inspiration. They result from various political alliances and contingent combinations of different repertoires and discourses. Of course, and although their exact composition may differ from case to case, recent occupy movements were no exception to this. According to Jonathan Smucker, for instance, two very different tendencies were at play within the movements. Whereas one focused on prefigurative experiments with participatory democracy, the other was more strategically oriented and aimed towards the establishment of discursive hegemony and institutional power in the long run (Smucker 2017: 118–25). In a similar vein, Paolo Gerbaudo argues that the occupy movements were the product of a contingent 'marriage' between 'the neo-anarchist method of horizontality and the populist demand for sovereignty' (Gerbaudo 2017: 7). Prefigurative democracy may indeed be understood to emerge from a combination between a participatory or 'horizontal' view of democratic organisation and decision-making on the one hand, and an attempt to represent or symbolically 'stand for' a larger social group (such as 'the 99%') on the other. As Arendt and Laclau are both prominent exponents of these two opposite sides of the radical-democratic spectrum, their respective oeuvres offer valuable resources from which to derive a theory of prefigurative democracy that combines them.

Structure of the Book

In order to establish a theory of prefigurative democracy, the following steps will be taken in the course of this book. In Chapter 1 I engage with the political thought of 'classical' anarchists such as Mikhail Bakunin and Peter Kropotkin in order to reconstruct the history of what is now called 'prefiguration' or 'prefigurative politics'. I argue how this conception of revolutionary change has been closely intertwined with the history of anarchism since its commencement as a radical tradition in the late nineteenth century. In anarchist theory, prefiguration is often understood as a principle that prescribes a high measure of consistency between the means and the ends of political practice. This was originally phrased as an attempt to 'build a new society in the shell of the old': within the organisational structures of a revolutionary movement, or in one's everyday life and social environment. I argue that the anarchist idea of prefiguration has a number of limitations. Most importantly, it is underpinned by the assumption that a prefigurative politics must eventually lead towards the ultimate end of a post-political society, which is devoid of political conflict. I claim that, as a consequence, the anarchist idea of prefiguration fails to grasp the radical potential of contemporary prefigurative movements and practices. Engaging with the political thought of Claude Lefort, I argue why prefiguration may instead be understood as an attempt to change the political institution of society (rather than to found it anew).

If prefigurative action does not necessarily imply an ultimate, predefined end, then how exactly do its means and ends relate to each other? In Chapter 2 I explain why Hannah Arendt's political thought may give rise to a different understanding of prefigurative democracy as a politics *without ends*. This is so, for a number of reasons. First, the concrete ends or objectives of prefigurative experiments may often be unknown to those involved in these practices. Prefiguration should instead be understood as a deliberately open-ended and experimental process. But, seen from Arendt's perspective, there is also an important experiential aspect to prefigurative democracy that renders it particularly meaningful to those engaged in it: prefigurative experimentation entails an immediate experience of political freedom. It thus is questionable to what extent the practitioners of a prefigurative politics really wish to see their movement or practices come to an end (Cooper 2014: 223). They rather seek to prolong their prefigurative experiments as long as possible.

This gives rise to the question how prefigurative democracy can acquire a more durable, institutional form in the long term, whilst retaining its distinctive open-ended or experimental character. This question will be addressed in Chapter 3, in which I ask if it may be possible to imagine a distinctively prefigurative form of government? Many recent occupy movements were initially self-organised in public assemblies. But what distinguishes the public assembly as a typically prefigurative form of organisation, and could it also give rise to a more durable prefigurative institution? I briefly discuss a number of recent theorisations of the assembly-form, and conclude that it has a fleeting and temporary character: sooner or later, public assemblies tend to disperse. Is there an alternative form of government that may emerge from the public assembly and durably accommodate prefigurative democracy? Returning to the work of Hannah Arendt (and to Rosa Luxemburg as one of her main sources), I argue that a radical council system may best provide a more durable, institutional form for prefigurative democracy in the long term.

Prefiguration is often closely associated with participatory democracy. Recent occupy movements, such as OWS and 15-M, also seem to have had a strong critique of electoral-representative democracy in its current state. But this does not evidently mean, as is often argued, that these movements dismissed any form of political representation per se. They clearly stood for a much larger support base – even though they were never formally mandated to speak or act on the behalf of others. How can the representative role of these movements – as manifested by slogans such as 'We are the 99%' and 'This is what democracy looks like' – be appreciated from a prefigurative point of view? In Chapter 4 I engage with Ernesto Laclau's constructivist theory of representation to argue that prefigurative democracy is by no means devoid of popular representative claim-making. In fact, it presupposes a very specific mode of representation that is not based on a formal mandate and instead is open to anyone. I argue that the rhetoric and practices of recent occupy movements, and the representative claims that they implied, had a typically synecdochal form. The synecdoche is a figure of speech in which one of the constitutive parts of a larger whole takes upon itself the task to 'stand for' or embody this whole in its entirety. As it is underpinned by a different, non-mandated form or political representation, prefigurative democracy may thus be understood to offer a critique of electoral-representative democracy and its elitist and non-egalitarian implications.

Chapter 5 raises the question what happens on the 'day after', once the occupied squares have been evacuated and the protesters returned home. Recent occupy movements have often been criticised for their perceived inability to establish any significant political changes in the long term. But can social movements so easily be judged on the basis of their immediate outcomes? What renders prefigurative democracy 'successful' or 'a failure' – and are these terms at all suitable to make such an assessment? Or is there another way in which it may be understood to have a lasting impact? I return once more to both Arendt and Laclau, and reconstruct two geological metaphors for political change that they employ in their own work: Laclau's concept of 'sedimentation' and Arendt's notion of 'crystallisation'. These metaphors allow us to imagine how prefigurative practices of the past may continue to have political relevance or potential for the future, long after the protesters have returned home.

In the concluding chapter, finally, I establish how 'prefigurative democracy' enables us to better appreciate the democratic relevance and radical potential of protest movements today. This may leave the reader wondering what is the exact purpose of this book. Does it merely seek to provide a descriptive analysis of prefigurative politics, in light of its recent manifestations on public squares around the world? Or is its aim to present a normative argument on democracy and the relevance of protest and social movements? Do I seek to contribute to a better and more informed understanding of protest and its democratic relevance or legitimacy today? Or am I trying to propose a political strategy or alternative road map for radical change? And for whom is this book written: for political theorists and philosophers, for scholars of social movements, for political activists or perhaps for a much broader audience? The (admittedly rather unsatisfactory but most honest) answer to these questions is that I aspire to do all of this at once – and none of it in particular. The purpose of this book is to show why prefigurative democracy matters, and to better understand the place and relevance of protest, contestation and experimentation in a democratic society. This inevitably requires that I engage with my subject in an analytical as well as a normative way. There is no way to 'tell it like it is' without at least implying how things should be (and the other way around). By engaging with this subject, employing the political thought of theorists like Arendt and Laclau as philosophical tools, I hope to both acquire and contribute to such a better understanding – among activists, scholars, students and everyone else who cares about democracy.

Chapter 1
A New Society in the Shell of the Old

It is often held that '[p]olitics is about ends and means – about the values that we pursue and the methods by which we pursue them' (Isaac 2002: 32). One question that – explicitly or implicitly, directly or indirectly – seems to be at stake in nearly every debate in political theory and philosophy, then, is: how exactly do these means and ends relate to each other? Does the end justify any means? Or is there a limit to the methods that can legitimately be used to realise one's ends? Of all tendencies or schools in political theory, anarchism arguably takes the most radical position on this matter: namely, that the means of political action should be consistent with the pursued ends. Many anarchists have insisted that revolutionary movements should seek to embody or reflect their ideal image of a future society within their own practices and organisational structures. The difference between means and ends thus becomes negligible. As the anarchist feminist Emma Goldman wrote in 1924, reflecting on her recent experiences in the newly founded Soviet Union:

> There is no greater fallacy than the belief that aims and purposes are one thing, while methods and tactics are another. . . . All human experience teaches that methods and means cannot be separated from the ultimate aim. The means employed become, through individual habit and social practice, part and parcel of the final purpose; they influence it, modify it, and presently the aims and means become identical. . . . No revolution can ever succeed as a factor of liberation unless the MEANS used to further it be identical in spirit and tendency with the PURPOSES to be achieved. (Goldman 2003: 260–1)

Throughout the history of anarchist theory and practice, various terms and phrases have been used to pinpoint this particular view of political practice. Today, the term 'prefiguration' is often used in reference to this idea 'that the means be in accordance with the ends' (Franks 2003: 16). But traditionally, it has also been described as an attempt to 'build a new society in the shell of the old' (Graeber 2013: 232–3). In this chapter, I sketch a brief history of prefiguration as an idea of political practice, which outdates its use as a term, and retrace it to the commencement of anarchism as a distinctive political tradition. Anarchists have employed this idea of 'prefiguration' in two different, but related, ways. As a strategic principle, it originated from the conflict between Karl Marx and his anarchist rival in the International Workingmen's Association, Mikhail Bakunin. By the end of the nineteenth century, it was taken up and further developed by revolutionary syndicalist movements. However, in the course of the past century and a half the anarchist idea of prefiguration also acquired a more ethical or micro-political connotation. Peter Kropotkin, that other great Russian anarchist, promoted the idea that one should not only strive to establish radical change at a structural or organisational level within one's revolutionary movement, but also within one's own living environment and interpersonal relationships. This insight has greatly influenced anarchist and New Left movements in the second half of the twentieth century.

Having reconstructed anarchism's strategic and ethical articulations of prefiguration, I argue that both are underpinned by the ideal-image of a post-political society in which (the possibility of) conflict has no legitimate place. The establishment of this 'new society' is perceived as the 'end' of a revolutionary politics. The question, however, is whether such a depoliticised ideal-image of 'society' is either possible or desirable. Engaging with the democratic thought of Claude Lefort, I argue that prefiguration should be conceptualised not as a gradual process of 'building a new society in the shell of the old', but rather as an experimental attempt to change its political form. Such a radical-democratic conception of prefigurative politics better corresponds with the experiences of contemporary occupy movements.

Bakunin and the Origins of Prefiguration

Much ink has been spilled on the question of where and how the origin of anarchism must be located. 'Anarchism', broadly construed, may be regarded as a synonym for 'anti-authoritarianism' – in which case it arguably has existed throughout the history of mankind

(Marshall 1993). One may also refer to Pierre-Joseph Proudhon as the first social theorist to explicitly identify himself as an 'anarchist' – which, until then, was used as a pejorative term – in 1840 (Proudhon 1994: 205). However, as a distinctive political movement or tradition anarchism arguably commenced at the moment when a split emerged within the International Workingmen's Association (or the 'First International') between Karl Marx and his followers on the one hand, and his great anti-authoritarian counterpart Mikhail Bakunin, on the other. Although 'prefiguration' was not used as a political term at the time, the historical break between Marxists and anarchists has everything to do with this particular view of revolutionary practice (Maeckelbergh 2009: 59).

In order to appreciate the origin of the conflict between Marx and Bakunin, we may need to briefly turn to the latter's intellectual background. Born to a noble Russian family in 1814, the young Bakunin went to Berlin in 1840 to study Hegelian philosophy. In 1842, Bakunin published a polemical essay, titled 'The Reaction in Germany', in which he developed an alternative reading of Hegel's dialectics (Bakunin 1974c). The latter is often believed to have a typically 'triadic' logic as the dialectical tension between 'thesis' and 'anti-thesis' is understood to resolve in a moment of *Aufhebung*. The two sides are then 'sublated' (that is, simultaneously negated and transcended) into a new, qualitatively different stage. Bakunin developed a different, typically 'dyadic' or 'ant-thetic' dialectics (Leier 2006: 101; McLaughlin 2002: 50). In his view, there could be no reconciliation between the two dialectical sides.

The Young Hegelian Bakunin asserted that truth 'is present only as Positive and Negative, and these mutually exclude each other to such an extent that this mutual exclusion constitutes their whole nature' (Bakunin 1974c: 46). The Negative, which constitutes the revolutionary or progressive side of each opposition, seeks to change or disrupt the status quo. It is both creative and restless. The Positive, on the other hand, seeks to maintain the status quo and thus is characterised by passiveness and unproductiveness. This means that the Positive effectively 'excludes the Negative from itself, [and thus] it excludes itself from itself and drives itself to destruction' (Bakunin 1974c: 49). The relation between the Positive and the Negative thus is essentially a negative one: it can only be resolved in the destruction of the Positive and its reabsorption in the Negative. Dialectical contradiction should eventually lead to the full negation of one of its sides – that is, the passive Positive (Angaut 2007: 77).

Abstract as this dialectical thought may seem, it has significant political implications. For if the contradiction between two dialectically opposed sides cannot be resolved without the annihilation of one of its two sides, then the Negative must already contain or bring about the new that it will set in its place. Any struggle against the status quo, in other words, also immediately implies the actualisation of its alternative. Of course, this is a *bestimmte Negation*: its content is determined by the nature of the Positive that it seeks to negate. But it nevertheless is the Negative that proactively brings forth a new order that – in and through struggle – will eventually replace the old one. Hence the often-quoted, and generally misinterpreted, concluding words in Bakunin's early essay: 'The passion for destruction is a creative passion, too' (Bakunin 1974c: 58). Evidently, Bakunin did nor argue that destruction in and of itself is a creative act, but rather that it always and necessarily coincides with the creation of something new.

It seems that Bakunin's later, more explicitly anarchist, political thought was still underpinned by this 'anti-thetic' ontology (Angaut 2007: 107; McLaughlin 2002: 51). This becomes most clearly visible in one of his later texts, where Bakunin explains how he arrived at his anarcho-collectivist worldview:

> Even the most rational and profound science cannot divine the form social life will take in the future. It can determine only the *negative* conditions, which follow negatively from a critique of existing society. Thus, by means of such a critique, social and economic science rejected hereditary individual property and, consequently, took the abstract and, so to speak, *negative* position of collective property as a necessary condition for the future social order. In the same way, it rejected the very idea of the state or of statism, meaning the government of society from above downward . . . Therefore, it took the opposite, or negative, position: anarchy, meaning the free and independent organization of all the units and parts of the community and their voluntary federation from below upward. (Bakunin 1990: 198)

Thus, collectivism and anarchism, the guiding principles in Bakunin's later political thought, are not the products of utopian speculation (Nettlau 1996: 105). The hypothetical conditions of the future society are articulated negatively. They emerge out of an analysis of the status quo, which is characterised by capitalist exploitation and state repression. This means that the very forms of repression and exploitation with which revolutionaries (that is: the Negative) are confronted most directly, in many respects prescribe the content of its radical alternative. As Murray Bookchin would later put it, '[w]e find forms of affirmation that follow from acts of negation. With the inversion of a "social question" there is also an inversion of the social dialectic; a "yea" emerges automatically and simultaneously with a "nay"' (Bookchin 2003: 7). Or, in the words of the autonomist Marxist John Holloway, '[w]e negate, but out of our negation grows a creation, an other-doing' (2010b: 3).

It was this fundamental insight on radical social change that would eventually fuel the conflict between Bakunin and Marx and their supporters. Ultimately, Marx and Bakunin had a shared political end: a stateless society, devoid of any class distinctions or division of labour. They nevertheless had a radically different philosophical and strategic understanding of how this goal should be pursued. This theoretical difference manifested itself in two ways. First, Bakunin's view of radical politics was significantly more immediatist or decisionist (Schmitt 1985: 66). The only legitimate goal for a revolutionary movement, he held, was the 'immediate, direct, *definitive, and complete* economic emancipation of the workers' (Bakunin 1971a: 170). His ideal image of the revolutionary subject was not the historical class that will rise when the time is ripe, but the eternal rebel or outcast who *chooses* to resist their current conditions. It was the bandit or brigand, who rebels against patriarchal power relations in the Russian *mir* (Bakunin 1990: 211); the 'rabble' or 'riffraff' whom Marx pejoratively called the *Lumpenproletariat* – but which, according to Bakunin, is 'almost unpolluted by bourgeois civilization' (Bakunin 1971c: 294); Adam and Eve, the first to defy the laws of their creator, or even Satan himself – 'that eternal rebel, the first freethinker and the emancipator of worlds' (Bakunin 1974a: 112). For the anarchist Bakunin, resistance was not inspired by a complex theory, a comprehensive agenda or a historical predisposition (Bakunin 1974b: 198), but rather by the desire to see immediate change 'through practical action' (Bakunin 1971a: 167).

This difference also had important implications at a strategic level. Marx (2010b: 355) argued that state power should be appropriated and employed as a political instrument until the class distinctions between proletariat and bourgeoisie had gradually disappeared. The immediatist Bakunin, instead, insisted that the state had to be dismantled 'on the first day of the revolution' (1992: 130). He also advocated the immediate abolition of hereditary law

(Leier 2006: 237–8) – this much to the annoyance of Marx, who stressed that revolutionary struggle should be directed against the very structural basis of capitalism and private property, and not its superficial mechanisms such as the state or hereditary law (Marx 2010c; see also Eckhardt 2016: 19–23). But Bakunin insisted that political struggle must itself contain the very seeds of the radical alternative that it seeks to bring about. How could Marx, who advocated the establishment of a 'dictatorship of the proletariat', expect this newly founded 'people's state' to gradually wither away, rather than to constitute yet another class society? Liberty, Bakunin claimed (1990: 179), 'can be created only by liberty, by an insurrection of all the people and the voluntary organization of the workers from below upward'. And this meant that any radical workers' organisation, such as the International, should aspire to realise its alternative to the status quo on its own terms – rather than to pursue state power. A certain measure of consistency was required between the means employed in revolutionary struggle and the ends that were negatively articulated in this struggle.

This resulted in the so-called 'embryo hypothesis' – the idea that the International, as a workers' organisation, should seek to embody its ideal of a future society within its own practices and organisational structure (Nettlau 1996: 196; Schmidt and Van der Walt 2009: 21). The International, Bakunin argued, should consist of various international sectors, uniting revolutionary workers within the same trade. These trade sectors would be so organised that they could be the 'living seeds of the new society which is to replace the old world' (1971b: 255). One of the best expressions of this view can be found in the *Sonvillier Circular*, a pamphlet published in 1871 by the Jura Federation within the International, which was spearheaded by Bakunin:

> The society of the future should be nothing other than the universalization of the organization with which the International will have endowed itself. We must, therefore, have a care to ensure that that organization comes as close as we may to our ideal. How can we expect an egalitarian and free society to emerge from an authoritarian organization? Impossible. The International, as the embryo of the human society of the future, is required in the here and now to faithfully mirror our principles of freedom and federation and shun any principle leaning towards authority and dictatorship. (Jura Federation 2005: 97–8; see also Eckhardt 2016: 107–9)

In 1872 the General Council of the International, which was in Marx's hands, expelled Bakunin and his Jura Federation from the International. This marks the beginning of anarchism as a distinctive revolutionary tradition. But in the idea that 'the International was to provide the organisational basis for a postrevolutionary society and, therefore, that the means adopted by the workers must be consistent with their end' (Graham 2015: 176), we also find the origin of a particular view of radical change that is now referred to as 'prefiguration'. As I will argue in the next section, this idea of a prefigurative revolutionary strategy was taken up and further developed by the syndicalist movement in the late nineteenth and early twentieth century.

Syndicalism and the 'Embryo Thesis'

Bakunin and his Jura Federation were not the only ones to argue that a revolutionary movement should try to resemble a future society in embryonic form. In his address to the 1868 congress of the First International in Brussels, the Belgian socialist delegate César De Paepe argued that workers' associations and trade unions would have to fulfil a double revolutionary role. Their task was not merely to organise strike actions in order to enforce better working conditions in the long term. In the meantime, they should also prepare to take control of the means of production and organise an international workers' movement (quoted in Graham 2015: 92). In the event of a revolution, this movement should have the institutional means available to replace the capitalist state with an international, federated system of workers' self-management. De Paepe (2018) argued that the International should itself bear 'the seeds of all the institutions of the future. Let a section of the International be established in each commune; the new society will be formed and the old will collapse with a sigh.'

This idea was formative to the syndicalist tradition that emerged in the late nineteenth century.[1] Syndicalists held that a new society and its institutional form should not be created after the revolution, but should instead be constituted within and against the current capitalist order. This in many respects echoes Bakunin's view of revolutionary change (Damier 2009: 5–6; Schmidt and Van der Walt 2009: 153), but syndicalists insisted that a central role was to be played specifically by trade unions. As the syndicalist theorist Rudolf Rocker (2004: 57) argued, the union should serve both as 'the fighting organization of the workers against the employers' and as 'the school for the intellectual training of the workers' that would prepare them to '[take] the socio-economic organism into their own hands and [remake] it according to Socialist principles', after the revolution.

In France, this idea of the prefigurative revolutionary union was defended most avidly by the shop assistant and syndicalist activist Émile Pouget, who argued that 'the task of the trade unions is to lay the groundwork for the future' (2005: 435). Together with Émile Pataud, Pouget co-authored a utopian novel titled *How We Shall Bring About the Revolution*, in which the authors laid out a strategic plan for how the syndicalist movement could effectively acquire control over the means of production and replace the bourgeois state with a revolutionary, union-based apparatus (Pataud and Pouget 1990; see also Damier 2009: 25). Pouget also played a prominent role in the syndicalist Confédération Générale du Travail, still one of the largest trade unions in France, which states in its 1906 Charter that 'the union, today a resistance group will be, in the future, a group for production and redistribution, the basis of social reorganization' (CGT 2012).

A similar strategy was implemented by syndicalist unions during the Spanish civil war of 1936–9. The Confederación Nacional del Trabajo (CNT) not only had to wage battle against General Franco's fascists – but it also, at the same time, tried to radically reform economic relations within their own territories. Although the union's leadership was reluctant to implement a prefigurative strategy while a civil war was raging through the country, the CNT's rank and file continued to collectivise land, farms, factories and public services. In thousands of businesses, from small enterprises to the railways and telephone services, the CNT militants implemented new forms of workers' self-management and collective ownership (Mintz 2013).

The most famous and profound syndicalist expression of a prefigurative strategy, however, was given by the Industrial Workers of the World (IWW). Founded in 1905, 'the Wobblies' had 150,000 members at its peak in 1917. Although the lion's share of its members was based in North America, this internationalist union used to have branches in every corner of the world (Cole et al. 2017). In the preamble to its constitution, the IWW pinpointed its own revolutionary strategy as follows:

> It is the historic mission of the working class to do away with capitalism. The army of production must be organized, not only for everyday

struggle with capitalists, but also to carry on production when capitalism shall have been overthrown. By organizing industrially we are
forming the structure of the new society within the shell of the old.
(IWW 2021)

This last phrase is often perceived as the most profound expression
of the idea of prefiguration (Schmidt and Van der Walt 2009: 21).
A new society, based on principles of equality and freedom, gradually grows within the belly of the beast – the old society, defined by
exploitation and repression. Like an embryo, slowly developing all
the features that it needs to survive outside of the womb, this new
society waits for the right moment to be born. In its forms of organisation and collaboration, it gradually shapes a new order that will
soon break through the old one and establish itself in its place.

This image has continued to speak to the imagination of radical theorists throughout the twentieth and twenty-first century. In
the 1970s, the Quaker and anti-war activist George Lakey set out
a comprehensive strategy along similar lines. He proposed to gradually set up a vast network of radical democratic councils. These
'Groups for Living Revolution', as Lakey called them, should not
only seek to engage with various social struggles, but could also
serve to politicise public institutions such as cooperative stores and
local schools, thus turning them into counter-institutions that may
eventually replace the contested order. 'As these institutions grow,'
Lakey argued (1987: 48), they would 'become part of the unfold-
ing new society. The people transfer allegiance from the discredited
institutions of the past to these new institutions.' Lakey's revolutionary strategy and his views on consensus-based decision-making have
significantly influenced the repertoire of American social movements
until today (Cornell 2011; Graeber 2009: 235; 2013: 194–5). The
IWW and its distinctive prefigurative strategy was also an important source of inspiration for Italian autonomist Marxist movements
of the 1960s (Tarì 2011: 104–5; Wright 2002: 190–6). It continues to resonate in the work of Antonio Negri and Michael Hardt,
who use similar terms to describe how the emergence of new forms
of biopolitical production and networked communication give rise
to non-capitalist relations of property, and to new platforms of
political organisation within and against empire (Hardt and Negri
2000: 207; 2009: 8). Within the current capitalist order, they claim,
'we can already recognize . . . the makings of a new society in the
shell of the old' (2009: 301).

What exactly would a transition of power, from the old society to the new one, look like in practice? At what point will the new society burst through the shell of the old, so to speak, and what is needed to enforce such a breakthrough? In order to further this moment of collapse, most syndicalists promoted the tactic of 'direct action', work strikes and sabotage (Trautman 2014). Such actions both served to enforce short-term demands for the improvement of working conditions, and, in the longer term, to mobilise and empower a growing unionised movement 'within the shell' of a capitalist society. A General Strike in every trade and branch of industry would eventually give capitalism its deathblow (Pouget 2010: 175). It appears, however, that syndicalists often had no idea of when this tipping point might happen (Damier 2009: 124). In any case, and apart from a few short-lived successes in revolutionary Spain, such a triumphant moment never occurred in the history of syndicalism. Some contemporary anarcho-syndicalists have thus altogether discarded the idea of one great revolutionary moment. As the British anarcho-syndicalist Solidarity Federation today argues, '[t]he libertarian communist revolution is a process. It is a movement. It will likely develop and blossom from strike waves to expropriations over a period of years. This isn't a "transitional phase", it is what the revolution is' (Solidarity Federation 2012: 110). What remains, however, is a strong commitment to the idea that the current society and its political institutions must gradually be replaced with a radically new and revolutionary structure.

We thus may conclude that, from its inception in the break between Marx and Bakunin in the First International, the anarchist and syndicalist tradition was underpinned by a particular revolutionary strategy. Anarchists insisted that their revolutionary movement should seek to embody, within its own organisational structure and political practices, the kind of society that it wished to establish in the future (Boggs 1977a: 100). It must be stressed that this view was first and foremost informed by practical considerations. The idea was that the means employed in revolutionary struggle inevitably determine the course of action and its possible outcomes. Ensuring consistency between means and ends was preferred because it was deemed strategically advantageous (Graeber 2013: 190–1). In conclusion, this early form of prefiguration was still rather consequentialist: it was in light of the perceived outcome that a political means or course of action should be legitimised (Gordon 2018: 529).

However, in anarchist theory and practice the meaning of 'building a new society in the shell of the old' has shifted in the course of the twentieth century. Andrew Cornell argues that whereas most pre-Second World War anarchists and syndicalists sought to prefigure the new world within their own organisational structures, a post-war generation of anarchists sought to create the desired social relations within their everyday lives and living environment. Their 'prefigurative lifestyles and communities were less and less embedded in broader working-class traditions and neighborhoods, and they were not paired with confrontational class struggle' (Cornell 2016: 208; see also Boggs 1977a: 119). A strong measure of consistency between means and ends was preferred not merely for its strategic merits, but also because it was considered morally preferable to act in accordance with one's ends and values, or more liberating to pursue radical change within one's own living and working environment. How could this second concept of prefiguration spring from the same anarchist tradition and come to predominate over the more strategic one? In order to answer this question, I will first return to the work of another classical anarchist theorist: Peter Kropotkin.

Mutual Aid and Cooperation: Kropotkin's Affirmationist View of Prefiguration

If Bakunin is often depicted as a passionate propagator of revolutionary violence whose ideas were 'luridly illuminated' by 'the destructive vision of blood and fire' (Woodcock 1963: 171), then the other great Russian champion of anarchism, 'prince' Peter Kropotkin, is often presented as his more moderate counterpart, who 'showed an extraordinary mildness of nature and outlook' (Woodcock 1963: 172; see also Avrich 2005: 27). This benign image obscures the fact that Kropotkin did recognise the legitimacy and inevitability of revolutionary struggle (Kinna 2016a: 13–18). And although they never met in person, Kropotkin was in many ways influenced by Bakunin and his intellectual and political heritage (Kropotkin 1899: 311; See also Marshall 1993: 311). There are, however, significant differences between the two key theorists of the anarchist tradition. If Bakunin provided a first philosophical framework for the anarchist movement and then continued to become its international figurehead, Kropotkin laid the empirical groundwork for a more scientific anarchism (Leier 2006: 72–3; Mac Laughlin 2016: 155) and further developed its ethical framework.

Kropotkin's most famous work is *Mutual Aid,* published in 1902, in which he presented a counter-narrative to social Darwinism. This current, which was fashionable at the time, reduced every aspect of both human and natural life to a function of the evolutionary 'struggle for survival'. It claimed that 'the struggle for the means of existence, of every animal against all its congeners, and of every man against all other men, was "a law of Nature"' (Kropotkin 2006: xiii). Kropotkin, however, contended that war and competition are by no means the 'normal state of existence' (Kropotkin 2006: 94). Mutual aid or solidarity between members of the same species is no less significant as an evolutionary principle. As a matter of fact, mutual aid has been a much more important factor of evolution than competition – not least because a large part of animal species are social beings that tend to live in groups (Kropotkin 2006: 25). This applies to many species of mammals, birds and insects – but also, Kropotkin insists, to *Homo sapiens.* Our ability to live together peacefully, and to establish a durable social, economic and political order, is not merely the product of civilisation. It is ingrained in our human nature and social instinct, and it has played an important role in the establishment of human society at various stages of its evolution. Kropotkin showed how communities of 'savages', 'barbarians', the medieval city and modern trade unions or cooperatives were all based on the same principle of mutual aid (Morris 2018: 155–6). Why, then, do we still find ourselves in a world characterised by exploitation and oppression? Kropotkin argued that, throughout the history of mankind, various mechanisms have corrupted this potential for peaceful cooperation and mutual aid. The centralised and authoritarian state has 'systematically weeded out all institutions in which the mutual-aid tendency had formerly found its expression' (Kropotkin 2006: 186). In spite of its best efforts, however, the state has not managed to root out solidarity in all its forms. Mutual aid has always 'reappeared and reasserted itself in an infinity of associations which now tend to embrace all aspects of life' (Kropotkin 2006: 243).

Kropotkin in fact believed that, in his own time, mutual aid and cooperation had become more widespread than before, and that a durable society founded on such principles was already within reach. 'We can already catch glimpses of a world in which the bonds which bind the individual are no longer laws, but social habits,' he stated optimistically (Kropotkin 2015: 35). As he established in two other major works, various technological and economic developments indicated that the 'existing societies . . . *are inevitably impelled in the direction of communism* (Kropotkin 2015: 31). In *The Conquest of Bread*, published in 1892, Kropotkin sketched the image of a future anarchist-communist society in which both the means of production and its products are held in collective ownership. Capitalist divisions of labour are done away with, and society as a whole secures each individual's right to well-being (Kropotkin 2015: 18). In his 1898 collection, *Fields, Factories and Workshops*, he moreover showed how recent agricultural innovations allowed his contemporaries to grow sufficient food on relatively small patches of soil, even within urban environments (Kropotkin 1985: 106). Before long, he speculated, a few hours' work a day should suffice to provide ample means for everyone, so that the remaining leisure time could be devoted to study, arts and handicrafts (Kropotkin 1985: 187). These ongoing developments suggested that mankind would soon be able to abolish capitalist exploitation and statist control, if 'the voluntary associations which already now begin to cover all the fields of human activity would take a still greater extension so as to substitute themselves for the State in all its functions' (Kropotkin 1970a: 284).

This aspect of Kropotkin's radical thought has been of significant influence in twentieth-century anarchist theory – especially in the work of so-called 'practical anarchists'. Colin Ward, for instance, opens his famous book *Anarchy in Action* with the following, ironic question: 'How would you feel if you discovered that the society in which you would really like to live was already here, apart from a few little, local difficulties like exploitation, war, dictatorship and starvation?' (Ward 2008: 23). David Graeber seems to take a similar view when he asserts that in many ways – and in most aspects of our normal, everyday lives – we *already are* anarchists and communists. All social systems, including capitalism, 'have always been built on top of a bedrock of actually existing communism' (2011: 95; see also Scott 2012: xii). Manifestations of such a 'baseline communism', as Graeber calls it, can be encountered in the most everyday moments and circumstances. It arguably can also be found in nearly every social, cultural or historical context. This why many anarchist theorists, and particularly those inspired by Kropotkin, eagerly search for traces of less hierarchical and more egalitarian forms of organisation in prehistoric or indigenous societies

(Gelderloos 2016; Scott 2017). But another example would be the forms of mutual aid and solidarity that emerge in the aftermaths of both natural and human-inflicted disasters. Rather than rush to the assistance of their citizens, governmental institutions often tend to withdraw from such situations and to abandon the needy. When they are left to themselves, however, citizens often succeed in setting up their own infrastructures for mutual aid and crisis management (Solnit 2009). Scott Crow describes how, after Hurricane Katrina struck New Orleans, anarchist and anti-racist activists set up a collective for mutual aid in one of its poorest neighbourhoods. The absence of the state and its institutions did not limit this emergence of mutual aid – in fact, it was its very precondition (Crow 2011). Seen from Kropotkin's point of view, these examples prove that a society without the state and authoritarianism is not only possible: in fact, new social forms immediately emerge as the state ceases to exist (Marshall 1993: 325).

Kropotkin's substantive ideal of a radically egalitarian and free society was in many ways comparable to that of Bakunin. Yet, he arrived at this conclusion via a rather different theoretical route. According to Bakunin, as we have seen, it is in opposition to current social and political relations that its radical alternative can be imagined. His ideal of a stateless, federated political order and a collectivist economy should gradually take shape within and against the status quo. Kropotkin, on the other hand, found the seeds for a future society not primarily in struggle, but in already-existing social practices and relations throughout the (natural) history of mankind. His aim was not merely to build a 'new society in the shell of the old', but rather to liberate these already-existing forms of mutual aid and self-organisation, and to finally break the shell that restrains them (Kropotkin 1992: 81). In that respect, his view of social change was distinctively affirmationist. The objective of social struggle, to put it in Ward's terms, would thus be to 'so enlarge the scope and influence of [existing] libertarian methods that they become the normal way in which human beings organise their society' (Ward 2008: 163). However, Kropotkin disagreed at a more substantive level with the syndicalists. He was not convinced that the trade union could, in and of itself, be the 'embryo' of a new society (Nettlau 1996: 277–8; Schmitt and Van der Walt 2009: 134). Union politics had a tendency to become bureaucratic and it often 'lacked anarchism's breadth of vision' (Kinna 2016a: 172). If anything, it was the social commune that could serve as the constitutive basis of a future social order (Kropotkin 1992; Morris 2018: 275).

In Kropotkin's anarchist thought we can thus see the emergence of a second conception of prefiguration *avant la lettre*. It is centred on the same idea that in order to establish radical social change, a high degree of consistency must be observed between the means and ends of revolutionary practice. '[A] conception of human progress and of what we think desirable in the future,' he argued, 'leads us inevitably to our own special tactics in the struggle' (1970c: 184). However, this view of prefiguration also pertains to overcoming long-established habits and social conventions, and cultivating virtues such as solidarity and cooperation, courage and devotion (1970b: 108). As Ruth Kinna (2016a: 165) argues, Kropotkin's moral framework is ultimately based on an assertion of the famous Golden Rule: 'Treat others as you would like them to treat you under similar circumstances.' One should adhere to elementary principles such as freedom and equality with the highest possible standard of consistency:

> We do not wish to be ruled. And by this very fact, do we not declare that we ourselves wish to rule nobody? We do not wish to be deceived, we wish always to be told nothing but the truth. And by this very fact, do we not declare that we ourselves do not wish to deceive anybody, that we promise to always tell the truth, nothing but the truth, the whole truth? We do not wish to have the fruits of our labor stolen from us. And by that very fact, do we not declare that we respect the fruits of others' labor? (Kropotkin 1970b: 98–9)

This does not mean that being virtuous or morally consistent, in and of itself, will be sufficient. Kropotkin was still a social revolutionary. But it does follow that consistency between means and ends is not only – or not even primarily – of strategic relevance. We can thus see how, already in Kropotkin's anarchist thought, the focus started to shift towards a more ethical conception of prefiguration. In the next section, we will see how this development was completed in the second half of the twentieth century. In the discourse of many post-war anarchist movements, 'prefiguration' was regarded first and foremost as an ethical or micro-political principle, which may at times be in tension with its more strategic use. In fact, some anarchists would start to read prefiguration as an explicitly *anti*-strategic principle.

Prefiguration, Ethics and Micro-politics in Contemporary Anarchism

Several developments seem to have contributed to this shift towards a more ethical or micro-political form of prefiguration in the second half of the twentieth century. A first, and arguably most important, factor was the experiences with authoritarian socialism in the course of the previous decades. According to the anarchist moral philosopher Benjamin Franks, many of the atrocities committed by self-proclaimed socialist regimes evinced a typically consequentialist understanding of revolutionary practice in which the end 'justifies the means, even if the methods are autocratic' (Franks 2003: 23). Lev Trotsky (1973: 42), for instance, held that 'the revolution itself is a product of class society and of necessity bears its traits' – and that, as a consequence, the struggle for a just society cannot be of the same nature as this new society itself. He concluded that in revolutionary struggle, 'the means are subordinated to the end' (Trotsky 1973: 55) and that there will inevitably be a tension or discrepancy between them.

Franks argues that anarchists, instead, have always refused to legitimise their conduct with a reference to its perceived outcomes. For them, the means of radical politics must always be 'in accordance with the ends' (Franks 2003: 18). This fundamental insight places 'anarchism outside of instrumentalist political traditions like Leninism and social democracy in which authoritarian methods are justified if they meet libertarian-egalitarian goals' in the long run (2014: 703). The problem with a consequentialist view of revolutionary change, such as the Bolshevists promoted, is that it perceives political action merely as an instrument, whose purpose is entirely external to itself. In consequence, it also reduces individual actors or political movements to mere tools or resourses that political parties or leaders could use as they see fit (Franks 2006: 103). A consequentialist outlook on politics moreover implies that any act or organisational practice can only be appreciated in light of its ultimate, revolutionary end. But what, Franks asks (2003: 24), if this distant end is never fully realised? What if the great 'millennial revolution' never occurs? Should radical political practice not also serve to improve our own, everyday lives in the here and now? Franks admits that a prefigurative approach may not always be the most efficient way to establish durable, systemic change. But, he contends, it does 'produce the very forms of social relationship, albeit in miniature, that [its practitioners] hope to achieve in the longer term' (Franks 2010: 146). It should thus not surprise us that the experiences with authoritarian socialist regimes in the first half of the twentieth century not only led to a revival of anarchism in the 1960s and 1970s (Hobsbawm 2007b), but also to an increased interest in its distinctive prefigurative view of radical change (Maeckelbergh 2011b).

Another important factor that contributed to this turn to a more ethical or micro-political idea of prefiguration in the twentieth century was the emergence of the 'New Left' in the 1960s and the gradual rise to prominence of feminist, anti-racist, LGBTQIA+ (lesbian, gay, bisexual, transgender, queer/questioning, intersex and asexual/ally), environmentalist and animal rights movements in the second half of the twentieth century (Breines 1989: 14; see also Epstein 1991: 268–9; Kauffman 2017: 13–15). Whereas in the late nineteenth and early twentieth century, anarchism had been primarily oriented towards class politics, its distinctive critique of hierarchy and systemic power thus acquired a broader application. Anarchists grew more conscious of the various ways in which they continued to reproduce racism, sexism and heteronormativity within their own practices and forms of organisation (Milstein 2012). Prefiguration thus became more strongly associated with the prominent feminist idea that 'the personal is political' (Rowbotham 1979: 133). For many anarchists today, a prefigurative view of radical change necessarily implies that one engages in a myriad of struggles at a broader societal as well as a more personal level (Raekstad and Gradin 2020).

At the same time, 'prefiguration' also came to be strongly associated with the lifestyle choices of individual activists and their communities. Think, for instance, of changing one's consumption pattern by following a vegetarian or vegan diet, restricting oneself to using organic and fair trade goods, or buying from local cooperative stores rather than major supermarkets (Wilson 2014: 191). Some anarchists promote a total abstention from the consumption of addictive goods such as drugs, alcohol and tobacco (Kuhn 2010). Others advocate collective living or polyamory as ways to challenge the patriarchal ideal of the nuclear family as the cornerstone of society (Dixon 2014: 85). Even the endorsement of a countercultural aesthetic has been promoted as an important form of prefiguration as it challenges the hegemony of the culture industry and the homogeneous standards of beauty, health or success that it tends to impose on us (Portwood-Stacer 2013). In short, as well as establishing a radically different society, many contemporary anarchists also seek 'to liberate *themselves* to the greatest degree possible' (Gordon 2008: 39; see also Crass 2013: 23; Holloway 2010a: 153–4).[2]

This turn towards a more 'lifestylist' or micro-political form of prefiguration has also been subject to critique. Murray Bookchin (1995b) famously warned that the adaptation or facilitation of alternative lifestyles is unlikely to lead to systemic or durable change in the long term. Some activists, however, have precisely endorsed a prefigurative approach because of its perceived anti-strategic character. In her studies of the New Left in the 1960s, Wini Breines draws a distinction between a strategic social movement politics, which is 'committed to building organization in order to achieve major structural changes in the political, economic and social orders' (Breines 1989: 7), and prefiguration, which she defines as an 'essentially anti-organizational politics' (Breines 1989: 6). This does not mean that the advocates of a prefigurative approach within the New Left were not concerned with revolutionary strategy. But, Breines holds, 'they were in fact making a moral as well as an organizational statement' (Breines 1989: 39), which indeed meant that the capacity to consistently embody one's future ideals in the here and now was equally important as establishing structural change in the long term (Epstein 1991: 17).

Finally, another significant shift in the prefigurative politics of anarchist movements is that it has acquired a more spatial – and, by virtue of that, also often a more temporary and local – character. At a fundamental level, anarchism challenges the way in which space is divided by national borders and appropriated by means of capitalist property rights. Anarchists have always sought to 'dissolve any such categorization and classification schemas that promote spatiotemporal permanence' (Springer 2016: 62). But the turn towards a more micro-political form of prefiguration arguably did render anarchist practice a more localist character. Prefigurative experimentation not only requires a physical space in which people can engage in open debate and collective organisation, but also the ability to wrest oneself from established power mechanisms and the social space controlled by them. This means that it often entails the occupation of streets, squares and parks, endangered nature reserves, abandoned houses, factories or public buildings (Dee 2016; Epstein 1991: 83; Hammond 2013). The anarchist author Hakim Bey (2003) famously coined the term 'Temporary Autonomous Zone' (TAZ) in the 1980s, in reference to these kinds of liberated spaces or 'free enclaves', which emerge when people engage with prefigurative politics

(Day 2005: 35–6). Critics, however, warn that these kinds of occupied spaces are 'understood and built as explicitly temporary – not spaces for sustained change or the working-out of concrete alternatives, let alone ambitious competitors to global capitalism' (Srnicek and Williams 2015: 34). The temporal enactment of a new society may not pose any significant challenges to the current one in the long term.

It could thus be argued that, in these respects, the politics of contemporary anarchists 'is only in small part a continuation of the nineteenth and early twentieth-century anarchist movements' (Gordon 2008: 5). The early anarchists and syndicalists sought to gradually unfold the organisational structures that must eventually replace the capitalist state. As we have seen in this section, however, since the second half of the twentieth century the focus of many anarchists seems to have shifted to a more ethical or micro-political form of prefiguration (Bray 2013: 248). I nevertheless contend that at least one aspect runs like a red thread through the history of this tradition since its inception in the conflict between Bakunin and Marx. And this is precisely the idea that the means of radical politics should be consistent with its ends, and that a 'new society' (be it the organisational structures or the social habits and relations that constitute such a society) can and must be formed 'in the shell of the old'.

Prefiguration and Contemporary Occupy Movements

In the past years, many anarchist and social movement scholars have sought to place recent occupy movements such as OWS and 15-M in this anarchist tradition of prefigurative politics (Bray 2013; Graeber 2013; Hammond 2015; Van de Sande 2015). It is striking, however, that both the strategic conception of prefiguration, and its more ethical or micro-political variant, are interchangeably invoked in this field of literature. Most sources focus on the latter, and interpret the activist tent camp as an attempt to create a 'utopian microcosm' (Smucker 2017: 118) '[I]n classic prefigurative fashion,' L. A. Kauffman argues, these occupation movements 'were organized with the hope that they might serve as models for self-managed societies run through directly democratic means' (Kauffman 2017: 169). In other words, rather than as concrete steps towards the gradual establishment of a 'new society', these square occupations are generally seen as attempts to temporarily enact this new society in the here and now (Butler 2015). It is precisely for this reason that these movements' prefigurative tendencies have also been criticised as a-strategic or politically ineffective (Gerbaudo 2017: 179; Mouffe 2013; Smucker 2017; Srnicek and Williams 2015). But at the same time, some sources seem to suggest that these square occupations also served a more strategic purpose. David Graeber, for instance, describes the movement's original strategy as follows:

> The idea would be to occupy a . . . public space to create a New York General Assembly, which could, like its European cousins, act as a model of genuine direct democracy to counterpoise to the corrupt charade presented to us as 'democracy' by the U.S. government. The Wall Street action would be a stepping-stone toward the creation of a whole network of such assemblies. (Graeber 2013: 42–3)

And indeed, this is precisely what many occupation movements set out to do. In the summer of 2013, after Istanbul's occupied Gezi Park had been cleared out, the movement continued to set up different assemblies and councils in all of the city's neighbourhoods, thus creating a vast network of small, local public assemblies (Roos 2013). Under the slogan 'Toma los barrios' ('Take the neighbourhoods'), the Spanish *Indignados* also set up local assemblies in every part of Madrid, which all reported back to a central Asamblea Interbarrios. From these local assemblies, which often closely collaborated with already-existing neighbourhood committees, a multitude of action groups and campaigns sprang forth (Sánchez 2012; see also Flesher Fominaya 2020: 118–22). OWS was arguably less successful in the pursuit of this strategy. But whereas it may not have established a durable network of assemblies, a manifold of new local action groups and networks, such as Occupy Our Homes and Occupy Sandy did emerge in its wake (Gould Wartofsky 2015: 221; Manilov 2013). We may thus conclude that many of these occupy movements sought to gradually and durably unfold a new political structure in the long term – albeit with varying results.

In short, it is not difficult to recognise how various anarchist ideas of prefiguration have directly or indirectly informed the practices of recent occupy movements. At the same time, the originally anarchist notion of prefiguration does not sufficiently grasp their radical potential and democratic relevance. In the next section, I flesh out a number of objections to this originally anarchist view and propose that we reimagine prefiguration as a distinctively radical-democratic form of politics.

The Political Institution of Society

Why draw a distinction between anarchism and radical democracy in the first place? After all, it may as well be argued that anarchism is part of a more encompassing, radical-democratic tradition. Anarchists have always advocated self-organisation and participatory decision-making both within their own movements and as the founding principles of a future society. On an ontological plane, however, there seems to be a significant difference between contemporary radical-democratic theory on the one hand, and 'classical' anarchism on the other – which has important implications for our understanding of prefigurative democracy and its radical potential today. I specifically take issue with the (essentially depoliticised) concept of 'society' or 'the social' that I claim is implied in the anarchist idea of prefiguration as 'building a new society in the shell of the old' (in its strategic as well as its more ethical or micro-political articulations). It should be stressed that some contemporary (post-) anarchists have become more critical of this original anarchist notion of society. But as I will argue below, even their idea of radical social change appears to be underpinned by a depoliticised idea of social division and conflict – and, in consequence, of society per se.

The anarchist ideal of a future, post-revolutionary society is essentially a depoliticised one in the sense that it is primarily based on voluntary association, mutual aid and collaboration between social groups and its individual members. A prefigurative process should thus culminate in the establishment of a 'new society' that is devoid of social division and political conflict: or, essentially, a postpolitical society. This was never a fundamental point of disagreement between the Bakuninist and Marxist factions within the First International (Hobsbawm 2007a: 81). Friedrich Engels famously argued that, after the revolution and the subsequent withering away of the state, 'the government of persons [would be] replaced by the administration of things' (Engels 1987: 268).[3] Anarcho-syndicalists had a similar aspiration, as they sought to gradually replace the current society and its political institutions with an essentially administrative system of workers' councils. Both Kropotkin's idea of a social order based on an ethics of mutual aid and cooperation, and the aspiration of contemporary anarchists to live consistently with one's moral values, seem to be underpinned by the – often explicit, sometimes more implicit – ideal image of a harmonious society which holds no legitimate place for political conflict (Critchley 2007: 129).

Emma Goldman (1969: 67) even described anarchism as 'the theory of social harmony'. Thus, the end of prefiguration, as anarchists have it, arguably is also the end of politics *tout court*.

It is questionable to what extent this ideal image of a society without social or political division is either realisable or even desirable. The democratic thought of Claude Lefort can help to problematise this social ideal. One of its key features is Lefort's insistence that the social is always politically instituted. In order to understand this, we first need to be able to distinguish between what Lefort calls 'politics' (*la politique*) and 'the political' (*le politique*). Our everyday use of the term 'politics' suggests that there exists a particular institutionalised sphere in which political debates, procedures and conflicts have their proper place: the sphere of Parliament, city councils, political parties, workers' councils and so forth. This is what Lefort refers to as 'politics' (*la politique*). This distinctive political realm, then, is understood to exist alongside other spheres such as the 'economic, the juridical, the aesthetic, the scientific or the purely social' (Lefort 1988c: 11). According to Lefort, however, the very distinction between these spheres (and the various features or characteristics ascribed to each of them) already presupposes a particular political investment, 'because the very notion of society already contains within it a reference to its political definition' (Lefort 1988b: 217). One simply cannot speak of 'the social' or 'society' without acknowledging that a specific political form is implied – not only in its very structure, but at a more fundamental level in any notion that society has of itself. This is what Lefort calls society's *mise en forme*: a 'shaping whereby a society institutes itself as *this* society' (Breckman 2013: 150). Lefort stresses that 'no elements, no elementary structures, no entities (classes or segments of classes), no economic or technical determinations, and no dimensions of social space' can possibly exist without implying such a political form (Lefort 1988c: 11). 'The political' (*le politique*), then, is the ontological level at which this formative process takes place.

The political shaping of a social space (its *mise en forme*) requires that 'society' gives meaning to itself. This is what Lefort calls its *mise en sens*: the particular way in which a social space distinguishes between 'the real and the imaginary, the true and the false, the just and the unjust, the permissible and the forbidden, the normal and the pathological' (1988c: 11–12). In order to represent itself to itself, moreover, this social space must also stage itself in a particular way, which is what Lefort refers to as its *mise en scène* (1988b: 219;

1988c: 12). He stresses that these *mise en forme, mise en sens* and *mise en scène* inevitably take shape against a background of social division, and that they will always be subject to antagonism and dispute (Marchart 2007: 98). Any social order thus is already ingrained by particular divisions, conflicts of interest and inequalities that are *constitutive* precisely of what we call 'society', and which 'bear the mark of a formation' or its *mise en forme* (Lefort 2007: 112). 'Politics' is the distinctive institutional space of power on which such conflicts and divisions can be projected. In a truly democratic society, however, this sphere of 'politics' also forms the stage on which such conflicts on the institution of society can be openly performed, and where in this way 'conflicts of "politics" themselves make up "the political"' (Ingram 2006: 36). Precisely for this reason, democracy should be perceived – and, moreover, must perceive itself – as radically open-ended (Lefort 1988a: 39; see also Abensour 2011: 109). As Martin Breaugh (2013: 28) puts it, 'democracy thrives on conflict and on the endless questioning of the law. In fact, it could not exist without the presence of a multiplicity of conflictual discursive sources incapable of exhausting its meaning and its orientations.'

This brings us back to the anarchist ideal of a post-political society. On a descriptive plane, Lefort argues, this is a naive ideal since a society devoid of political conflict and social division would not be able to perceive itself as a society in the first place. To imagine a society without a distinctive political sphere in which conflicts can be staged thus is effectively impossible. More importantly, it is also potentially very dangerous:

> Whoever dreams of an abolition of power secretly cherishes the reference to the One and the reference of the Same: he imagines a society which would accord spontaneously with itself, a multiplicity of activities which would be transparent to one another and which would unfold in a homogeneous time and space, a way of producing, living together, communicating, associating, thinking, feeling, teaching which would express a single way of being. (Lefort 1986: 270)

As far as Lefort is concerned, this qualifies as totalitarianism. Most regimes seek legitimacy in an external source that does not coincide with society itself (such as a divine order, a particular concept of justice, or – in the case of modern democracy – an 'empty place of power'). A totalitarian regime, on the other hand, presents society as an organic totality that is fully transparent to itself. It does not need an external source of legitimacy, but claims to fully embody the interests of an entire class or race. The problem is not merely that totalitarianism represses any form of opposition within and against itself, but rather that such a society is unable to conceive of itself as divided in the face of a position external to it. The divisions, inequalities and conflicts of interest that constitute any society have by no means disappeared: they have become invisible – and, thus, unnameable. One may argue that the anarchist ideal of a post-political society would have similar, distinctively totalitarian, features.

It should be granted that some contemporary anarchist and post-anarchist theorists have long abandoned this 'classical anarchist' ideal of a perfectly harmonious, post-political society. Uri Gordon, for instance, argues that contemporary 'anarchist discourse lacks both the expectation of eventual revolutionary closure and the interest in utopian blueprints for a "postrevolutionary" anarchist society' (Gordon 2008: 40). The inevitable diversity or plurality of any society thus always leaves it 'open to change and challenge from within' (Gordon 2008: 46). As individuals will continue to have conflicting preferences, beliefs or interests, an anarchist society must always continue to accommodate agonistic debate (Springer 2016: 146–7). Such a more complex and less harmonious idea of an anarchist society is also presented in twentieth-century anarchist fiction. Ursula Le Guin's science fiction novel *The Dispossessed*, for instance, narrates the story of planet whose social structure is based on anarchist principles. At the same time, this 'ambiguous utopia' it is by no means devoid of conflict, poverty or scarcity (Le Guin 1974).

In the next chapter, I will engage with the attempts of contemporary anarchists and post-anarchists to develop a more open-ended idea of prefiguration. For now, however, it is important to stress that not just any form of conflict or disagreement should necessarily be qualified as *political*. Some contemporary anarchists may acknowledge that a perfectly harmonious society without any form of interpersonal conflict may never be possible. However, to the extent that it pursues a social order that is devoid of political conflicts between social groups – and that, in consequence, is not constituted by any formal political institutions in which such conflicts can be staged – anarchism often does continue to be informed by the ideal of a post-political society. Even many contemporary and less utopian-minded anarchists thus fail to acknowledge the degree to which division or antagonism between social groups are precisely co-constitutive of these groups' shared discourses and identities.

Although such antagonisms can never be fully institutionalised (Marchart 2018: 89), I assert that they do require democratic institutions in which they can be staged and articulated in a politically meaningful way. As Cornelius Castoriadis argues, 'a society without [a] State is possible, conceivable, and desirable. But a society without explicit institutions is an absurdity into which both Marx and anarchism lapsed' (Castoriadis 1997: 1; see also 1993: 267).

This brings me to a second objection to the anarchist idea of prefiguration, and the social ideal by which it seems to be underpinned. As we have seen above, there are various ways in which a substantive idea of this 'new society' may be acquired. Bakunin employed a negativistic or 'anti-thetic' methodology: by reversing the contested status quo, he arrived at a hypothetical idea of a future society. Kropotkin, on the other hand, used a more affirmationist approach as he derived his ideal image of the post-capitalist society from already-existing forms of solidarity and mutual aid. This ideal society may be distant, and perhaps not realisable in the short or in even the long term. Or, as some contemporary anarchists insist, it may well be within reach on a small scale – in the sense that one may seek to prefigure alternative social habits and relations within one's own life or social movement. Either way, the suggestion is that a prefigurative process should ideally culminate in the realisation of a particular predefined end – and that, in the meantime, one must try to act consistently with it. This implies that one can have a rather circumscribed idea of what this end entails. Again, this is by no means an exclusively anarchist idea – it arguably is implied in most, if not all, revolutionary tendencies that originated in the nineteenth century. But it is particularly problematic in the context of a discussion of prefigurative politics and its radical potential today. Not only is it impossible to provide a, more or less detailed, image of the future society without resorting to speculation. But more importantly, the suggestion is that one is able to imagine a point beyond which this prefigurative politics is no longer necessary – or even no longer possible. Should prefigurative politics be imagined to have a definitive 'end' at all? Or is it rather a radically open-ended politics, whose aims and objections are continuously challenged and rearticulated throughout the process? I will return to this question in the next chapter.

Finally, a third objection to the anarchist idea of prefiguration as 'building a new society in the shell of the old' concerns the conditions in which this 'new society' should come about. The original slogan conveys that an alternative social order can and must take shape independently from all existing political institutions and the social relations or public discourses constructed or maintained by them. However, if it is hard to conceive how this was possible in the late nineteenth and early twentieth century, it may be almost impossible to imagine what this might look like in our own times. Today, 'the shell of the old society' comprises not only the state and its repressive institutions such as the police and prisons, but an extensive network of public services and infrastructures, healthcare and social welfare institutions, public media, schools and universities. And as every part of social reality has been subsumed under a capitalist mode of production in the course of the past centuries, one may indeed conclude that 'capitalism is so well integrated into every aspect of life that there is no getting away from it completely' (Portwood-Stacer 2013: 147). Is it possible at all to consistently prefigure a radically different society in a social environment that is incompatible with, or even hostile to, its foundational principles (Wilson 2014: 175)? And, to stick with the metaphor, is there any 'empty space' left within the 'shell' of the old society that can gradually be filled with 'new' forms of organising, production and cohabitation? One may indeed doubt if capitalism and its relations of power and control can still be imagined as a 'shell' at all, since it arguably has neither 'outside' nor 'inside'. We are all interpellated by the dominant capitalist ideology, which we actively reproduce at our schools and in the media, in our interpersonal relations and in our use of language. As Louis Althusser (2014: 262–3) put it, 'those who are in ideology believe themselves by definition outside ideology'. In the same fashion, it is questionable if one could prefigure, or even imagine, a 'new society' that is wholly unaffected or 'uncontaminated' by the old one.

Prefigurative Democracy: Towards a Radical-Democratic Perspective

I have presented three points of critique against the anarchist conception of prefiguration. First, the anarchist ideal of a post-political society that holds no institutional place for political conflict or social division may be impossible as well as politically undesirable. Second, the idea that a prefigurative politics has a predefined end implies that one must have a rather detailed image of what the 'new society' must look like (even if the definitive realisation of such a 'new society' is not understood to be within reach). And third, it is questionable to what extent prefiguration may still be imagined as a process of 'building a new society in the shell of the old' in a time when capitalism and the state have permeated nearly every aspect of social and everyday life. If we return to the context of recent social movements, we can see certain tensions emerge between this original anarchist notion of prefiguration and contemporary practices. The temporary occupants of Tahrir Square, Puerta del Sol, Zuccotti Park or Gezi Park clearly did not share a detailed understanding of what a future society should look like – let alone, of how to get there (Gerbaudo 2017; Juris 2012; Kotsev 2013; Mensahawy 2020: 130). As a matter of fact, this question was continuously and explicitly at stake in their prefigurative experiments themselves. Rather than a 'model' of the future society, the occupied square should be perceived as a laboratory in which a continuous experiment could take place (Flesher Fominaya 2020: 314). The anarchist idea of prefiguration as a process of 'building a new society in the shell of the old' may thus not suffice to understand their radical potential and relevance.

What, then, would an alternative radical-democratic conception of prefiguration look like? Rather than as a process of 'building a new society in the shell of the old', I propose to conceptualise prefiguration as an experimental attempt to change the political form of society. Thus perceived, prefigurative democracy takes place within, and in engagement with, this existing social space. Its aim is not to live a 'pure' and radically consistent life in the here and now or to form an embryonic and sterile 'new society', but instead to contest and alter its political form, meaning and staging. It does not pursue the establishment of a post-political society, but rather seeks to politicise certain aspects or areas of our everyday life and social environment that were not hitherto perceived as legitimately political. Its aim, in other words, is not to eradicate political conflict or social division per se, but to create new political forms and meanings that allow us to understand or stage such conflicts in a different way. Critics may object that this implies giving up the revolutionary pretension of prefigurative politics. Indeed, seen from a radical-democratic perspective, prefigurative politics does not necessarily establish a durable break with the status quo in its every aspect. But it is also not reformist in that its aim is to challenge and alter the structural and discursive roots of a society. A radical-democratic theory of prefiguration must thus seek to present an alternative to both revolutionary and reformist conceptions of political change.

There evidently are also key aspects of the originally anarchist conception of prefiguration that need to be maintained. One of its defining features is that it challenges the often-made distinction between the means and ends of political practice. At the same time, as argued above, a radical-democratic conception of prefiguration implies that this is an open-ended process, whose goals and objectives are continuously at stake. It thus follows that prefiguration can no longer simply be defined as the principled insistence that one's 'means be in accordance with the ends' (Franks 2003: 16). How, then, must the relation between means and ends of prefigurative democracy be understood? This question will be addressed in the next chapter.

Chapter 2
Beginnings Without Ends

If politics is essentially about 'ends and means', then this implies that political actors must always have a clear end in sight (Dewey 1973). But is this necessarily the case? Recent occupy movements such as Occupy Wall Street (OWS), the Spanish 15-M movement and Nuit Debout were met with great scepticism. What, it was asked, were these movements actually for (Frank 2013)? Why did they often refuse to present an implementable agenda or strategy (Mirowski 2013: 327)? However, many of these occupy movements explicitly rejected such an instrumentalist logic.

How, then, should the relation between the employed means and the pursued ends of radical politics be understood from a prefigurative perspective? This relation has been conceptualised in a number of ways. In the following sections, I discuss three of these conceptualisations and critically assess them in the context of contemporary protest movements. First, in anarchist theory the principle of 'prefiguration' is often taken to prescribe a high measure of consistency between the applied means and the ultimate ends of revolutionary politics (Franks 2003: 16). But this implies that participants always act with a clear end in sight, which often is not the case. Alternatively, prefiguration could be conceived of as a 'rehearsal', the ends of which are open to continuous reformulation. Prefiguration then is viewed as an experimental attempt to act 'as if' the desired change is already in place – for instance, in order to gain a better understanding of the exact change that one wants to see in the future. However, by interpreting prefiguration as a rehearsal of future ends, one risks downplaying the immediate experience that it entails for those involved. Another possibility, which is more open to this experiential character, would be to argue that prefiguration caters to a plurality of (individually held) ends, rather than a single, common end. The problem with this interpretation, however, is that it tends to overlook the political and collective character of prefigurative democracy. I therefore propose a fourth option: rather than redefine the relation between means and ends, prefigurative democracy may be understood to refute this category altogether. Drawing on Hannah Arendt's understanding of political action, I argue that prefigurative politics should be conceived as a beginning *without* ends. Such an open-ended conceptualisation of prefigurative democracy sheds a different light on the practices of contemporary social movements.

Beyond Consistency: Rethinking the Relation Between Means and Ends

The idea of prefiguration is often associated with an attempt to live or act consistently with one's ideal image of what a future society should look like. Take, for instance, this fragment by the anarchist scholar and activist Cindy Milstein:

> We're not putting off the good society until some distant future but attempting to carve out room for it in the here and now, however tentative and contorted under the given social order. In turn, this consistency of means and ends implies an ethical approach to politics. How we act now is how we want others to begin to act, too. We try to model a notion of goodness even as we fight for it. (Milstein 2010: 111)

As this fragment suggests, prefiguration is often understood as an 'ethical' way to pursue radical change (Breines 1989). The idea is that one must aspire to 'be' or embody the desired change within one's own movement or private life. Alongside such ethical considerations, however, one may also pursue consistency between means and ends simply because it is necessary. As Audre Lorde (1984: 123) famously put it: 'the master's tools will never dismantle the master's house'. As we have all been conditioned in a society based on various forms of oppression and marginalisation, it follows that we have internalised many habits and ideas that are harmful to ourselves and others. Effective radical change thus not only requires the prefiguration of alternative social structures and living conditions, but is also a matter of changing oneself. For example, one may think of upholding non-violence as a guiding principle. Pacifist anarchists have always dismissed the use of revolutionary violence, as this would be inconsistent with the end of establishing a peaceful society devoid of conflict and domination (Thaler 2019). As the Dutch anarcho-syndicalist Bart de Ligt (1883–1938) asserted, there 'appears a flagrant contradiction between such means and the goal in sight' (1989: 72). Seen from this perspective, then, an essential part of a prefigurative politics may be to enact a non-violent movement culture 'that works within and acts against a dominant society by upholding criticism, dialogue, and nonviolent actions' (Vinthagen 2015: 287).

However, this focus on consistency also gives rise to a number of practical and theoretical problems. To begin with, one inevitably operates in an environment that is hostile to one's own ideas and principles (Wilson 2014: 175). This arguably means that one often cannot be fully consistent. Discussions on the use of violence may well serve to illustrate this. Even though most practitioners of a prefigurative politics would probably agree that the ideal aim is to establish a peaceful society, this unfortunately does not mean that non-violence can always be consistently observed in practice – for instance, because one needs to defend oneself against violent opponents or a repressive state (Crow 2011; Gelderloos 2007). An obvious example would be the occupation of Tahrir Square during the Egyptian revolution of 2011. Surely, the activist tent camp that emerged on this iconic square had significant prefigurative features (De Smet 2016; Van de Sande 2013), but it was also under siege by Mubarak's supporters and state security forces. Whilst the idealised image of a 'utopian republic of Tahrir' (Khalil 2011: 247) has often been reproduced in the media, it tends to be forgotten that many Egyptian revolutionaries lost their lives defending the square (Abul-Magd 2012). One may of course aspire to be consistent, even when it comes to the deployment of self-defence. But when push comes to shove, under these circumstances it arguably is impossible to act consistently with the ideal society that one seeks to establish in the long term.

Another problem with consistency as a key criterion for prefigurative politics is that one may not always have a clear idea of the pursued ends. As Dan Swain argues, '[i]f one is to match means to ends, one needs fairly substantive agreement on ends'. But this suggests 'that the ends are in fact in view, that is, specified to a greater or lesser degree' (Swain 2019: 53). As we have seen, however, it is far from evident what the end of a prefigurative politics should entail. There obviously are practical limitations to our ability to imagine a perfect society (after all, our imagination is fallible), but also more principled ones. As we have seen in the previous chapter, the ends and foundations of a democratic politics can never be taken for granted, and must always be open to scrutiny, contestation and rearticulation. As Claude Lefort argues, democracy 'is instituted and sustained by the dissolution of the markers of certainty' (1988c: 19). It may thus make more sense to understand prefiguration as a radically open-ended practice (Gordon 2008: 40–6) that challenges the 'established institution of society' (Castoriadis 1993: 263) and seeks to politically reconstitute it – without knowing in advance where or when (if ever) it should come to a close.

This gives rise to the question how exactly are the means and ends of prefigurative democracy related, in a time when the 'markers of certainty' have indeed disappeared and the ultimate ends of politics are often unclear? In the following sections, I briefly engage with a number of possible solutions to this problem: prefiguration as a rehearsal or acting 'as if' the desired social conditions are already in place; prefiguration as an ethics that serves a plurality of different (and often individually held) ends; and finally, prefiguration as a radically open-ended politics.

Acting 'As If': Prefiguration as a Rehearsal

How can the means and ends of a prefigurative politics be related, if there is no certainty about the ends that must be pursued in the first place? One possible solution to this problem is that the ends of a prefigurative politics must be continuously rearticulated throughout the process itself. Prefigurative politics should then be understood as the temporary, and inevitably imperfect, realisation of a hypothetical end. One deliberately acts *as if* the conditions for establishing a radically different society are already in place.

Such a conception is proposed by Brecht De Smet and Dan Swain, who employ the pedagogical theories of the Soviet psychologist Lev Vygotsky and his conception of 'proleptic learning' in order to better appreciate the open-endedness of prefigurative politics. According to Vygotsky, a pedagogical process can only be effective when it foreshadows or anticipates future attainments in the process itself. In De Smet's formulation (2015: 52), proleptic learning thus 'anticipates or imagines competence through the representation of a future act or development as already existing'. By pretending to have already acquired a certain level or skill, one projects oneself at a more advanced stage – and thus gradually obtains said level or skill in practice. Swain (2019: 58) associates this idea of 'proleptic learning' with a rehearsal. One repeatedly enacts the pursued ends in practice, thus gradually working towards a better performance. Acting 'as if' the desired change can already be put into practice thus serves a certain didactic function. But, Davina Cooper adds, it also grants a certain legitimacy to one's actions. In a prefigurative politics, 'action is set so that a social, scientific, ethical and political "otherwise" justifies, validates, normalises and holds up the actions undertaken' (Cooper 2020: 896–7).

This 'proleptic' reading of prefiguration has a number of advantages. First, it allows us to understand prefiguration as a distinctively experimental process (Raekstad and Gradin 2020: 37; Swain 2019: 56), in which the stated end is a hypothesis as to what a radically different form of society might look like. That is to say that the concrete ends of prefigurative practices must be subject to continuous revision and reformulation throughout, and after, the process. It also follows that any attempt to prefigure radical change will inevitably be imperfect and fall short of its ultimate objectives. As a consequence, and unlike some anarchist conceptions of prefiguration, proleptic learning is not primarily aimed at moral consistency: there inevitably 'remains a difference between the attempt at enactment and its successful realisation' (Swain 2019: 58). The point, in other words, is not to 'get it right' the first time, but continuous practice may lead to a more refined understanding both of the ends that are to be pursued, and the way to realise them in practice. Samuel Beckett's famous phrase – 'Ever tried. Ever failed. No matter. Try again. Fail again. Fail better' – may well apply to this particular reading of prefiguration (Thaler 2019: 1012).

Although experimentation is indeed a particularly relevant feature of prefigurative politics (Van de Sande 2013: 230; 2015: 189), this idea of prefiguration as a form of 'proleptic learning' or 'rehearsing' has a number of shortcomings. As any musician or actor is well aware, rehearsing not only entails the continuous repetition and refinement of one's performance. In most cases, one also has to follow (or even memorise) a script or sheet music. The outcomes of each attempt may vary to some degree, and the point of the exercise may not necessarily be to 'get it right' the first time. But there usually *is* a rather specific idea of what the eventual performance or recording of a piece should look or sound like. Thus, it is still implied that a future end must be 'already in place' (Cooper 2020: 908), in the sense that some shared agreement on its intended form and content is already presupposed. It is questionable, however, to what extent this applies to recent prefigurative movements, such as OWS or 15-M. Not only were they politically diverse, but they also often lacked a shared understanding of what their protest should lead to. This question was continuously at stake in their prefigurative experiments.

Another problem with this conception of prefiguration is that it remains oblivious to its more immediate *experiential* value. Prefigurative experimentation may not only lead to a better or more refined understanding of one's ends, but it also has a strongly emancipatory or empowering character in the here and now. The wish to live a better or more fulfilling life in the present has always been an important motivation to engage with prefigurative politics. Imperfect and short-lived as these experiences may be, Lynne Segal (2017: 206) stresses, what truly matters 'is primarily the consciousness acquired through the exhilarating joy of resistance itself, the sense of shared agency expressed in helping to build any alternative, autonomous space, for as long as they might last'. Although the value of experience is acknowledged in comparisons between prefiguration and proleptic learning (De Smet 2020: 12; Swain 2019: 52), it is still mostly appreciated in light of its distant end. This also implies that there must be a qualitative difference between this ultimate end and its prefigurations in the present. However, prefiguration may also be experienced as something that has intrinsic value or meaning to those engaged in it – no matter what its eventual outcome may be. Seen from this perspective, a prefigurative experience might in no way be inferior to its projected future. As well as its experimental character, then, a theory of prefigurative democracy should also account for this more immediate, experiential meaning. To stick with the music analogy: rather than the rehearsal of a classical orchestra, perhaps prefiguration could be imagined as an open-ended jam session (by amateur musicians). Its success is not based on the ability to execute a pre-set script or score; improvisation is key, and although one may of course aspire to develop one's musical skills through practice, it does not serve a predefined end external to itself.

A Plurality of *Teloi*: Prefiguration as Virtue Ethics

Another possible way to reimagine the relation between means and ends in a prefigurative politics is to argue that it caters to a wide variety of different ends or interests. Such a conception of prefiguration is promoted by contemporary post-anarchist theorists. Although the term is used in various ways (Franks 2007), what 'post-anarchists' such as Saul Newman, Andrew Koch and Todd May have in common is the aspiration to combine key aspects of anarchist political thought with elements of post-structuralist philosophy. They thus tend to take the term 'anarchism' rather literally: ἀναρχία should not merely be translated as the absence (ἀν-) of a leader or government or ἀρχός – but, more fundamentally, as the complete lack of any first principle or ἀρχή (Newman 2001: 161; see also Bey 2003; Schürmann 1987: 6). In short, post-anarchists not only pursue the classical anarchist ideal of a stateless and classless society, but reject the idea that society could be based on a moral or ontological foundation (such as 'universal truth', 'the good' or 'human nature'). Post-anarchists also typically refute any attempt to provide a political or symbolic representation of 'society' (Jun 2012: 105; Koch 1993; May 1994: 47–8). In this respect, post-anarchists significantly deviate from their 'classical' forebears such as Bakunin and Kropotkin:

> We can no longer sustain the idea, present in classical anarchism, of the uprising of an already constituted rational and ethical body against the external encumbrance of power. . . . [T]his social totality no longer exists, which is why contemporary insurrections need to invent new forms of solidarity and being-in-common. (Newman 2016: 65)

It thus follows that post-anarchists reject the idea of a shared social, moral or political *telos*. They instead advocate an ethical framework that allows us to appreciate an endless plurality of meanings, principles, goals and aspirations that we have as singularities (Koch 1993: 346). Seen from this post-anarchist perspective, then, prefiguration implies 'a refusal of strategic politics' as it eschews any long-term ends and instead 'takes place in the immediacy of the present, in the here and now, without being determined by a particular future end or *telos*' (Newman 2016: 65). It is exactly this aspiration, Newman holds, that renders it a distinctively ethical outlook on radical political practice (Newman 2016: 64).

But what would a post-anarchist ethics look like in practice, and how may it relate to other (normatively and ontologically founded) moral theories? Benjamin Franks, an anarchist philosopher and critical fellow traveller of the post-anarchist tendency, has dealt most extensively with this question. As established in the previous chapter, Franks initially counterpoised prefiguration to consequentialist theories of revolutionary politics (2003: 23–4; 2006: 102–3). But if prefiguration is not compatible with a consequentialist view of radical politics (as some of the early anarchists and syndicalists thought), then how exactly must the relation between its means and ends be understood? One option may be to turn to that other prominent school of normative ethics: deontology. Unlike consequentialism, deontology assesses the morality of an action on the basis of the rules or duties to which it should adhere. Moreover, Immanuel Kant's famous imperative that other human beings should never be treated merely as a means to an end corresponds well with the anarchist intuition that one should always seek to act in accordance with one's ends (Franks 2006: 108). The problem with this deontological framework, however, is that it still presupposes at least some ontologically founded and universalist conception of 'the good' or 'the just'. This is something that Franks, like many contemporary (post-)anarchists, eschews, as 'it would foreshorten the possibilities for moral subjects to determine their own ends' (2008: 141).

Franks's solution is to associate prefiguration with a third important school of normative ethics. The 'prefigurative characteristic of creating and maintaining fulfilling social practices that are co-operative, non-hierarchical and generate or perpetuate similar activity,' he argues, 'makes practical anarchism particularly congruent with virtue ethics' (Franks 2010: 141). There are a number of reasons why a virtue ethics seems to cater well to a prefigurative politics. First, virtues are typically exercised 'without regard to consequences' (MacIntyre 1985: 198). A course of action is not prescribed by its perceivable outcomes, but rather appeals to a concept of virtuous conduct. In the context of prefigurative practices, this means that one is not primarily focused on the free or just society that a revolutionary politics should ultimately bring about – but rather on the forms of solidarity and social cooperation that can already be realised in the present (Franks 2010: 146).

Another advantage of virtue ethics is that it allows activists to come to grips with the difficulties of pursuing moral and political consistency within a social context that is incompatible with, or even hostile to, their own political ideals. Rather than a claim to full consistency between means and ends, prefiguration then may also be read as a way to 'foster both a sense of responsibility' and an attempt 'to begin working through ways of responding to ethical conflicts' (Wilson 2014: 195). One may argue that the ground for its legitimacy lies neither in the ability to give a detailed account of its ends, nor in the capacity to consistently act in accordance with these ends, but precisely in the mutual correspondence between these means and ends (Jun 2012: 238–9). Such legitimation thus can only be given in light of the concrete context in which one acts.

But most importantly, adherence to one virtue does not necessarily imply the dismissal of others. Different virtues can be pursued alongside each other. Franks asserts that virtue ethics also does not necessarily presuppose a universalist concept of human nature or of the good life – or, for that matter, of what constitutes a sound political strategy (Franks 2010: 150–1). Instead, virtues refer to goods that 'are inherent in social practices, [and] have their own rules, which are negotiable and alter over time' (Franks 2008: 147). This also means that, unlike a deontological or consequential ethics, Franks's prefigurative virtue ethics does not necessarily require a single, fixed *telos* or end – nor does it presuppose that one *telos* is prioritised or hierarchised over others. Instead, a prefigurative ethics should cater to the various goals or *teloi* that different actors or collectives may have, even within the context of a single social movement. This is where Franks parts ways with his post-anarchist interlocutors: whereas '[r]ejecting a single universal (*telos*) is . . . epistemologically, ethically, and ontologically consistent with anarchism', he also asserts that 'rejecting all goals would undermine valuable social practices and make anti-hierarchical prefiguration impossible' (Franks 2018: 40).

How, then, may this anti-instrumentalist idea of prefiguration as a virtue ethics be employed in the context of recent occupation movements such as OWS or the Spanish 15-M movement? One advantage of Franks's proposal is that it allows us to appreciate the radical open-endedness of these movements. As we have seen before, these movements were typically pluralistic and their individual participants often had very different reasons or motivations to join them (Juris 2012; Kotsev 2013; Mensahawy 2020: 130). Imagining prefiguration as informed by a plurality of *teloi* or motivations allows us to understand how the concrete articulation of its ends is always immediately at stake in a prefigurative politics. It also entails a better appreciation as to why prefiguration is so meaningful for those who take part in it.

At the same time, it is questionable whether this idea of prefiguration as virtue ethics is specific enough to understand what is at stake in a radical-democratic politics. Most liberals would readily agree that one's acts should 'encapsulate the values desired in their preferred goals' (Franks 2008: 137; 2010: 114). Perhaps, Luke Yates (2015: 18) argues, 'as a qualifier of prefiguration the "means–ends equivalence" idea is simply not precise enough'. Moreover, recent prefigurative movements often sought to make a *collective* intervention by experimentally shaping a new institutional form of society. They articulated new, shared political discourses and sought to establish systemic change in the long run. Surely, a prefigurative social movement pertains to more than a sum of individuals, who each pursue their own ends. This post-anarchist idea of prefiguration as informed by a plurality of *teloi* may end up downplaying its distinctive political or collective characteristics – or, at least, for it to be employed in the context of recent social movements.

In the previous pages I have reconstructed three different conceptualisations of the relation between means and ends in a prefigurative politics. According to its classical definition, the means of prefigurative action are deemed to be fully consistent with its ends. But this implies that it is always possible to act consistently and that one has a positive (and rather detailed) understanding of the ends that one seeks to realise. An alternative option would be to see prefiguration as a 'rehearsal', but this still fails to grasp both its open-endedness and its experiential character. Finally, the post-anarchist idea of prefiguration may cater to a variety of (individually held) *teloi*, but this arguably obscures the political and collective character of prefigurative democracy. We thus need a fourth way to conceive of this relation between the means and ends of prefigurative democracy. This should allow us to integrate several features of the various conceptions discussed above. First, prefigurative democracy is a radically open-ended and experimental process, meaning that it is not necessarily informed by a predefined idea of its intended outcomes. Second, it has a typically non-instrumentalist and experiential character in the sense that it entails a concrete and inherently meaningful experience on the part of its practitioners. And third, prefiguration must be understood as a distinctively political practice, in the sense that one pursues radical change at a collective (and not merely an individual) level. As I show in the remainder of this chapter, the political thought of Hannah Arendt may well inform such a notion of prefigurative democracy.

Hannah Arendt's Conception of Political Action

One distinctive feature that Arendt's philosophical conception of political action has in common with the originally anarchist idea of prefiguration is that both originated in a critique of Marxism. Upon finishing her famous *Origins of Totalitarianism* in 1951, Arendt embarked on a research project with the aim of showing how certain aspects in Karl Marx's political thought would eventually be instrumental to the emergence of totalitarianism (Weisman 2014; Young-Bruehl 2004: 278–9). This project would never be completed, but among the various philosophical works that indirectly sprang from it was her opus magnum *The Human Condition*. Arendt's aim in this book was 'to think what we are doing. . . . It deals only with the most elementary articulations of the human condition, with those activities that traditionally, as well as according to current opinion, are within the range of every human being' (Arendt 1958: 5). In order to establish this, Arendt employs her trusted methodology of the conceptual distinction (Arendt 2018b: 473–4). 'What we are doing', then, is classified into three distinct categories: that of 'labour', 'work' and 'action'.

It is often held that this categorisation corresponds with another of Arendt's famous distinctions: that between a private and a public sphere. The private sphere, which is confined within the walls of the household, and is characterised by the hardships of everyday life, typically is the realm of labour. It revolves around the maintenance of biological life or *zōē*. This is counterposed to the public sphere, which is where our public life, or *bios*, takes place. The public sphere is shared with, or constituted between, others. And so one's political actions and interventions are witnessed and judged by these others (1958: 97). It is often claimed that such a rigid division between the private sphere of labour and the public sphere of political engagement has rather problematic gendered implications (Butler 2015: 86–8). But without intending to downplay the oblivion to gendered or racial inequality that is manifested throughout Arendt's oeuvre (and in this distinction between the private and the public realm in particular), I assert that another reading of her classification between work, labour and action is possible. Arendt can help us to better appreciate what renders political engagement worthwhile and meaningful – for instance, in the context of contemporary social movements. However, this implies that we do not understand 'labour', 'work' and 'action' as distinct categories, each with their own corresponding realm or 'territory', but instead approach them as 'the fraught conjunction of two different pairs of concepts – labor and work, and work and action' (Markell 2011: 18).

We can be relatively brief about the first of these pairs, as it is arguably one of Arendt's best-known arguments. What distinguishes labour on the one hand from action and work on the other, she argues, is that the former is characterised by necessity – and, in consequence, its inherent repetitiveness and endlessness. Only labour is 'unending, progressing automatically in accordance with life itself and outside the range of wilful decisions or humanly meaningful purposes' (Arendt 1958: 105–6). We daily perform labour in order to sustain our biological life. The products of labour are typically meant for consumption, meaning that they 'appear and disappear' continuously (Arendt 1958: 94). Work, on the other hand, is the kind of activity that results in objects with 'worldly permanence' (Arendt 1958: 143). By producing durable artefacts, we furnish the world around us and thus grant to our temporary presence here some measure of stability and durability. In this way, work transgresses the realm of mere necessity. The same could be said of political action: although it does not lead to durable products or results, as we will see below, action is equally characterised by an absence of necessity (Arendt 2005a: 119). It is often assumed that Arendt frowns upon labour. But a more accurate reading may be that labour consists of the 'repetitive, mundane activities that sustain a trust in life' (Gündoğdu 2015: 138), and thus realises the elementary preconditions for both work and public engagement. Labour may not always be the most fulfilling or inherently meaningful activity, but it has its own proper place and function in the reproductive cycle of life.

A second feature that Arendt ascribes to political action can be found when we counterpose labour and action on the one hand to work on the other. Work, or the activity of making something, is fundamentally characterised by the relation between means and ends (1958: 143). It not only requires a particular plan, model or blueprint – a detailed idea of the artefact or object in which the work process eventually is supposed to result – but also the use of means (tools and instruments) to obtain these ends. Work is the activity that mediates between tools, raw materials and the products into which they eventually are reshaped. It is a distinctively instrumentalist category: in work, 'the end justifies the means; it does more, it produces and organizes them' (Arendt 1958: 153). This has several consequences for our understanding of work vis-à-vis labour. Labour is 'caught in the cyclical movement of the body's life process', and thus 'has neither a beginning nor an end' (Arendt 1958: 144). Work, on the other hand, is distinct from all other human activities precisely in that it has 'a definite, predictable end and a definite, predictable beginning' (Arendt 1958: 143). Writing in English, Arendt deliberately exploits the double meaning of the word 'end' in this context (Arendt 2018d: 299). First of all, the 'end' is what results from a production process: the thing or object that such a process is intended to bring forth. But at the same time, the 'end' of a production process is also the projected moment when this process comes to a close. Any work will eventually be finished. Of course, one can start anew and aim to re-establish the same end. But the next production process (and, thus, its point of conclusion) will always differ from the former – as much as its product will be a different product. No two 'ends' of work are exactly the same.

Action, then, resembles the labour process in this last respect. Both typically lack an 'end' in this double sense of the word – albeit for different reasons. Labour, on the one hand, is endless due to its inherently repetitive or circular process. Action, on the other hand, is endless because its outcomes simply cannot be foreseen (Arendt 1958: 233). Arendt presents two related arguments in support for this statement. First, as we have seen, one always acts in a world that is shared with many others, who each have their own motivations and intentions. Any action can set into motion a 'new chain of happenings' (Arendt 2006b: 59–60). Due to this 'infinitude of intersecting and interfering intentions and purposes' (Arendt 1968a: 147), it is often impossible to grasp the aims and motives of individual actors. What is more, such motives tend to remain ambiguous or unclear to these actors themselves (Arendt 2006a: 88). Not only are those who engage in political action uncertain about the outcomes of their own deeds, but they often 'know not what they do', or why they do it (Arendt 1968a: 148). It is only afterwards, with the benefit of hindsight, that one may be able to ascribe a particular 'end' to one's actions and political engagements in order to make sense of it. This also means that an action can never be judged on the basis of its intended outcomes. 'Every good action for the sake of a bad end,' Arendt claims, 'actually adds to the world a portion of goodness, and every bad action for the sake of a good end actually adds to the world a portion of badness' (Arendt 1968a: 148).

In short, a political deed cannot be assessed on the basis of its 'ends' since the intentions behind it often remain unclear – not least to the actors themselves – and because its concrete outcomes are always unforeseeable.

Why is Arendt so invested in this conceptual distinction between action and work? She asserts that in modern political thought and philosophy, the two have often been confused. As *Homo faber* has come to determine our entire relation with the world around us, political action is often mistaken for a fabrication process (Arendt 1958: 305–6). This instrumentalist tendency in the philosophical tradition culminates in the work of Marx – who, Arendt holds, conceived of '"making the future" and "building and improving society" as though one were talking about making chairs and building and improving houses' (Arendt 2005b: 58). This is not only problematic at a conceptual level, but it has also had disastrous consequences. In fact, this instrumentalist aspect in the tradition of Western political thought was arguably one of the elements that would eventually give rise to totalitarianism. When our understanding of action collapses with that of making – a realm in which 'everything is judged in terms of suitability and usefulness for the desired end, and for nothing else' (Arendt 1958: 153) – it follows that the ends justify any means. It moreover implies that those who engage in political action merely serve as the instruments of political change or historical progress: that one 'cannot make an omelette without breaking any eggs' (Arendt 1994b: 283–4). Those who appeal to this rationale, Arendt argues, tend to confuse political action with violence – a realm that 'is ruled by the means–end category, [and] whose chief characteristic, if applied to human affairs, has always been that the end is in danger of being overwhelmed by the means which it justifies and which are needed to reach it' (Arendt 1972a: 106). Nothing, Arendt holds, could be further removed from what makes political action and public engagement truly meaningful to those involved in it.

Let me pause for a moment, and briefly summarise what can be concluded from our reading of Arendt so far. I have established two (or two pairs of) conceptual distinctions that Arendt develops in *The Human Condition* and other works from the late 1950s and early 1960s. First, as opposed to labour, political action presupposes that one is free from necessity. Second, as opposed to work, action is essentially open-ended and cannot be assessed by instrumentalist standards (Meade 1997: 119). But if political engagement is not primarily aimed at the relief of necessity or the pursuit of specific predefined ends, then what *is* at stake in politics? Why, in other words, would one engage in political action at all? Before we can apply our findings in the context of prefigurative protest movements, I will first turn to another part of Arendt's oeuvre in order to address these questions.

Freedom: Arendt on the Meaning of Politics

In addition to her planned book on Marx, in the late 1950s Arendt also embarked on a second project. Her plan was to write an 'Introduction into Politics' that should provide a 'more systematic examination of those spheres of the world and human life which we properly call political, that is, of the public realm on the one hand, and of action an [*sic*] the other' (Arendt 1993: 201). The unfinished manuscript, which is originally written in German and was published posthumously, comprises several unsuccessful attempts to commence the project over the course of years. Eventually, Arendt decides to employ a more experiential or phenomenological approach. Rather than reconstructing the conceptual meaning of 'political action', she asks: what does politics mean to those who take part in it? What is the purpose of politics for them? And is it still possible to meaning-fully engage with politics at all? (2005a: 96–108).

This phenomenological approach allows Arendt to immediately answer her own question. 'The answer is: the meaning of politics is freedom. Its simplicity and conclusive force lie . . . in the existence of politics as such' (Arendt 2005a: 108). Freedom, she states further on in manuscript, 'most certainly was and is not the end purpose of politics, that is, something that can be achieved by political means. It is rather the substance and meaning of all things political' (Arendt 2005a: 129). Again, Arendt deliberately exploits the various uses and meanings of a term – this time of 'meaning' (*Sinn*) itself. The meaning of something is always intrinsic in the thing itself. Unlike ends, which only emerge once an activity has come to its point of conclusion, meaning only properly exists in the moment of action (Arendt 2005a: 194). Thus, freedom is the 'meaning of politics' in the double sense that it is both its purpose or raison d'être – the very reason why we engage in politics in the first place – and that it best describes this 'field of experience' for those engaged in it (2006f: 145). As Arendt states in her famous essay on freedom, people 'are free . . . as long as they act, neither before nor after; for to *be* free and to act are the same' (2006f: 141). This experiential intepretation of political action evidently corresponds with Arendt's critique of instrumentalism. Freedom, as the meaning of politics, is not an end product that results from a political fabrication process (Topolski 2015: 65; Vergara 2020: 191). Quite the opposite: it is precisely due to this lack of blueprints, models and rigid procedures and protocols that one finally is free to act in a political context. In politics, the question what it is we are doing, and why we do it, is always on the table. And it is precisely this radical open-endedness and the lack of necessity – in short: the fact that we do not know what we do – that renders political action free (Bowen-Moore 1989: 59).

Bringing together these two aspects in Arendt's political thought – her conceptual distinction between 'labour', 'work' and 'action' on the one hand, and her experiential reading of freedom as the meaning of politics on the other – allows us to rethink the relation between the means and ends of prefigurative democracy. In fact, employing Arendt in this context gives rise to the question whether this category of means and ends can be employed in this context at all. If labour 'has neither a beginning nor an end' (Arendt 1958: 144) and work typically has 'a definite, predictable end and a definite, predictable beginning' (Arendt 1958: 143), then political action may as well be construed as a beginning *without* ends. One initiates something new, without knowing where this will lead in the long term. This also implies that it entails a certain risk or insecurity (Lorey 2015: 79). Arendt consistently relates the human potentiality for making new beginnings to the condition of natality. This is not merely a metaphor: it is not *like* the way we are born, but precisely *because* we were once born into a world shared with others, that we all have an innate capacity to make an intervention, begin something new – and, thus, be free (Arendt 1996: 55; Bowen-Moore 1989: 26). 'Because he *is* a beginning, man can begin; to be human and to be free are one and the same' (Arendt 2006f: 166). Our ability to be free is ingrained in our capacity as human beings to make an intervention and begin something new.

What renders such new beginnings so radical is that they seem to emerge out of nothing. Political action typically establishes a break with the status quo. It – quite literally – 'takes place' as an exceptional or extraordinary moment and creates the conditions in which something radically new can appear. A new beginning must carry its own source of legitimisation and offer its own foundation (Pitkin 1998: 281) and thus has 'nothing whatsoever to hold on to' outside of itself (Arendt 2006a: 198). In short, there arguably is something extraordinary or even miraculous about political action (Arendt 2005a: 114; Arendt 2006f: 168; Marchart 2005: 68; Virno 1996: 208–9). Political action is meaningful: not in light of its eventual outcomes, but precisely because it entails a seemingly miraculous break with the present – and, for those immediately involved in it, a direct experience of freedom.

This also explains Arendt's fascination with the history of revolutions and the moment of political founding or constitution that they entail. She is keen to stress that the Latin concept *principium*, from which our term 'principle' is derived, also translates as 'beginning' (2006a: 205). What is more, the ancient Greek *archê* (ἀρχή) does not coincidentally bear exactly the same double connotation. The political act of foundation thus establishes two related things: it begins something new, and it gives expression to a set of principles or 'criteria according to which all public actions are judged and which articulate the whole of political life' (Arendt 2018a: 53). It is constitutive both of the public space that action requires to emerge *and* of the very principles that are enacted in it (Arendt 2006f: 151). Ultimately, its source of legitimacy lies in the constitutive moment itself (Arendt 2006a: 205; Habermas 1996: 453; Kalyvas 2008: 242). The very etymology of 'constitution' illustrates that this is inevitably a collective – and by no means an individual – practice: it involves 'a plurality of actors coming together to *co-institute*, to establish jointly' (Kalyvas 2018: 105).

Arendt claims that only in such collective and constitutive moments of foundation is one free to experiment with new procedures of decision-making, new forms of organisation, new divisions of responsibility and distributions of power. This is also why, in her controversial comparison between the French Revolution and the American Revolution, Arendt favours the latter. Unlike the French revolutionaries, who primarily sought to liberate the people from poverty, misery or toil, their American counterparts sought to establish a new political space in which the enactment of freedom and making a beginning would always remain a possibility (2006a: 133). True equality, she states, is not so much related to justice but rather inheres in the ability of citizens to co-constitute and freely act and speak within a political space as each other's equals – what the ancient Greeks referred to as *isonomia* (ἰσονομία, see Arendt 2005a: 118). It is precisely this distinctive open-endedness, the intrinsic experience of freedom, and the ability to act as equals that together characterise Arendt's understanding of foundation as a political act par excellence.

Beyond the Means–Ends Distinction: An Arendtian Reading of Prefiguration

How can the means and ends of prefigurative democracy be understood to be related if there are no 'markers of certainty' to give us direction along the way? Arendt's political thought has only rarely been referenced in the literature on prefigurative politics (Disch 1997). However, her conception of political action may help us to see this means–ends relation in a different light. Rather than a full consistency between means and ends, or a 'rehearsal' of the eventual ends, or a means that serves to a plurality of different *teloi*, prefigurative democracy can also be understood to challenge the very category of means and ends. This allows us to develop an anti-instrumentalist understanding of prefigurative democracy that meets the three criteria set out in the discussion above. First, prefiguration is radically open-ended and has an experimental character; second, it entails a meaningful experience to those immediately engaged in it (which means that its value or significance cannot be reduced to its eventual outcomes); and third, it is a distinctively political and collective practice. I will address the first two of these aspects below and return to the third point in the final section of this chapter.

To start with, let us see how Arendt's distinction between 'labour', 'work' and 'action' may inform a more open-ended conception of prefiguration. It is important to recall that we should not read this conceptual distinction as a strict division between mutually exclusive categories, each 'belonging' to their own realm or territory. It is also not quite Arendt's point that one activity should be prioritised over the other, or that they are not all part of what it means to be human (Topolski 2015: 57). However, she does argue that confusing these various forms of human activity may have undesirable consequences. Most important, in this context, is the often-made confusion between work (which is typically underpinned by an instrumentalist logic) and action. It easily feeds into the idea that, in politics, the ends justify the means – that 'in order to break an omelette, one has to break a few eggs'. As we have seen, this is precisely the rationale that many advocates and practitioners of a prefigurative politics seek to challenge. They typically insist on maintaining consistency between means and ends. As discussed above, however, this would imply that the ends of a prefigurative practice are already known in advance. It is debatable whether this is desirable or even possible in a radical-democratic politics, where the purposes of political process are constantly subject to scrutiny and rearticulation. Our engagement with Arendt arguably leads to a radically different understanding of the means–ends relation in politics. Political actors may often not have any predefined end at all. It thus follows that the real meaning of a political deed, what renders it intrinsically meaningful to those involved, is not determined by its eventual or projected outcomes. Rather than to argue for a perfect consistency between the means and ends of political practice, one could also see prefiguration as a critique or dismissal of this very instrumentalist category (or, at least, when it is applied to politics). Along the lines of Arendt's conception, we may reimagine prefigurative democracy as a beginning *without* ends.

Such a non-instrumentalist and radically open-ended conception of political action also resonates with how prefigurative politics is often perceived in practice. It is implied, for instance, in a famous slogan of the Mexican Zapatista movement: 'preguntando caminamos' ('we walk while asking') or 'caminar preguntando' ('asking while walking'). For the Zapatistas, arguably one of the most long-standing and influential prefigurative social movements of the past decades (Stahler-Sholk 2019), a lack of certainty about the possible outcomes of a process by no means detracts from its meaning or relevance. Quite the opposite: its end or purpose must deliberately and repeatedly be at stake along the way (Sitrin and Azzellini 2014: 38–9). According to John Holloway, who is actively involved in the Zapatista movement, their famous slogan underlines how prefigurative politics 'must be understood as both explanatory and open' (2010b: 44). It is not hard to recognise a similar open-endedness in the practice of many occupy movements such as OWS or the 15-M movement (Douzinas 2013: 163–4). Their squares and activist tent camps were 'laboratories of democracy in which shared understandings of democracy [could] develop: what "good" or "real" democracy might look like, and what is required for it to work' (Flesher Fominaya 2020: 13). In other words, these movements sought to make a new beginning, without having a clear idea of where and when this would end. This may also explain their reluctance to formulate any short-term demands (Bray 2013: 103–4). What was at stake in many of these movements' prefigurative practices was not to find an immediate solution, or to always act consistently with their projected ends or objectives. The real issue, rather, was to figure out in what direction their politics should take them. As Verónica Gago, speaking from the perspective of feminist assembly movements in Latin America, puts it: 'when we don't know what to do, we call an assembly' (2020: 164–5).

This brings us to a second important feature of prefigurative democracy: its experiential character. Applying Arendt's critique of the means–end distinction to the prefigurative politics of such social movements urges us to rethink the temporality between the present and the future. Political action does more than interrupt the status quo. It can also break with our chronological experience of time itself. In modern times, we are used to thinking of time as a gradual process: it is perceived as the measurable distance between two moments on a linear scale. But this is not the only possible conception of time. It may also be thought of as a moment or instance that cuts across this chronology – a conception of time that the ancient Greeks referred to as *kairos*. What is distinctive about this *kairotic* conception is that it allows us to understand chronologically remote moments as being 'simultaneous-along-time' (Anderson 2006: 24). Walter Benjamin referred to this conception of time in his 'Theses on History', whose first English edition was posthumously published by Arendt. Benjamin uses the term *Jetztzeit* (literally: 'now-time') to describe this sense of proximity between different historical events (Löwy 2016: 88–9). Revolutions, for instance, are typically experienced by their participants as the incarnations of previous historical events. They 'make the continuum of history explode' (Benjamin 1968b: 261). Rather than pursue a future end, one seeks to hold on to such an extraordinary moment as long as possible. Benjamin narrates how, in the July Revolution of 1830, the Parisian revolutionaries even fired at the city's tower clocks in an attempt to make them stop running (Benjamin 1968b: 261–2).

One may of course object that such a – seemingly anachronistic – conception of time has little resonance with the experiences of social movements today. Yet, this critique of chronology implicitly re-emerges in contemporary forms and definitions of prefiguration. In Marianne Maeckelbergh's formulation, 'practising prefiguration means removing the temporal distinction between the struggle in the *present* toward a goal in the future; instead, the struggle and the goal, the real and the ideal, become one in the present' (2009: 66–7).

A similar idea was conveyed by the faux street sign of Tahrir Square, to which I referred in the Introduction. It is as if, by putting this up in the heart of London's financial district, one tried to give expression to a sense that 'Tahrir Square is here too'. Much like Benjamin's revolutionary Parisians, the participants of Occupy LSX sought to break through 'the continuum of history'. This non-chronological conception of time also seems to resonate with the experiences of recent indigenous movements that have engaged in prefigurative experimentation (Coulthard 2014: 159). These movements often took inspiration not from an ideal-image of the future but from the experiences of their ancestors in the past. As Nick Estes, a citizen of the Lower Brule Sioux tribe, argues:

> Indigenous notions of time consider the present to be structured entirely by our past and our ancestors. There is no separation between past and present, meaning that an alternative future is also determined by our understanding of our past. (Estes 2019: 14)

One example is the indigenous #NoDAPL movement of 2016. In an attempt to stop the construction of an oil pipeline near the Standing Rock reservation in the United States, and to protect its water sources and sacred burial grounds, this indigenous movement erected several tent camps in the reservation. Estes argues that 'the spirit of #NoDAPL, enacted daily in camp life, embodied a brief version of what Native life could be' (Estes 2019: 57).

This *kairotic* conception of time, which underpins the conception of prefigurative democracy that I seek to advance here, has a number of significant implications when we apply it to contemporary social movement politics. First, it follows that the meaning of such practices cannot be determined by its specific outcomes. Whatever happens next in no way detracts from the value of this experience. Second, as we have seen, in the experience of those engaged in political action, the future may not be as distant as is often assumed from an external point of view. Finally, the *kairotic* conception of time implies that there is an inherent tendency in political action to *oppose* its own point of conclusion. The very last thing that political actors want is to see their practices coming to a close. One rather tries to hold on to it and to prolong or expand the experimentation, continuous evaluation, conflict – and, above all: the experience of freedom – that it entails. As Davina Cooper (2014: 223) argues, '[a]s experiments in living that necessarily involve prefigurative practice . . . everyday utopias assert the importance of maintaining and sustaining what *is*'.

Again, this last feature – the urge of its participants to extend the political moment as long as possible – can easily be recognised in the practices of recent prefigurative movements. David Graeber and his fellow OWS founders saw the occupation of Zuccotti Park as 'a stepping-stone toward the creation of a whole network of such assemblies' (Graeber 2013: 43). In Turkey and Spain, networks of local neighbourhood assemblies emerged in the wake of the Gezi Park and 15-M movement (Roos 2013; Sanchéz 2012). It must be stressed that the question why or how a prefigurative practice can be extended is often itself a matter of debate. In the aftermath of some recent prefigurative movements, there were several, and at times competing, attempts to prolong or revive the experiment after its momentum had passed (Flesher Fominaya 2020: 146–7). Of course, this urge to hold on to the political moment also gives rise to new questions and dilemmas. How could one give a more durable form to such prefigurative moments, whilst retaining its distinctive open-ended, experimental and experiential character? And what sort of organisational or institutional form may be required to establish this? I return to these questions in the next chapter.

Let me first address another possible objection to the Arendtian conception of prefigurative democracy advanced here. If prefiguration must indeed be imagined as a beginning without ends – then what is still being prefigured? Does Arendt not condemn us to a rather sterile or empty idea of politics, in which one merely acts for the sake of acting? Is there still a future left for us to pursue? However, it must be stressed that just because action has no pre-defined ends, it does not necessarily follow that it cannot be inspired or driven by certain hopes, ideals and aspirations for the future. Alongside the difference between the meaning (*Sinn*) and ends (*Zwecke*), Arendt also introduces another relevant conceptual distinction in her unpublished 'Introduction into Politics': namely, that between ends (*Zwecke*) and goals (*Ziele*). The latter may be defined as the 'guidelines and directives by which we orient ourselves and which, as such, are never cast in stone, but whose concrete realizations are constantly changing' (Arendt 2005a: 193). A goal is 'not contained within the action itself, but, unlike ends, neither does it lie in the future. If it is achievable at all, it must remain constantly present, and precisely during times when it is *not yet* achieved' (Arendt 2005a: 198). Thus, unlike Giorgio Agamben, who has developed a 'gestural' conception of politics as 'means without ends', Arendt maintains that action can be inspired by an ideal or aspiration that is not yet fully attainable in the present. It would be a mistake to assume that in political action 'nothing is being produced or acted, but rather something is being endured and supported' (Agamben 2000: 57). Seen from Arendt's perspective, political action inevitably does project beyond itself – or, indeed, prefigures an unattained goal, which is simultaneously 'not not' and 'not yet' realised (Swain 2019: 58). Her distinction between 'ends' (*Zwecke*), 'meaning' (*Sinn*) and 'goals' (*Ziele*) may help us to understand how prefigurative democracy can be both radically open-ended in the sense that it strives towards an uncertain and unrefined goal; and at the same time methodical in that one must continuously seek to overcome problems and obstacles in the pursuit of this horizon (Dietz 1994: 880–2). As Oliver Marchart argues in a similar vein, '[p]refigurative activists never move in straight lines toward a clearly defined goal; they move in staggering, tottering ways on noncircular lines toward an obfuscated goal' (Marchart 2019: 188).

Such a radically open-ended and anti-instrumentalist conception of prefigurative democracy also corresponds with its distinctive experiential features: precisely because a prefigurative politics does not strive towards a future end that is external to itself, those involved in it will typically seek to hold on to this moment of experimentation as long as possible. One may add to this that prefiguration entails a radically different sense of time, as present and future – or the means and the goals of political action – are experienced to coincide in the moment itself. But does Arendt's theoretical framework also meet the last criterion set at the beginning of this section? Her concept of action may be distinctively open-ended and receptive to the experiential aspect of political action, but is it also sufficiently political? Let me address this last question in the next section.

Prefiguration as Politicisation

If political action does not necessarily serve to meet certain predefined ends – and if, moreover, political action typically takes place in a public realm that must be distinguished from our social and private environment – then what exact issues or topics can still be addressed in politics? What can politics possibly be about, if not the solution of societal issues or the implementation of an economic agenda (Arendt 2018b: 454–8)? It has been argued that Arendt's idea of the political is 'devoid of determinate social content' (McNay 2014: 38) and that she promotes an 'exceptionalist' idea of politics (Apter 2018). True political action, then, would only occur in the rare event of a Grand Historical Moment. And even in these rare cases, Arendt's notion of politics and the public sphere would categorically exclude everyone with a (re)productive function in society, as their concerns or grievances would be deemed insufficiently political or not worthy of public scrutiny (Bargu 2013; Wolin 2016: 240–1). It is understandable how Arendt's thought – and specifically her distinctions between 'work', 'labour' and 'action'; between the 'social' and the 'political'; or between the French and the American Revolution – gives rise to such interpretations. But I nevertheless contend that her conception of political action may be read and employed in a less rigid fashion. Rather than one side of a categorical distinction between different 'realms' or 'forms of doing', it may also be understood precisely as a transgression of such boundaries.

For a start, although there may be something 'exceptional' about political action, this does not quite mean that it should only rarely occur. Political action is exceptional in the sense that it establishes a break or interruption, after which nothing will ever be the same again. For those involved – either in an immediate sense, as participants, or indirectly as audience or bystanders – it entails a new beginning. But such a break could arguably occur anywhere and at any time. As an intervention, it transgresses the distinction between what is deemed 'properly' political, and that which is excluded from the political sphere or debate. Rather than a rigid categorical distinction, the boundary between the political on the one hand and the social or the private on the other is then understood as a 'line drawn in the sand . . . calling out agonistically to be contested, augmented, and amended' (Honig 1995: 146). In that case, as Richard Bernstein (1986: 122) puts it, 'the question whether a problem is itself properly social . . . or political is itself frequently the central political issue'. Politics thus entails the reframing and reclaiming of particular issues as sufficiently political. And it is precisely this reframing and reclaiming that establishes an intervention in the status quo. 'Political action' could then be read as a process of *politicisation*, or the rearticulation of conventional distinctions between 'the public' and 'the private', 'the political' and 'the social', and so on (Gündoğdu 2015: 56–7). As Andrew Schaap puts it, Arendt is 'primarily preoccupied not by the challenge of emancipation but civility – that is, how the public realm can be constituted in order to arrest those social processes that lead to people being made super-fluous' (Schaap 2021: 42). Such acts of politicisation may evidently occur on the grand stage of History, but they may equally well happen in a more mundane or everyday context.

Seeing the politics of contemporary prefigurative movements through an Arendtian lens, this concept of 'politicisation' is particularly fruitful. Evidently, the experiments that took place on Tahrir Square, Zuccotti Park, Puerta del Sol and many similar places did not merely pertain to democratic decision-making and the organisation of public assemblies. There was also an important practical side to everyday life in the occupied square. Within these spaces, food was being prepared and distributed (Gordinier 2011); laundry was done and toilets were being cleaned (Gessen 2011); internet cafés and stages with amplification for debates and musical performances were set up (Khalil 2011: 247); teach-ins, workshops and lectures were organised (Pickerill and Krinsky 2012); and well-being or mental health work groups endeavoured to create a socially safe and inclusive environment (Howard and Pratt-Boyden 2013). These mundane or everyday activities did not merely form the infrastructure to support another prefigurative experiment with General Assemblies and consensus-oriented decision-making. Instead, they were part and parcel of the prefigurative experiment itself. As Cristina Flesher Fominaya (2020: 138) argues, the most important politicisation that these movements established 'resulted not from Habermasian exchanges of rational arguments extolling the virtues or challenges of democracy in the general assemblies . . . but rather from the shared experience of resolving the *practical* organization of life in common'.

Indeed, Judith Butler argues that there was something 'Arendtian and counter-Arendtian' about these everyday practices within the occupied square. On the one hand, by occupying and reorganising public space these protesters gave expression to their grievances and demands. On the other hand, their public statement largely pertained to 'maintaining themselves as persisting bodies with needs, desires, and requirements' (Butler 2015: 97). Even the most mundane or everyday activity suddenly acquired political meaning. By sleeping, eating, cooking and studying on the streets, Butler holds, these protesters transgressed the boundaries between the private and the public – thus politicising both (Butler 2015: 71). If it is true, as Arendt herself states, that 'whatever occurs in this space of appearance is political by definition, even when it is not a direct product of 'action', then arguably cooking and sleeping in Gezi Park or Tahrir Square became the most political thing to do (Arendt 2006f: 153; see also Lorey 2015: 77).

Approaching prefiguration as a process of politicisation also offers us a better understanding of why it is a distinctively political concept (and not primarily an ethical one, as some contemporary post-anarchists seem to hold). The point of prefigurative democracy is not so much to 'be the change you want to see' at an individual level, or to live a virtuous life behind closed doors. It is undeniably admirable if one manages to live in accordance with one's social and political ideals (although the ability to do so consistently may evince some measure of privilege). But there is also an important difference between moral consistency at a personal level and the need to collectively experience freedom in practice. As second generation feminists have rightly pointed out, 'the personal' can be political. Romantic and sexual relationships, gendered divisions of labour, personal safety and domestic violence all have important political implications. However, in order for them to be sufficiently politicised, they first need to be made 'public' in one sense or another. (This is not quite the same as saying that they need to be visible for everyone, but rather that they must somehow be addressed in a collective practice shared with others.) For social movements, experimenting with new forms of organisation, decision-making, cohabitation, planning, production and distribution and so forth may be a viable way of politicising such issues. This is precisely what we have seen in the everyday practices of the occupy movements of the past decade. What renders the establishment of a field kitchen or the distribution of clothing equally political as the organisation of a General Assembly is the fact that these experiments are part of collective practices, which both challenge and reshape the political and organisational form of society.

Epilogue (By No Means a Conclusion)

I commenced this chapter with the question how prefigurative democracy may be imagined in a time when all markers of certainty have disappeared. Originally, in anarchist theory and practice, prefiguration was often perceived as an attempt to act in full consistency with one's ends. But it may not be quite evident how to do this, if the very content of these ends is unknown – or, to be more precise, when this is continuously debated and rearticulated within one's political practice itself. Not only is a prefigurative politics radically open-ended, as the practices of recent social movements suggest, but it also has strongly experiential and collective features. An Arendtian conception of political action may help us to reimagine the relation between means and ends in a prefigurative politics. What really is at stake here is not the ability to act consistently with one's ends, but rather the attempt to make a new beginning *without* ends. This explains why square occupation movements such as 15-M, OWS or Nuit Debout often lacked a clear agenda, and why they sought to prolong or expand their practices as long as possible. What is prefigured does not merely lie in a distant future: instead, it is realised and experienced in the political moment itself.

It could be objected that such an 'end-effacing' (Swain 2019) reading of prefiguration essentially deprives it of its revolutionary potential. After all, if one acts without a clear end in sight, then how is it at all possible to establish durable and systemic change in the long run? The point, of course, is not to argue that prefigurative democracy cannot have significant impact or outcomes. But if radical change is established in the here and now, rather than the future, this implies a different understanding of 'change' itself. As stated above, one of the main concerns of those engaged in a prefigurative practice is to hold on to the moment of beginning. In their experience, 'change' is not gradually established or measured by a chronological standard but continuously prolonged and expanded over time and space. This also means that, in order to last, prefigurative democracy must eventually acquire a durable institutional form. In the next chapter, I therefore turn to the question of what kind of political institution or governmental form could accommodate it in the long term.

Chapter 3
From the Assembly to Council Democracy: Towards a Prefigurative Form of Government?

Against the anarchist reading of prefiguration as a process of 'building a new society in the shell of the old', prefigurative democracy may also be understood as an attempt to challenge and reshape society's political form. This gives rise to the question whether prefigurative democracy also implies a particular, substantive idea of what such a political form should look like. Is prefiguration merely a formal concept, which could be applied in the context of any social movement, irrespective of their concrete political aspirations (Raekstad and Gradin 2020: 36)? Or is it also underpinned by a distinctively prefigurative view of democratic organisation or government? To speak with Claude Lefort, does prefigurative democracy imply a particular *mise en forme*, *mise en sens* and *mise en scène*?

There is also another reason to raise this question at this point. In the previous chapter I interpreted prefiguration as a politics without ends. I argued that its practitioners are not primarily concerned with the question how, or when, their practices will eventually come to a close. This also means that prefigurative movements often seek their own continuation: they typically try to prolong and expand their own practices as long as possible. But, as political theorists have argued in the wake of recent occupy movements, if prefigurative democracy is to sustain over time it will need to acquire a more durable organisational form and structure (Hardt and Negri 2017: 224). This leads to a certain tension. For how can a democratic politics that is characterised by its open-endedness and spontaneity, its experimental and experiential character, and its immediate experience of freedom be formalised without compromising on precisely these aspects? Might any attempt to institutionalise prefigurative democracy not also entail the loss of precisely these distinctive features?

What might a more durable institutional form for prefigurative democracy look like? In order to answer this question we may first need to ask what kind of institutions, policies and procedures can already be seen to be taking shape within the practices and structures of contemporary prefigurative movements. One form of organisation that has been widely employed by many recent movements is the public assembly. A number of key features have been be attributed to the assembly form. The assembly is a public encounter between people with different experiences and perspectives. But precisely by virtue of this, it challenges established hierarchical relations and forms of leadership. The assembly also has an important bodily aspect in that it lays claim to public space through the act of physical assembling. It is a notably prefigurative form in that it entails the enactment of new social and political conditions. The public assembly is also often regarded as a symbolic expression of the popular will. In being so, however, it precisely inscribes the established idea of 'the people' with a new meaning. At the same time, such assemblies have a rather temporary and fleeting character: sooner or later, they disperse again. It thus is questionable to what extent it may resolve the elementary tension between the open-endedness of prefigurative democracy on the one hand, and its need for a more durable institutional form on the other.

How might a more permanent, institutional shape be given to prefigurative democracy? Is there a way to retain some of its prefigurative features, or might it even give rise to a particular kind of democratic government? As we will see below, several recent social movements eventually turned to another institutional form, in an attempt to achieve precisely this. They sought to establish durable networks of democratic councils or neighbourhood assemblies that would outlive the temporary public assemblies on their occupied squares. In order to better understand this move towards the establishment of council democracy, I return to Hannah Arendt. Drawing from Arendt's idea of a 'council system' (and from some of her most important sources, most notably Rosa Luxemburg), I argue how political councils may accommodate prefigurative democracy and give it a more durable form in the long term.

Contemporary Social Movements and the Public Assembly

As we gather together in solidarity to express a feeling of mass injustice, we must not lose sight of what brought us together. We write so that all people who feel wronged by the corporate forces of the world can know that we are your allies. (New York City General Assembly 2012: 148–9)

Thus begins the 'Declaration of Occupation', which was unanimously accepted by OWS's General Assembly on 29 September 2011. The declaration then continues to list the many wrongs and injustices of the capitalist order and its democratic deficits, and finally calls upon the 'people of the world' to 'assert [its] power':

> Exercise your right to peaceably assemble; occupy public space; create a process to address the problems we face, and generate solutions accessible to everyone. . . . Join us and make your voices heard! (New York City General Assembly 2012: 148–9)

This declaration can be read in two complementary ways. On the one hand, it is a founding document that proclaims 'the assembly' as a political space or body. Thus conceived, the assembly is a self-constituent body that is itself assembled of different bodies – it is in a state of being assembled. In this declaration, the assembly bestows upon itself a certain authority to speak on behalf of a larger group or constituency. On the other hand, OWS's declaration can also be read as an appeal: members of the public are invited to join the assembly, and to take part in its continuous process of collective deliberation and decision-making. The assembly could thus also be understood as a practice or activity of assembling. It is both a political body that authors and authorises its own declaration, and, at the same time, the continuous practice that this declaration calls for. Indeed, in the course of the past decade many social movements around the world have answered this call by organising their own public assemblies. But what explains the prominence of this particular organisational form in the practices of these recent movements? How does it cater to, and why does it often seem to emerge from, a prefigurative view of democracy?

In the wake of these occupy movements, many radical political theorists have sought to conceptualise the public assembly as a democratic expression or practice as well as a form of organisation. Judith Butler (Butler 2011b, 2015; Butler and Antanasiou 2013) has employed their performative theory of gender in the context of what they call 'assembly movements' in order to better understand their constitutive and symbolic relevance. Verónica Gago (2020) engages with the assembly in the context of feminist movements

in Latin America and stresses their radically pluralist and ontologically diverse composition. In a similar fashion, Michael Hardt and
Antonio Negri (2012, 2017) understand the assembly as the organisational form of the 'multitude' and recommend how this form
could acquire more durability and strategic effect in the long term.
Isabell Lorey (2014, 2020) presents the assembly as a distinctively
'presentist' form of democracy, which is devoid of political representation and its imputed hierarchies. Approaching the public assembly
from a more historical perspective, however, Jason Frank precisely
interprets it as 'a distinctive – and distinctively powerful – mode of
democratic representation' (2021: xiv). In short, not only has the
assembly been analysed in different ways, but various (and at times
incompatible) features and functions have been ascribed to it in the
recent debate. Let us briefly flesh out a number of these key aspects
and show how various accounts of the public assembly deviate from
each other.

A first feature of the public assembly is that it creates an encounter – or, to be more precise: that it *is* an encounter – between a
wide plurality of social groups or individuals who may share particular grievances or concerns, but who nevertheless have very different experiences or identities. According to Hardt and Negri, it
is informed by a 'logic of assemblage', which combines or brings
together its various parts not on the basis of shared characteristics,
but on the basis of possible connections between them (2017: 295).
Recent assembly movements thus 'affirm a beating heart of plural
ontology' in that they 'create a model of constituent democracy in
which differences are able to interact and together create new institutions' (Hardt and Negri 2017: 69). The assembly establishes a
common ground between various conflicts and struggles, and broadens the understanding of its participants and their ability to identify
with each other, without ignoring or nullifying the significant differences between them (Gago 2020: 156). According to some sources,
this suggests that the assembly form is underpinned by a typically
feminist critique of political representation. Sara Ahmed (2017: 30)
explains how feminist analysis of sexism in both its structural and
everyday forms starts with collecting individual stories and experiences and establishing the various connections between them. In a
similar fashion, Gago defines the assembly as a 'mobile structura-
tion of a political process led by a multiplicity of subjectivities that
traverse different conflicts' (2020: 176). It refutes any form of political representation – which, according to some feminist scholars,

is inherently masculine as it is majority-based and establishes at least some measure of hierarchy and exclusion (Lorey 2020: 148–9). According to Isabell Lorey, the assembly instead exemplifies a 'presentist' and essentially open or undetermined form of democracy (Lorey 2020: 196–8). It neither has a predetermined organisational form or structure, nor does it 'stand for' a particular circumscribed 'people' or 'nation' (Lorey 2014: 60; 2020: 17–18). Being a radically pluralist and inclusive encounter, in the assembly no experience or identity is subordinated to another.

A second, and related, characteristic that is often ascribed to the assembly is that it challenges traditional forms of hierarchy, rulership and vertical leadership. Many recent public assemblies typically employed participatory and consensus-oriented forms of democratic decision-making. Initially, they thus were widely regarded as the exponents of a distinctively 'leaderless' or 'horizontalist' form of democracy (Hardt and Negri 2012; Mason 2012; Sitrin 2012; Tormey 2015). But this initial interpretation of the assembly as a 'leaderless' form of organisation has also been challenged from various perspectives. To begin with, and notwithstanding its strong appeal, the accuracy of this image is disputable. Many recent public assemblies arguably did depend on, and gave rise to, certain forms of political leadership (Nunes 2014; Smucker 2017). The idea of 'leaderlessness' may thus render invisible certain power relations or inequalities that nevertheless do emerge within a social movement. This could easily feed into what Jo Freeman (1972) famously called a 'tyranny of structurelessnesss'. When formal leadership roles are lacking in a social movement, those who are de facto in powerful positions cannot be held accountable. It may therefore be more productive and informative to ask how the assembly gives rise to alternative, more fluctuating and diverse forms of leadership. Paolo Gerbaudo (2012: 39–44) has compared the assembly with a choreography, which is scripted, casted and staged in advance by movement organisers on social media and other digital platforms. Rodrigo Nunes, in turn, argues that the assembly serves to 'distribute' leadership roles, which can be 'occupied by different agents at different times' (2021: 180). Rather than imagining the democratic social movement as being 'leaderless' it may thus be more descriptively accurate as well as politically empowering to construe them as intrinsically leaderful (Smucker 2017: 186). Hardt and Negri agree that, in order to effectively pursue radical change at a structural and institutional level, some forms of 'tactical leadership' may need to be formalised. However, they maintain that the assembly could continue to play an elementary role in determining the long-term aims and strategies of the multitude (2017: 19). Can the public assembly be imagined at all as a durable democratic institution? I will return to this question further below.

A third important feature of the assembly, which is stressed most markedly by feminist scholars, is its bodily aspect. Although social media have come to play a prominent role in the mobilisation and practical organisation of social movements (Castells 2015; Gerbaudo 2012; Swann 2018), the physical aspect of public assembling clearly has also retained its relevance over time (Frank 2021: 1–2). Judith Butler thus theorises the assembly as 'bodies in alliance', which has two important implications. On the one hand, it means that the assembly can only emerge between bodies that are gathered in public and that, in the act of assembling, lay claim to public space. Following Arendt in this respect, Butler thus attributes an important constitutive function to collective political action. Both as a political practice and a physical gathering, the assembly realises the conditions for its own emergence (Butler 2015: 71). At the same time, this also means that the assembly constitutes itself *as* a gathering of bodies – each with their own physical or material needs, vulnerabilities and deprivations. As we have seen in the previous chapter, the everyday aspects of daily life in the occupied square are by no means of secondary importance. Instead, Butler argues, it was precisely by 'sleeping and eating in the public square, constructing toilets and various systems for sharing the space' – in short, by 'maintaining themselves as persistent bodies' – that its participants gave expression to their grievances and demands (Butler 2015: 97). It would thus be a mistake to assume, as is often done, that assembly movements such as OWS or 15-M did not make any demands. It is precisely by performing aspects of their daily life in public that these movements enacted the kind of 'relations of equality that are lacking in the economic and political domain' (Butler and Antanasiou 2013: 102).

This brings us to a fourth, and related aspect of the public assembly: it both enacts and creates the conditions that are needed to overcome the contested status quo. Butler employs their performative theory of gender in order to explain this. Gender is performative in that it is constituted by its enactment in practice. Specific gendered features in one's behaviour or appearance are thus not merely the manifestations or expressions of an already-existing identity, but are themselves co-constitutive of the very way in which someone is gendered (Butler 1990: 34). Much in the same way, Butler argues, the public assembly may be understood as a performative enactment of the social and political change that it pursues. First, as we have seen, it performs the physical and material conditions that the establishment of a more just and equal society requires. Second, the assembly enacts new conceptions of the good life and the principles on which it can be based (Butler 2015: 218–19). Finally, the assembly is also a performance of popular sovereignty. It is the enunciation of a 'we the people' (Butler 2011a). In fact, Butler stresses, 'the assembly is already speaking before it utters any words', in that merely by its coming together in public 'it is already an enactment of a popular will' (2015: 156). Oliver Marchart (2019: 176–88) speaks in a similar fashion of the assembly as the 'pre-enactment' of how activists imagine an alternative future.

A final element that is sometimes ascribed to the assembly form is its aesthetic or symbolic function. Jason Frank has reconstructed the historical role of popular assemblies in the imagination or representation of 'the people' in modern democracies. Whilst 'the people' is generally held to be the ultimate source of political authority in a democracy, it is only rarely (if ever) visible as such. But throughout the past centuries the assembly has often been perceived as the most tangible manifestation of popular sovereignty, especially in revolutionary moments and times of political crisis (Frank 2021: 40). It presents a 'living image' of the people, to itself as a people. However, the assembly does more than simply represent 'the people' – it also reinscribes it (and whatever understanding it has of itself) with new meaning and content. As 'both the authorizing source and the effect of representation', it sets 'into motion the condition for the emergence of new collectivities and political subjects' (Frank 2021: 9). A paradox thus seems to inhere in the form of the assembly: on the one hand, it is historically taken to be the most immediate expression of a popular will; and on the other hand, this popular will is also at least partially formed or articulated by the assembly itself. Frank insists that this is not merely a juridical problem, as is often assumed in theoretical debates on constituent power, but also an aesthetic one. How is it possible that a numerical minority, as gathered in, for instance, Tahrir Square of Zuccotti Park, can legitimately and convincingly present itself as the embodiment of an entire population and its shared grievances or aspirations (Frank 2021: 70)?

I have thus identified a number of aspects that have been ascribed to the assembly form in the wake of its repeated emergence in the past decade. The assembly establishes a radically pluralistic encounter between various experiences or perspectives; it challenges traditional forms of hierarchy and vertical leadership; it emerges between bodies that, in the act of gathering, lay claim to public space; it implies a performative enactment of the very social conditions that allow its emergence in the first place; and finally, the assembly inscribes the idea of 'the people' as the ultimate source of popular sovereignty with a new meaning or content. There clearly are tensions between these various aspects and theorisations of the public assembly. For instance, whereas Lorey conceptualises the assembly as an example of 'presentist' democracy, Frank insists that it fulfils an elementary role in the symbolic representation of 'the people'. As I will argue in the next chapter, the widespread idea that recent social movements such as OWS or 15-M embodied a 'presentist' or even an explicitly anti-representative idea of democracy relies on a limited conception of 'representation' to begin with. Prefigurative democracy does, in fact, require at least some forms of representative claim-making. At the same time, public assemblies do typically emerge in times of democratic crisis, when the legitimacy of representative institutions, or their ability to fulfil this role in practice, is widely disputed. So, if the public assembly can at all be understood to represent 'the people', then it does so in a different way than the forms of representative government whose legitimacy it seeks to contest.

One question that has not been addressed, however, is whether the public assembly can also acquire a sufficiently durable institutional form to accommodate prefigurative democracy in the long term. As I argue in the next section, the experiences of contemporary social movements suggest that it cannot. Many of these movements eventually turned towards a different organisational form: that of the council.

A Prefigurative Form of Government?

The public assembly is typically prefigurative in that it establishes a political form and enacts social conditions that may characterise a radically different, future society in the here and now. However, as is also suggested in several of its theorisations discussed above, assembling is not a continuous practice. If only for practical reasons, it cannot be endlessly maintained. But arguably also at a more conceptual level, assemblies have a fleeting and temporary character. Butler describes them as 'anarchist moments or anarchist passages' that emerge 'when the legitimacy of a regime or its laws is called into question, but when no new legal regimen has yet arrived to take its place' (2015: 75). They 'form unexpectedly and dissolve under voluntary or involuntary conditions' (Butler 2015: 7). A public gathering must inevitably disperse at some point. Although the General Assembly and consensus-oriented decision-making procedures in Zuccotti Park were inspiring examples of prefigurative experimentation, OWS activist Astra Taylor reflects, 'I never believed I had joined a credible example of a better form of government. I had read enough about the history of protest movements to know that the assembly would break down' (Taylor 2019: 50).

This is not to say that such public assemblies cannot lead to meaningful political or societal change. The assembly does intervene in ordinary politics: it mobilises or politicises its participants, informs political debate or public discourse, and provides 'the people' with new sources of identification. It may remind us of the fact that 'another world is possible' and possibly stimulate the imagination of what this 'other world' might look like. To this extent, public assemblies not only have a prefigurative character but they can also have a significant and lasting impact. What the assembly does not do, however, is durably intervene in the institutional form of society in order to reshape it. It does not give rise to new institutional and organisational forms that have the capacity – let alone the pretension or aspiration – to outlive the moment of assembly. But prefigurative democracy must arguably go further than a mere (pre-)enactment of an alternative society in the here and now. Although it does, indeed, have an important performative or aesthetic aspect, prefigurative democracy does more than merely reimagine or enact what a radically different society might look like. As Hardt and Negri argue (2017: 69), a social movement worth its salt should not only seek to 'animate and incarnate new human relationships but also to participate from below in the construction of new institutions'.

Indeed, this is precisely what many recent prefigurative movements set out to do. Although many of them initially emerged in the form of a public assembly, those that were not swiftly repressed often continued to look for a more permanent institutional form. Various examples could be given. In Spain, several branches of the

15-M movement sought to institutionalise at a local level by setting up neighbourhood councils (Flesher Fominaya 2020: 144–6).
Others chose to participate in municipal elections, in an attempt
to democratise the existing representative institutions from within
(Ordónez et al. 2018). In the wake of Nuit Debout and the Yellow
Vest (Gilets jaunes) movement in France, hundreds of so-called 'citizens lists' or 'participatory lists' have emerged on the ballots for
local elections (Dau 2020). Many of them have also been organised
in a nationwide network with the ultimate aim of creating a new and
federated structure for democratic governance alongside established
institutions (Legros 2020). In revolutionary Syria, activists have set
up community councils to both coordinate resistance against Assad's
regime and eventually replace it after its withdrawal (Yassin-Kassab
and Al-Shami 2016: 68–73; Aziz 2013).

The most telling example of such attempts to institutionalise prefigurative democracy is offered by OWS. In the course of October
2011, the occupiers of Zuccotti Park decided to replace their General
Assembly (GA) as its most important body of decision-making with
a 'spokescouncil'. In the first weeks of OWS's existence, all decisions
with respect to both the movement's strategy and the organisation of
daily life within the occupied square were formally taken in a daily
meeting within the occupied square itself. Everyone present was wel-
come to participate in the deliberation – and, in principle, everyone was able to veto any decision. Working groups with different
thematic focuses and responsibilities would work out proposals for
deliberation in the GA and implement its eventual decisions. It soon
became clear that, notwithstanding its strong mobilising potential
and symbolic appeal (Cornell 2011), the GA was unfit for long-
term strategising and efficient organisation (Bray 2013: 88–91). The
occupiers thus turned to a different organisational model, in which
every working group would be represented by an appointed delegate or 'spoke' in a so-called 'spokescouncil'. Delegation rotated
on a regular basis. During council meetings each delegate would
be seated with their own working group members who could provide input to the spokes (Graeber 2013: 232), but only designated
delegates would be allowed to directly address the meeting (Bray
2013: 88). Of course, the introduction of this spokescouncil system
did not remain uncontested. Some members of OWS feared that this
shift would render the decision-making process less accessible and
inclusive, or that the movement would gradually come to resemble a
political party (Gould-Wartofsky 2015: 125; Gray 2011).

One striking feature all of these examples have in common is that, in one way or another, they eventually all opted for a similar institutional form: the council. Some movements and activists tried to engage with already-existing representative councils (mostly at a municipal level) in an attempt to change them from within. Others instead tried to set up their own council system outside of the established liberal-democratic institutions. There are many more examples of recent social movements with prefigurative inclinations that have also employed the council as an institutional form. The EZLN or Zapatista Movement in south Mexico is organised from the bottom up through local 'Good Government Councils' (Oikonomakis 2019: 129). And during the past decade, the Kurdish independence movement has pursued the establishment of confederated council systems against and outside of the nation-state in Turkish (TATORT 2013) as well as north Syrian territory (Knapp et al. 2016: 51–3). In South African shack settlements, citizens organised in local councils or *amakomiti* have established dual power alongside the formal institutions of the state or municipality. As many of these settlements were illegally erected, its inhabitants initially had no choice but to organise themselves. Today, some of these committees operate in conjunction with state or ANC (African National Congress) officials, whereas in other cases the relationship with public offices remains more antagonistic. According to Trevor Ngwane (2021: 146), they may give at least a partial impression of what a democratic workers' state might look like. Another recent example on a much smaller scale is Cooperation Jackson, a network of worker cooperatives in Jackson, Mississippi, that seeks to establish a solidarity-based economy and democratic self-determination for the impoverished black community (Akuno and Nangwaya 2017). At an institutional level, Cooperation Jackson has pursued different complementary strategies: on the one hand, several of its leaders have successfully taken part in municipal and mayoral elections. At the same time, the organisation has also set up durable 'people's assemblies' that give input to city-wide policy debates and provide a platform for participatory democracy and the bottom-up organisation of various cooperatives.

These various examples suggest that, in the long term, the institutional form of the democratic council better caters to a prefigurative democracy than the public assembly. But why would this be the case? In the next section I return to the political thought of Arendt. Throughout her oeuvre, she too grapples with this problem of how the distinctive freedom, open-endedness and spontaneity of political action could survive its own institutionalisation (Kalyvas 2008: 192). In an attempt to resolve this problem, Arendt discusses various historical forms of government – ranging from the ancient Greek *polis* to the early US Republic. In the next section, I briefly reconstruct a number of features that she attributes to these various governmental forms. Arendt eventually hypothesises that only one organisational form is able to resolve the tension between action and institutionalisation: that of the council, which emerged in various revolutions throughout the nineteenth and twentieth century.[1]

Between Action and Institution: From the *Polis* to Revolutionary Councils

Arendt's conception of political action is radically open-ended and characterised by an immediate experience of freedom. But this also means that there is always a certain fleetingness to it: the impact or outcome of one's deeds and words can never be foretold. We inevitably act in a condition of uncertainty about where, when and how our political practices will come to an end. Political action thus is precarious in the sense that it has nothing but its own 'actuality' to hold on to (Arendt 1958: 206). Consequently, those engaged in political action often seek to sustain practice as long as possible. But how can such a fleeting moment be kept alive? And how have others tried to resolve this tension between the open-endedness of political action and its need for a durable institutional form?

A first historical form of government that Arendt often engages with is the *polis*. It is sometimes suggested that Arendt idealises the ancient Greek city-state. Upon closer inspection, however, it becomes clear that it is not so much the institutional form of the *polis* that intrigues her, but the idea of political action and community by which it is underpinned. According to Arendt, the ancient Greeks did not see their *polis* primarily as a material or juridical space. It rather was construed as a space that appears between people whenever they convene to act and speak in each other's presence. As Pericles put it, 'wherever you go, you will be a *polis*' (Arendt 1958: 198). What distinguishes the *polis* from other spheres, then, is that it was characterised by *isonomia* – or the principle that everyone is free to act as equals in the public sphere (Balibar 2014: 169). It is by virtue of a shared citizenship that, in this realm, no one could rule or be ruled (Arendt 1958: 32; 2005a: 118; 2006a: 20–1). Seen from this perspective, then, the formal laws and institutions of the *polis* merely served to accommodate and protect this space of freedom and equality. Arendt compares the ancient Greek conception of law (or *nomos*) with a city wall that encircles the political realm – thus giving the deeds and words of its citizens a less fleeting and more durable character. However, this 'wall-like law' was itself not considered a subject of political debate: constructing these boundaries of bricks and laws was a fabrication process, and not the matter of politics itself (1958: 194–5).

An entirely different conception of law, in this respect, is implied in the political structure of the Roman Republic. For the Romans, law (or *lex*) had the form of a contract or treaty that originated in the foundation of their body politic (Arendt 2005a: 183). It established a 'formal relationship between people rather than [a] wall that separates them from others' (Arendt 1958: 63n62). Whereas the Greek *nomos* primarily served to contain and protect a distinctive political realm, the Romans did not differentiate between a 'pre-*polis* experience' of political action on the one hand, and its accommodation or protection by law and institutions on the other. Instead, they continuously returned to the founding contract on which their Republic was based, and to the principles that 'inspirited' this original beginning (Arendt 2006e: 120).[2] The Romans were well aware, however, that in order to preserve this original foundation it had to be continuously amended, expanded and augmented (Arendt 2006a:194). Legislation thus was not seen as a precondition or by-product of politics, but instead as its very matter (Arendt 1958: 63).

This interest in law as a foundation of the body politic is echoed in modern republicanism, and especially in the early US Republic. Although the American revolutionaries deliberately placed themselves in the Roman tradition, what distinguished them is that they could not refer back to an original foundation that had been passed on from generation to generation (Gündoğdu 2015: 174–5). As they had to found an entirely new republic, they thus were forced to seek the source of its legitimisation within itself. For the first time, the foundation of a body politic had 'occurred in broad daylight to be witnessed by all who were present' (Arendt 2006a: 197). This becomes most apparent in one of the opening statements of the *Declaration of Independence*: 'We hold these truths to be self-evident, that all men are created equal, that they are endowed by their Creator with certain unalienable Rights, that among these are

Life, Liberty, and the pursuit of Happiness.' In Arendt's reading, the first words of this performative statement immediately save it from its own arbitrariness, whilst avoiding any appeal to an originary source of authority (Kalyvas 2008: 246–7; Negri 1999: 16). It was among the revolutionaries assembled that a certain truth could be *held* as 'self-evident' (Arendt 2006a: 184–5). Its foundational principles were given by neither God nor tradition, but 'rested exclusively in the power of the performative "We hold"' (Honig 1993: 107). This revolutionary moment thus contained 'two elements which to us seem irreconcilable and even contradictory' (Arendt 2006a: 214): the exhilarating experience of making an entirely new beginning on the one hand, and the need to found it in a stable and durable legal structure on the other.

However, even the American revolutionaries proved unable to sustain this precarious balance between action and institutionalisation over time. Prior to and during the revolution, many citizens had been able to engage in public deliberation and self-organisation through their townships meetings. Even though the revolutionaries were to found an entirely new body politic, they could draw from their previous experiences in local wards and councils to give it a stable and durable institutional framework (Arendt 2006a: 158; Kalyvas 2008: 227). After the revolution, however, the 'founding fathers' hurried to install a system of representative government – whose primary aim, according to Arendt, was not so much to facilitate public participation through delegation, but instead to establish 'a popularly controlled rule of the people's representatives over the people' (Arendt 2006a: 228). In the newly founded republic there thus 'was no space reserved, no room left for the exercise of precisely those qualities which had been instrumental in building it' (Arendt 2006a: 224). It deprived the Americans of their 'proudest possession': the ability to act politically, to engage in public affairs and to begin something new (Arendt 2006a: 231).

In short, none of these historical forms of government – the ancient Greek *polis*, the Roman Republic, or eventually the US Republic – was able to definitively resolve the tension between action and institutionalisation. This is why, in various places scattered throughout her oeuvre, Arendt turns to another form of government: that of the revolutionary council. From the local townhall meetings in revolutionary America and the *sociétés* or revolutionary clubs during the French Revolution of 1789, to the Paris Commune of 1871; and from the *soviets* during the Russian Revolution of 1905 and the February Revolution of 1917, to the Kronstadt Rebellion, the Spartacist *Räte* of 1919, and the revolutionary councils in Hungary in 1956 – in all these various events throughout the nineteenth and twentieth century, Arendt argues, the people 'have come forth, albeit never successfully, with another new form of government: the system of people's councils to take the place of the Continental party system' (Arendt 1958: 216; see also Arendt 2006a: 248). Although the council form has thus reappeared in virtually every important revolution of the past centuries, according to Arendt there is no immediate relationship between these revolutionary events. It emerged whenever the people were able to 'follow their own political devices without being spoon-fed by a party or steered by a government' (Arendt 2018c: 133).

Although Arendt rarely engages in speculation on the ideal political form of society, she nevertheless admits to having 'a romantic sympathy' with the revolutionary council (Arendt 2018b: 465), which she regards as one of the few appealing alternatives to electoral-representative government as we know it today (Arendt 1972b: 231). Various factors may have contributed to her preference for the council form. Arendt's mother had a great admiration for Rosa Luxemburg, who played a key role in the November revolution, and to whom Arendt would later devote an entire essay (Arendt 1968d; Young-Bruehl 2004: 27–8). Arendt's second husband, Heinrich Blücher, whom she met as a political refugee in Paris in the 1930s, had participated in the German revolution of 1918–19 as a member of Luxemburg's *Spartakusbund* (Muldoon 2016: 765–7; Young-Bruehl 2004: 124–5). It is also argued that Arendt's interest in councils and federalist forms of organisation were informed by her experiences with *kibbutzim* in Palestine, which she visited as an official for a Zionist organisation in 1935 (Muldoon 2016: 777). But it arguably was a historical event later on in her life that most aroused Arendt's interest in the council form: the Hungarian uprising of 1956 (Popp-Madsen 2021: 135–6). She included a new chapter on these events in the second edition of *Origins of Totalitarianism* (but again removed it from later editions), and returned to the phenomenon of revolutionary councils in several of her later writings, most notably in the last chapter of *On Revolution*. In these various places, Arendt draws the contours of what she calls a 'council system'.

In the following section I first reconstruct a number of key features that Arendt attributes to the revolutionary councils of the past centuries, and draw a comparison with the public assemblies of recent social movements. I argue that Arendt's council system provides a promising organisational form for prefigurative democracy as it has the potential to reconcile the freedom and open-endedness that inheres in political action with its need for institutionalisation.

A Lost Treasure: Arendt's 'Council System'

If Arendt's proposal for a council system is vague and sweeping (Canovan 1992: 237), this appears to be deliberate. Rather than to meticulously spell out the exact preconditions and features of the council form, she argues, 'it certainly is wiser to say with Jefferson, "Begin them only for a single purpose; they will soon show for what others they are the best instruments"' (2006a: 271). However, by reconstructing some of its key aspects it may nevertheless be possible to gain valuable insights about the possible form and role of institutions in radical democracy (Lederman 2019: 183). In some respects, the council may be understood to formalise or institutionalise certain features that we also encountered in recent public assemblies. First, Arendt claims that revolutionary councils emerge spontaneously and do not follow a pre-set plan. It is an intrinsically open-ended form of organisation that yields a high measure of spontaneity. Second, the council defies any form of hierarchy and rulership. In consequence, third, it implies a critique of traditional forms of political organisation, such as the political party. Fourth, Arendt attributes an important pedagogical function to the council. But there are also significant differences between the public assembly and the council form. A fifth feature is that the council does not serve a transitory or instrumental role, but is meant to outlive the revolutionary moment from which it emerges. Sixth, the council form can be employed in any social context and environment. It thus has an important politicising role. This also means, finally, that (unlike the public assembly) the council may strike a precarious balance between political action and its need for a durable institutional form. It may thus resolve the tension between action and its institutionalisation. Let me flesh out these various characteristics of the council form below.

A first feature of the revolutionary council, according to Arendt, is that it emerges spontaneously (Arendt 1972b: 231) and that none of its historical occurrences were planned or anticipated (Arendt 2006a: 248). Moreover, as much as the council is not the outcome of a pre-set plan, it does not serve to implement one, either. Arendt claims that in the Hungarian uprisings of 1956, 'no programs, points or manifestos played any role' (Arendt 2018c: 131). This inherent spontaneity and open-endedness of the council form stands in stark contrast with the theoretical model of revolution that would become dominant in the twentieth century: the idea that it was to be led by a professional organisation, which carried out a detailed programme (Arendt 2006a: 254). Arendt's insistence on the spontaneity and open-endedness of these revolutions resonates with one of Marx's observations on the Paris Commune of 1871. The Communards, he argued, had 'no ready-made utopias to introduce *par décret du peuple*' (2010a: 213). Their organisational form and political principles could only be found in political practice itself. In a similar vein, during the German revolution of 1918–19 many council communists held that the council form would naturally emerge as an evident form of self-organisation (Däumig 2012: 43; Gluckstein 2011: 33).

It must be stressed, however, that spontaneity or open-endedness should not be confused with a disdain for organisation per se (Breines 1989). As Rodrigo Nunes argues in the context of contemporary protest movements, they are rather two sides of the same coin. If one assumes that history does not run its inevitable course, and that the exact outcomes or consequences of one's actions can never be predicted, then the need for organisation in order to accommodate action becomes inevitable (Nunes 2021: 122). 'It is only by organising itself in however makeshift a way that any kind of spontaneous initiative can produce effects,' Nunes argues, 'yet it is only because an inclination to do something already exists that there is anything to organise' (Nunes 2021: 156). In a similar vein, Arendt refuses any such dichotomy between organisation and spontaneity. Rather, it was precisely the high rate of organisation within revolutionary movements and their ability to adapt to new situations that allowed these councils to spontaneously emerge in the first place.

A second characteristic of the council is that it defies any form of hierarchy or rulership. Arendt insists that in many of its historical occurrences, citizens 'were not content to discuss and "enlighten themselves" about measures that were already taken by parties or assemblies; they consciously and explicitly desired the direct participation of every citizen in the public affairs of the country' (2006a: 255). She thus draws a direct connection between the right to participate in debate and engage in public deliberation on the one hand, and the principle of self-organisation on the other. A formal right to free speech is meaningless as long as one is not also able to 'determine the political course' of society (Arendt 1972b: 232). This also implies that citizens must have the ability to speak and address each other as equals (Vergara 2020: 187–8). Thus perceived, the council may indeed be regarded as a modern realisation of the ancient Greek principle of *isonomia* – or 'to be free from the inequality present in rulership and to move in a sphere where neither rule nor being ruled [exist]' (Arendt 1958: 33; see also Balibar 2014: 173). It is also at this point that Arendt's idea of a council system differs most significantly from representative government as we know it today. The latter is merely based on the principle that 'the few rule, at least supposedly, in the interest of the many' (Arendt 2006a: 261). The council, on the other hand, establishes political space devoid of rulership. But this does not mean that it should be understood as an attempt to formalise or perpetuate a state of unruliness. More accurately, Arendt suggests that the council is based on an entirely different conception of 'rule' or ἀρχή – namely, the ability of citizens to determine and rearticulate the principles on which their political order is based (Arendt 2006a: 205; Markell 2006: 13).

It is also precisely for this reason that political parties, and other hierarchical forms of political organisation, hardly played any role in these revolutionary councils. This is a third feature of the council, which again is shared by the public assemblies of recent occupy movements. Arendt claims that the councils challenged 'the party system as such' (2006a: 257). In fact, as Oskar Anweiler (one of Arendt's most important sources on this subject) argues, the council form historically predated the emergence of the party as a revolutionary agent (Anweiler 1974). It was only after the October Revolution that the party came to be regarded as the revolutionary agent par excellence. In the Soviet Union, which derived its name from these early councils or *soviets*, the council form could only outlive the revolution because it was formally subsumed under the party-state (Boggs 1977a: 101). However, even after 1917 council communists continued to dismiss the party form as a remnant of the old bourgeois order (Popp-Madsen and Kets 2021: 168). Otto Rühle argued that parties merely served an electoral-representative role (Rühle 2021: 91). Whereas the revolution could only result from workers' self-organisation, parties would always try to claim it as their own (Rühle 2021: 95). Arendt shares this concern: the aim of political parties has never been to empower or activate people, but to muster their support and act in their stead (Arendt 2006a: 260–5). Whereas both public assemblies and councils spring forth from political action itself, parties tend to see the revolution as their own product, and will always seek to lead it in the name of the people.

Since Arendt is a prominent critic of representative government and party politics, it is often assumed that she rejects political representation *tout court*. However, she by no means dismisses any form of representation. In fact, Arendt acknowledges that councils fulfil a certain representative role as well (Arendt 2018c: 137; Kalyvas 2008: 282). She imagines her council system as a pyramidal, federated system whose participants are self-selected at the lower levels and delegated at the higher ones (Arendt 2006a: 269–70; Disch 2011a: 352).[3] In this respect, Arendt stands in a longer tradition that favours federated or bottom-up forms of organisation (Van Outryve d'Ydewalle 2019). However, since it is the primary task of a council system to accommodate public debate and deliberation, according to Arendt, it follows that the delegates at its higher echelons cannot simply transfer the opinions or preferences of their constituency. They must be able to engage in some level of deliberation and decision-making themselves, and to make decisions on their constituencies' behalf. In Arendt's conception, the council form thus arguably holds 'a middle ground between what is sometimes described as the distinction between representation and delegation' (Lederman 2019: 188).

A fourth feature of the council is that it fulfils an important pedagogical function. This insight is derived from Rosa Luxemburg, who had a strong impact on Arendt's idea of the council (Blätter and Marti 2005). Although Arendt clearly was not a Marxist, it is argued that she and Luxemburg at least shared a certain republican inspiration (Arendt 1968d: 54). This also implies a pedagogical view of citizenship. Since long before the October Revolution, Luxemburg consistently criticised Lenin's 'mechanistic' idea of revolutionary organisation – which, she held, was largely modelled after the existing state form, the military and the factory (Luxemburg 1961a: 90). Whereas the Bolsheviks assumed that a vanguard of experienced revolutionaries should politicise and lead the working class towards liberation, Luxemburg insisted that 'the organisation of revolutionary actions can and must be learnt only in the revolution itself, much like swimming can only be learnt in the water' (1974b: 524, my translation; see also Nixon 2018: 105). When, during the November Revolution of 1918, revolutionary workers' councils emerged in various German cities, Luxemburg immediately recognised their essential pedagogical function. It was often far from clear for what purpose these council systems had been established, or how they should be operated. Yet, she argued, 'this is not a lack, but rather the normal state of affairs. . . . The workers will learn in the school of action' (1971: 406).[4] Thus perceived, the council also caters to the ideal of what the ancient Greeks used to call *paideia* (παιδεία): the lifelong political education of citizens through participation and the exercise of critical thinking in the public realm (Bookchin 1995a: 63–4; Castoriadis 1997: 11). Recent public assemblies fulfilled a similar pedagogical function, albeit temporarily. But this is at the same time an important difference between the assembly and the council: if *paideia* must indeed be regarded as a lifelong and open-ended practice, then it arguably requires a more durable institutional framework in which learning practices can be nourished and sustained.

A fifth feature of the council is that it does not serve a transitory or instrumental role, but instead is often meant to outlive the revolutionary moment from which it emerges. In Arendt's reading, the council proposes itself as an 'entirely new form of government' (Arendt 2006a: 241; Gluckstein 2011: 45). This view of the council stands in stark contrast with that of most orthodox Marxists, who merely see it as a revolutionary instrument. Marx and Lenin interpreted the Paris Commune as a first attempt to establish a transitory proletarian state that should eventually give rise to a post-political, communist society (Lenin 1987: 312). The Bolsheviks, in turn, discarded the *soviets* as soon as their strategic purpose had been fulfilled (Anweiler 1974: 165). Rosa Luxemburg and the council communists, on the other hand, regarded their revolutionary councils as the prefiguration of a future workers' state (Muldoon 2020: 161; Nixon 2018: 52; Popp-Madsen and Kets 2021: 168–9). Arendt too insists that the federated council system, which emerged at so many different revolutionary movements throughout the past centuries, 'clearly intended to survive the revolution' (Arendt 2006a: 248). Its aim was not merely to topple the bourgeois state, but to replace it – or, in other words, to reconstitute society by imposing itself as its new political form. And it is also at this point that the council may be understood to differ from the public assembly. As discussed above, these assemblies are often precisely regarded as temporary organisational forms or 'anarchist moments' that briefly interrupt the political status quo. If these assemblies were prefigurative, it thus was mostly in a performative sense: they enacted the social and political conditions in which a radically different society might be able to emerge. The councils in Arendt's analysis, on the other hand, were also prefigurative in that they sought to provide an institutional framework through which society could be durably re-instituted. It should therefore not surprise us that many recent protest movements eventually shifted to the council as a form of organisation, in an attempt to prolong and expand their prefigurative experiment.

A sixth important feature of the council is that it can emerge in any social context and environment. Although, in principle, the assembly form is not limited to the street, in the context of contemporary social movements it is first and foremost associated with the occupation of public spaces. Ultimately, Butler (2015: 137–8) argues, the street or public square best accommodates the performative dimension of assembling. One of the central features that Arendt attributes to the revolutionary councils of the past century, on the other hand, is precisely that they have 'sprung up everywhere, completely independent of one another' (2006a: 258). They emerged in factories and workshops, but also in neighbourhoods and residential buildings, universities, coffee houses, public offices, military barracks and so on. 'Wherever people were together in whatever kind of public space, they formed councils, and the councils in each of these quite disparate groups transformed a merely haphazard coming together of people into a political institution' (Arendt 2018c: 138). Councils can thus emerge anywhere, at any time, and they are by no means mutually restrictive (Marchart 2005: 135–6; Schaap 2021: 17). Unlike the Republican Senate or bourgeois parliament, which does not tolerate a similar body alongside it, a single council does not claim exclusive jurisdiction over a territory or constituency. And unlike the Greek *polis*, it does not derive its political legitimacy from a law that immures and protects a uniquely political space. A single council, in other words, does not offer an exclusive or sufficient foundation on which an entire political order can be erected. It instead has the potential to politicise *any* activity, environment or shared occupation – any 'accidental proximity', as Arendt calls it (2006a: 259) – and to coexist with other, similarly politicised spaces. Whereas any other form of government implies the concentration of power in a limited set of institutions or offices, in a federated council system power can and must always be further divided. It ultimately derives its authority from its ability to organise from the ground – or, rather, from a plurality of grounds – upward (Arendt 1972b: 230–1).

It is at this point that Arendt's account of revolutionary councils also differs most emphatically from that of council communists (Popp-Madsen and Kets 2021: 173). Arendt is merely interested in the council as a political institution, and not in its economic functions. She claims that, in most cases, the councils were 'infinitely more interested in the political than in the social aspect of revolution' (Arendt 2006a: 258). In her analysis of the Hungarian uprising, for instance, she distinguishes between workers' councils, which focused on economic matters, and the revolutionary councils that served a political purpose – although she does acknowledge that the difference may not have been as clear-cut in reality (Arendt 2018c: 135). Arendt is not the only one to have developed such a political reading of the revolutionary council. Cornelius Castoriadis also argues that the Hungarian councils emerged in various contexts, and not merely in factories or other sites of production. 'Their exemplary character [did] *not* stem from their being *workers'* councils', he claims, but rather from their strongly participatory character (Castoriadis 1993: 260).

It is argued that this one-sided emphasis on the political features of revolutionary councils is historically inaccurate at best – or even borders on fiction (Muldoon 2020: 9–10; Sitton 1987: 97). But the Arendtian distinction between revolutionary and workers' councils is underpinned by a more encompassing theoretical view. Throughout her oeuvre, Arendt consistently maintains that politics and economics are of an entirely different nature. Economics is typically the realm of fabrication: it serves particular, predefined ends. The aim of economic management thus is to solve problems or overcome certain limitations towards the realisation of such ends. According to Arendt this may inevitably require a certain measure of verticality, and coordination or control from above. For this reason, she argues, 'the question of whether economic matters . . . can be handled by councils – whether, in other words, it is possible to run factories under the management and ownership of their own workers, we shall have to leave open' (2018c: 135). But politics, as we have seen, is distinctively open-ended, and should never be confused with management (Sitton 1987: 89). The aim of the latter is to ameliorate social relations, to settle economic differences, or to coordinate production processes. To put it in Arendt's terms, management is precisely ends-oriented, and typically belongs in a sphere of necessity (Arendt 2006a: 266). Politics, however, seeks to prolong itself over time, and implies that its participants act as equals among each other. Though historically contestable, what thus informs Arendt's distinction between economic and political councils is her wish to see the latter as durable institutional spaces in which political action can take place and where differences can be enacted. Their role is to politicise different 'accidental proximities' – or, a range of social contexts and environments (Vatter 2007: 78).

It must be stressed that this politicising function cannot be distinguished from its institutional form. One of the key insights that Arendt claims to derive from Luxemburg is 'the important idea that good organization does not precede action but is the product of it' (Nettl 2019: 504; also quoted in Arendt 1968d: 52). At various moments throughout the past centuries, revolutionary councils have emerged from practice. Their institutions and procedures were not drawn 'around an already existing public space', as we saw was the case in the Greek *polis* (Arendt 1958: 198). Instead, they 'were always organs of order as much as organs of action' – both form and content, the subject or moment of politics as well as its institutional space (Arendt 2006a: 25).[5] It thus follows that the institutional form, laws and procedures of these councils were continuously subject to debate and revision in political practice itself. In this respect, Arendt indeed sees the council as a radical exponent of the republican tradition. Politics pertains precisely to the formation, and continuous augmentation, of the institutional foundations of a community (Honig 1993: 112). The council thus best accommodates prefigurative democracy in that it perceives itself as an 'unfinished project' that always remains open to new beginnings (Kalyvas 2008: 278).

This brings us to the seventh and last important characteristic of the council: namely, that it has the potential to resolve the tension between the open-ended character of prefigurative democracy and its need to acquire a durable institutional form in the long term. As argued, one of the key problems that inform Arendt's political thought is how political action can give rise to a stable and institutional form without losing its distinctive open-endedness and spontaneity. The council offers a solution in that it remains open to continuous amendment or augmentation – thus keeping alive the revolutionary spirit from which it originally emerged. It mediates between constituent power and constituted power (Muldoon 2011: 398; Popp-Madsen 2021: 141). There is always a 'possibility of dis-ordering the existing order and reinventing new institutional frameworks, even if this may generate instability' (Tomba

2018: 116). At the same time, the council offers an institutional space in which this constant reinvention or augmentation can take place. It thus avoids the 'exhaustion of the constituent power in normal politics' on the one hand (Popp-Madsen 2021: 158), whilst stabilising or pacifying it in a more robust institutional framework on the other (Kalyvas 2008: 276). One may argue that, by striking a precarious balance between revolutionary openness and durable self-organisation, the council reconciles several key aspects that Arendt attributes to various historical forms of government. It combines the Greek principle of *isonomia*, or a political sphere devoid of rulership, with the republican practice of continuous augmentation and re-institutionalisation (Vergara 2020: 204). This may also explain why several recent social movements eventually turned from the public assembly to the council as a form of organisation. Whilst retaining several key features of the assembly (its open-ended, pedagogical and non-hierarchical character), it also allowed these movements to make a next step towards the durable institutionalisation of prefigurative democracy.

However, there is also one important feature of the council that remains largely overlooked in Arendt's account: namely, its symbolic function. As argued above, Arendt does recognise the representative role of councils (or, to be more precise, of its individual members). But this is merely at the level of decision-making and delegation. Something that she does not sufficiently address is how councils as political bodies may also symbolically stand for a larger social group – such as a neighbourhood, a body of workers or employees, or a social class. Such an understanding of the council as a symbolic body of representation can be derived from the work of Rosa Luxemburg.

Luxemburg has often been credited with being one of the few revolutionary Marxists who defended the right to free press, freedom of speech and democratic representation in her polemics against Lenin and Trotsky. According to the Bolsheviks, parliaments and other representative bodies could only reflect the popular will at the very moment of election. As their strategic use was limited, these bodies thus were to be discarded as soon as their revolutionary role had been played out (Luxemburg 1961b: 60–2). Although she was by no means a liberal democrat herself, Luxemburg instead maintained that there was a necessary and legitimate role for representative democracy within a revolutionary politics. She therefore insisted that her own party, the newly founded Communist

Party of Germany (KPD), continue to pursue an electoral strategy (Luxemburg 1971: 399; Nixon 2018: 45–6). Luxemburg's advocacy of representative democracy was underpinned by a rather idiosyncratic conception of political representation. According to her, representative bodies did not merely serve to voice or transmit the interests or preferences of their constituency. In addition to keeping a check on the 'pulse-beat of the political life of the masses' (Luxemburg 1961b: 62), they also embodied the popular will in a more symbolic or aesthetic sense, as 'the living fluid of the popular mood continuously flows around the representative bodies, penetrates them, guides them' (Luxemburg 1961b: 60). This also explains Luxemburg's appreciation for the soldiers' and workers' councils that emerged during the November Revolution. These councils represented their constituency in a direct or participatory fashion. Its elected members were recallable at any time, and stood in immediate contact with their support base in workshops and factories (Luxemburg 2012: 104; Tomba 2018: 108). But they also represented their support base in a more symbolic sense. 'Only in a permanent and lively exchange between the masses and their political bodies,' Luxemburg argued, 'can the state be filled with a socialist spirit' (Luxemburg 2012: 101). Luxemburg's conception of the council thus seems to be underpinned by a double conception of representation: on the one hand, it pertains to the election or delegation of representatives at various levels of decision-making; on the other hand, it also seems to refer to the way in which a representative body as such embodies the interests, grievances and identity of a social class. Luxemburg's councils also stood for something larger than themselves – in the same way as recent public assemblies in Tahrir Square or Zuccotti Park presented a 'living image' of the people that they claimed to represent (Frank 2021: 70). I will return to this specific aspect of representation and its relevance for prefigurative democracy in the next chapter.

Conclusion: Towards a Prefigurative Democracy

How can prefigurative democracy be institutionalised, and thus acquire a more durable form, whilst maintaining its distinctive open-endedness? Recent prefigurative movements often organised in public assemblies. This organisational form indeed has a number of important prefigurative characteristics, as the public assembly enacts the political form and social conditions of a possible future society.

Yet, as argued, the public assembly often has a temporary character. Various recent movements have therefore gradually turned to organise in spokescouncils, city councils and neighbourhood assemblies. Arendt's discussion of revolutionary councils throughout the nineteenth and twentieth century helps us to understand how prefigurative democracy may acquire a more durable and stable institutional form whilst preserving some of the key features that characterise the public assembly.

On the one hand, the council may be understood to nourish a number of features that have also been attributed to the public assembly: its distinctive open-endedness and spontaneous character, an absence of rulership and hierarchy, its disdain for electoral-representative government and political parties, and an important pedagogical function. But in addition to this, and unlike the public assembly, revolutionary councils seek to prefigure a durable political structure as they intend to outlive the moment of revolution. They also have a broader politicising role in that they can emerge in any social context or environment and serve to politicise these various 'proximities'. Finally, councils are 'organs of order as much as organs of action' (Arendt 2006a: 25), since they are open to continuous self-reform and augmentation. Council democracy may thus be understood to maintain a precarious balance between the extraordinary and insurrectionary moment of political foundation on the one hand, and a 'normal politics' that grants a certain measure of durability and stability to our public lives on the other. It combines key features that Arendt attributes to various historical forms of government, such as the ancient Greek principle of *isonomia* and the Roman idea of politics as a continuous augmentation of its own foundations.

My point is not to argue that, when left to itself, prefigurative democracy must necessarily give rise to a council system. Nor is it to claim that the council is the only possible institutional form through which it may acquire more durability and stability, or even to suggest that prefigurative democracy should necessarily seek its own institutionalisation. There may be good reasons not to prolong a prefigurative movement or practice. But there often appears to be a strong urge to retain the prefigurative moment and to institutionalise it in one way or the other. Moreover, as argued, there is a certain tendency in prefigurative practices towards the establishment of political councils. Arendt's political conception of the council may help us to look beyond the public assembly or the activist tent camp and imagine what a more durable prefigurative democracy might look like in the long term.

Of course, this inevitably also gives rise to new questions. Assemblies and councils do not only establish a public space that accommodates the exchange of ideas and public deliberation, as Arendt is keen to stress. They also embody a larger social group and speak on its behalf. How can such a political body represent something or someone that is larger than itself? One more feature that public assemblies and councils seem to have in common is that both present a symbolic image of the group or people that they claim to stand for. Although Arendt recognises the representative function of councils, this symbolic aspect of representation seems to escape her account. In order to understand this representative aspect of prefigurative democracy we need to draw on a different strand of radical-democratic thought. In the next chapter I therefore turn to Ernesto Laclau's theory of political representation.

Chapter 4
Embodiment: Prefiguration and Synecdochal Representation

When on 25 January 2011 Egyptian revolutionaries occupied Tahrir Square, no one could have predicted that the image of the occupied square would become such an important signifier for protest and contestation in the ensuing years. Throughout the following decade, the example of Tahrir Square would continue to inspire many occupy movements around the world: from the Spanish 15-M movement and the Greek anti-austerity movement to Occupy Wall Street (OWS), and from the Gezi Park protests in Istanbul and the so-called 'Umbrella Revolution' in Hong Kong, to Nuit Debout in Paris. Notwithstanding the obvious differences between these movements, they clearly did refer to each other – and to the iconic occupation of Tahrir Square in particular – as an important source of inspiration (Graeber 2013: 237). But obviously, the occupied Tahrir Square not only had an important symbolic value to many protesters around the world; for many Egyptian people, the 'Republic of Tahrir' and its temporary inhabitants also embodied the grievances and hopes of a significant part of their country's population. To them, the people assembled on this square were the true representatives of the popular will (Frank 2021: 70–1). One may argue that even Hosni Mubarak implicitly acknowledged this when he finally gave in to the protesters' demand and announced his resignation.

But if those assembled on Tahrir Square (or any other occupied square, for that matter) can indeed be understood to have represented the people at large, then what concept of representation was implied here? After all, they clearly did not have a formal mandate to speak or act on behalf of 'the people'. This is even more complex in the context of recent movements such as OWS and the 15-M movement, which were often very critical of electoral-representative democracy, as it prevents citizens from actively partaking in democratic politics.

As argued in the previous chapter, they sought to prefigure a more participatory and decentralised form of democracy. It is sometimes suggested that these movements were thus against political representation *tout court* (Lorey 2020; Sitrin and Azzellini 2014; Tormey 2015). However, it seems evident that their activist tent camps and prefigurative experiments also implied a strong representative claim in their own right (Saward 2010). These movements arguably did stand for something or for someone else – and arguably even spoke or acted for them. But this suggests that prefigurative democracy requires a very specific, non-mandated form of political representation.

How may prefigurative democracy be understood to challenge and alter our understanding of political representation? Although recent occupy movements such as OWS and 15-M were indeed very critical of electoral-representative government in its current state, this may not warrant the widespread claim that their prefigurative practices were entirely devoid of, or necessarily opposed to, any form of political representation. In the next section I first engage with this predominant reading of the occupy movements. Although many (but by no means all) of them indeed seem to have shared a critique of electoral-representative democracy in its current state, I argue, this should not be too easily equated with a dismissal of political representation *tout court*. But in order to appreciate this, we first need to gain more conceptual clarity on what exactly 'representation' means, since the term is used and defined in a myriad of ways. In the second section I therefore disentangle two different conceptions of representation. On the one hand, 'representation' is often understood as a relation in which one agent 'acts for' or on behalf of someone else – usually on the basis of a formal mandate. But on the other hand, it may also refer to a descriptive or symbolic relation, in which the represented acquires a particular meaning through the process of representation.

In the third section I apply these notions of representation as 'acting for' and 'standing for' to the politics of recent occupy movements, and argue why both are present (implicitly as well as explicitly) in their prefigurative practices and rhetoric. I then continue to develop a concept of non-mandated political representation as 'acting for' that is particularly important for our understanding of prefigurative democracy and the politics of recent occupy movements. Engaging with the political thought of Ernesto Laclau, I argue that this idea of representation has a typically synecdochal form. The synecdoche is a figure of speech in which a part is understood to 'stand for' a larger whole. Rather than being a mere symbolic or rhetorical form, the synecdoche also has an important political function in that it constitutes new shared discourses and identities. In the fifth section I further develop Laclau's concept of synecdochal representation in the context of recent occupy movements. I explore three features of prefigurative democracy that each have important synecdochal implications: the articulation of representative claims, the creation or reappropriation of commons, and the experimentation with participative democracy and decision-making. I reconstruct how these various features and their synecdochal implications played out in the rhetoric and prefigurative practices of recent occupy movements. These examples illustrate why synecdochal representation has a prefigurative function in its own right: whereas the whole is understood to be represented by one of its parts, it is this representative part that inscribes it with a particular meaning. Synecdochal representation thus takes as its referent the very social and political conditions that are co-constituted by the representative claim itself. In the concluding section I turn to contemporary debates on the relation between participatory or 'horizontalist' forms of democracy on the one hand, and representative or 'verticalist' forms on the other. Rather than belonging to one side of this dichotomy between horizontalism and verticalism, I argue, prefigurative democracy may instead be understood to combine these aspects. But first, let me engage with the contemporary theoretical debate on the representative role of recent occupy movements.

They Don't Represent Us? Occupy Movements and Representative Democracy

Consider this fragment from an 'FAQ' that was issued by the General Assembly of OWS:

> Occupy Wall Street is an exercise in 'direct democracy.' We feel we can no longer make our voices heard as we watch our votes for change usher in the same old power structure time and again. Since we can no longer trust our elected representatives to represent us rather than their large donors, we are creating a microcosm of what democracy *really* looks like. We do this to inspire one another to speak up. It is a reminder to our representatives and the moneyed interests that direct them: we the people still know our power. (New York City General Assembly 2011: 1)

This text, like many of the statements issued and slogans used by occupy movements, is open to various interpretations. According to many political theorists and social movement scholars, it suggests that OWS defies representative government. The statement instead appeals to an image of 'what democracy *really* looks like': a more participatory form of democracy, which is juxtaposed to electoral-representative democracy in its current (and, indeed, flawed) state. These occupy movements therefore sought to prefigure alternative forms of democracy in practice. They used consensus-oriented decision-making procedures and forms of public deliberation (Cornell 2012; Polletta and Hoban 2016), set up General Assemblies and spokescouncils (Bray 2013; Graeber 2013), and organised through various alternative, online and offline networks (Castells 2015; Swann 2018). Thus perceived, these activist tent camps shaped a 'microcosm' in which its inhabitants' ideal of an alternative democratic society could be enacted.

In this respect, it should indeed not surprise us that these occupy movements, and more specifically their attempts to prefigure alternative democratic structures and practices, have often been understood to imply a rejection of representative democracy per se. According to Michael Hardt and Antonio Negri, these protesters did not merely contest particular neoliberal policies or austerity measures in the wake of the financial crisis; their critique of democracy in its current state struck at a much more fundamental level, since 'representative structures and liberal governance regimes [were] all thrown into question' (2012: 43–4). Some claim that this critique was not limited to electoral-representative democracy in its current state, as it more broadly applied to the logic of political representation *tout court*. Isabell Lorey presents these occupy movements as the most recent exponents of a typically 'presentist' view of democracy. They did not give any 're-presentation of the whole, unified people nor of a normative political idea' (2014: 60; see also Lorey 2020: 14–15), but instead sought to establish a more inclusive and participatory democratic practice in the present. The underlying assumption here is that 'representative democracy' is essentially an oxymoron. Representation categorically precludes the people from immediate participation in the political process (Hardt and Negri 2004: 244–5; Rancière 2006: 53; Tormey 2015: 149). 'Real democracy', on the other hand, presupposes a horizontalist conception of organisation and a rejection of 'representative democracy and the empowerment of leaders that such delegation of authority [entails]'

(Sitrin 2012: 74). Seen from this perspective, then, these occupy movements were simply against any form of political representation. This would be evinced not only in their prefigurative experiments with participatory democracy and horizontal forms of organisation, but also by some of their most prominent slogans – such as 'This is what democracy looks like!', 'Real democracy now!' ('¡Democracia Real Ya!') and 'They don't represent us!' ('¡Que no nos representan!'). As Marina Sitrin and Dario Azzelini argue:

> 'They don't represent us!' has emerged as a powerful slogan in mobilizations all over the world. We hear it in the US, Spain, Greece, Brazil, Turkey, Slovenia, and even Russia. . . . The slogans are not phrased as rejections of specific political representatives, but as expressions of a *general rejection of the logic of representation*. (Sitrin and Azzellini 2014: 41, emphasis added)

Interestingly, a very similar analysis was made by some of these movements' most prominent critics. Chantal Mouffe argues that their reluctance to engage with any representative institutions or offices betrays a 'flawed understanding of politics' in general (2013: 78; see also Mouffe 2018: 20). Mouffe holds that a pluralist democracy simply 'cannot exist without representation', because political identities are the products of discursive articulation and representative claim-making (2013: 126). What these movements ought to challenge, she claims, is the fact that citizens today are no longer offered any alternatives to the hegemonic discourse – not representative democracy itself.

However, it is debatable to what extent the practices, slogans and aspirations of these movements were indeed underpinned by an unambiguous and principled rejection of any form of political representation (Flesher Fominaya 2020: 80). As we have seen in the previous chapter, even a renowned critic of representative democracy such as Arendt acknowledges that her 'council system' implies at least some forms of political representation and delegation (Kalyvas 2008: 282). What she, and arguably many recent occupy movements, take issue with is not so much political representation per se, but electoral-representative government in particular. As even some of its most prominent advocates insist, electoral representation is essentially elitist and inegalitarian since it requires 'the selection of representatives different from and perceived as superior to those who elect them' (Manin 1997: 149). This, Simon Tormey argues, is 'the metanarrative of representation: that our interests are best served if some represent and everyone else is represented' (Tormey 2015: 82). Electoral-representative government thus bestows upon some citizens the right to govern, whilst limiting the abilities of others to actively participate in politics (outside of the moment of election). It negates what Arendt calls *isonomia* – or the freedom of all citizens to partake in politics as each other's equals, without any form of hierarchy or rulership between them. What does not follow, however, is that a more participatory form of democracy must – or, indeed, could at all – be devoid of any form of political representation. Much like Arendt's and Luxemburg's revolutionary councils, these recent occupy movements arguably did stand for a larger 'people' or social group. Moreover, whilst slogans such as 'This is what democracy looks like!' or 'They don't represent us!' indeed suggest a critique of electoral-representative democracy in its current state, they arguably also imply a representative claim in their own right. Rather than a categorical dismissal of political representation, Paolo Gerbaudo argues, they should therefore 'be read as expressing a demand for better, and more direct and participatory representation to overcome the current "misrepresentation" of the people's will' (Gerbaudo 2017: 84).

What might such a more direct and participatory form of representation pertain to? Most likely, it should be more accessible or inclusive than electoral-representative government, which is inherently selective and hierarchical. Participation should be open to all, which also means that it must be based on a less formal and restrictive mandate than electoral representation. In the remainder of this chapter, I will reconstruct a conception of representation that is implied in prefigurative democracy and its participatory forms of organisation. But in order to do this we first need to acquire a better understanding of what exactly 'representation' means. As I will argue in the next section, this term tends to be employed in very different ways, which must be disentangled before they can be applied in the context of recent occupy movements.

Representation: The Various Uses of a Concept

What exactly *is* representation? As Hannah Pitkin argues in her seminal *The Concept of Representation*, the term tends to be used in very different ways, which are 'often intertwined, but their implications and consequences are very different' (1967: 59). Pitkin roughly divides the contemporary uses of the term into two different categories, according to a distinction that is made in some European languages, but not in others (Hofmann 1974: 19; Mulieri 2019; Sintomer 2013: 19–20; Spivak 1988: 276–7). In Dutch, German and Italian, for example, 'representation' may be translated as *vertegenwoordiging*, *Vertretung* or *rappresentanza*, respectively. This generally refers to the particular relation in which a representative (be it a politician, a delegate or a lawyer) speaks, negotiates, votes or even decides in someone else's stead. Pitkin calls this representation as 'acting for': 'the idea of substitution or acting instead of, the idea of taking care of or acting in the interest of, and the idea of acting as a subordinate, on instructions, in accord with the wishes of another' (1967: 139). Usually, representation as 'acting for' requires an explicit mandate – although there are also examples of non-mandated 'acting for' (Mansbridge 2003). In any case, it does require a certain degree of 'responsiveness': a representative 'must be responsive to [the represented] rather than the other way around' (Pitkin 1967: 140). Thus, the perceived legitimacy of a representative largely depends on their ability to adequately and accurately convey the opinions, grievances or interests of a particular group or constituency. This has two further implications. First, it follows that those represented must be understood to ontologically precede their representative – who, after all, is required to respond to the former's authentic grievances or interests. Second, it implies that there is a certain distance between representative and represented (Manin 1997). This concept of representation as 'acting for' is usually implied, for instance, in our common understanding of electoral-representative democracy.

However, all of the aforementioned languages also have a *second* term commonly translated as 'representation' – namely, *representatie*, *Darstellung* or *rappresentazione*. This is what Pitkin refers to as 'standing for', and it can be further divided into two subcategories. The first of these is descriptive representation. In this case, the aim of representation is to depict the 'original' in the most accurate way possible. A descriptive representation allows us to draw 'conclusions about the represented, gather information about the represented, because it is in relevant ways *like* the represented' (Pitkin 1967: 81). One may think of a pass photo or a map: although human faces or landscapes may of course be depicted in a variety of ways and for many different purposes, what these descriptive representations arguably have in common is their intention to show something 'like it really is'.

Another subclass of representation as 'standing for' is symbolic representation. Whereas descriptive representations tend to have a material referent, which can be represented in a more or less accurate way, symbols 'are often said to represent something, to make it present by their presence, although it is not really present in fact' (Pitkin 1967: 92). Think, for example, of a national flag: in most cases, flags do not clearly convey any concrete information about their referent (i.e. a nation-state, its citizens or territory, or a national identity). They rather serve to arouse certain feelings or emotions, or to invoke particular associations (Pitkin 1967: 99). In consequence, symbols may be understood to be co-constructive of their own referent: they bring something into being that did not exist as such, prior to (or independently of) its symbolisation. Pitkin's criterion of 'responsiveness' thus cannot apply here, since the represented as we know it at least partially originates in the representative relation itself. Whereas representation as 'acting for' and descriptive representation both imply that there is an objective and autonomous referent whose interests can be represented in a more or less accurate way, representation as a symbolic 'standing for' suggests that the referent does not exist independently, but is brought into being precisely through the articulation of a representative claim or relation (Disch 2011b: 106–9).

Not all European languages seem to make such a distinction between representation as 'acting for' and 'standing for'. English, Spanish and French only have one term to refer to both (*representation*, *representación* and *représentation*, respectively). Even in the (predominantly Anglophone) academic debate on political representation, these various concepts are regularly mixed up. However, both at a theoretical and a practical level, there are important reasons to maintain a conceptual distinction between them. Pitkin asserts that both descriptive and symbolic forms of 'standing for' are largely irrelevant for our understanding of representative democracy (Pitkin 1967: 107–11). In fact, she holds that symbolic representation is particularly dangerous as it does not require any kind of responsiveness between the representative and the represented. But representation as 'standing for' is arguably more elementary to our understanding of democracy than Pitkin suggests. In a parliamentarian context, for instance, a certain measure of descriptive resemblance between representatives and their constituency or support base may significantly contribute to the experienced legitimacy or effectiveness of democratic representation (Mansbridge 1999). And many radical democrats insist that the role of symbolic representation should also not be disregarded (Disch 2019; Laclau 2005a: 159–61). In fact, as I will argue below, this symbolic conception of representation as 'standing for' is of particular relevance for our understanding of contemporary protest movements and prefigurative democracy.

What is the political relevance of symbolic representation? Constructivist theorists of democracy such as Ernesto Laclau, Chantal Mouffe and Michael Saward have sought to understand how political representatives give rise to new political discourses and identities. As argued above, it is precisely this constitutive aspect that characterises symbolic representation: the representative relation partially precedes its own referent. Seen from such a constructivist perspective, then, representation is not a one-way street, but a back-and-forth between representatives and the constituency or support base. By articulating a particular image of 'whom' or what they stand for, representative agents precisely give rise to such a social group or constituency. This is why, according to Saward (2010: 15), 'the active making of symbols or images of what is to be represented' is even a 'central aspect' of political representation. Saward therefore conceptualises political representation as a claim, which is made in reference to a particular object and whose validity must be recognised by an audience in order to be effective (Saward 2010: 37). Pitkin's normative criterion of responsiveness hence does not apply here: rather than merely resembling an already-existing support base, representatives greatly contribute to the constitution of such groups. Since the legitimacy of a representative claim mostly depends on the extent to which it is acknowledged as such, no formal mandate is required for it to be recognised as valid. This also significantly broadens our understanding of representative agents. In principle, anyone can make such claims: politicians and political parties, but also activists, social movements, non-governmental organisations (NGOs), media pundits and personalities, or even commercial enterprises (Saward 2010: 16).

But if symbolic representation indeed plays an elementary role in the constitution or self-identification of the represented, as these constructivist theorists claim, then does this mean that the represented has no material reality or autonomy prior to the representative relation? Saward admits that, evidently, 'there is always a *referent*. But the real political work lies in the active constitution of constituencies – the making of representations' (Saward 2010: 51). It may thus be more accurate to say that symbolic representation is an articulatory process (Laclau 1990b: 38–9; 2007a: 98). Through its repeated use, a signifier gradually acquires a certain content and meaning and comes to inscribe a referent with a different meaning or new connotations. This is a distinctively political process, one may add, because there is always a competition between various possible articulations. The establishment of one discourse or collective identity inevitably comes at the expense of others. Or, to put it in Laclau and Mouffe's terms: any symbolic representation seeks to acquire political hegemony insofar as it comes to 'dominate the field of discursivity, to arrest the flow of differences, to construct a centre' (Laclau and Mouffe 2001: 112). It thus follows that no representative claim or demand can stand on its own. In order to be meaningful and politically effective, it must be absorbed into a broader range of claims, demands, agendas or identities that gradually come to presuppose or connote each other. This is what Laclau and Mouffe describe as the creation of an 'equivalential chain': a series of demands that together constitute a counter-hegemonic discourse. This chain is in turn represented by one particular signifier that has the potential to stand for or invoke all the others (Laclau 2005a: 131). This is, for instance, how the colour green could gradually come to stand for a range of different political demands or agendas: from concerns with climate change and deforestation, to vegetarianism and opposition to nuclear energy, or even pacifism. In itself, 'green' is an empty and politically meaningless symbol. It merely invokes loose associations with the natural environment, or with plants and forests in particular. Yet, in that capacity, it has effectively served to link these various demands into an equivalential chain and to establish a web of connotations, associations and alliances that did not hitherto exist. 'Green' thus plays a constitutive role in the establishment of this agenda – and, consequently, offers an important source of identification for those who subscribe to it (even though, at a more detailed level, they may still have very different conceptions of what it means to be 'green').

In short, whenever it is claimed – rightly or not – that the practices of recent occupy movements, or prefigurative democracy more generally, imply a critique of political representation per se (Sitrin and Azzellini 2014; Lorey 2020), then one question that should be raised is what exact conception of 'representation' is meant here. Are we speaking about representation in the sense of *Vertretung* or *vertegenwoordiging* – that is, 'acting for' someone else on the basis of a formal mandate? Or do we mean, instead, representation as a more

symbolic and often informal claim to 'stand for' someone or something else? Of course, in practice this distinction may not be as clear-
cut as presented above. Not only are representation as 'acting for'
and 'standing for' often employed in tandem, but one may even argue
that one often cannot do without the other: in order to effectively
act on behalf of someone else, one may also need to embody them,
at least to a certain extent. Conversely, a successful claim to 'stand
for' a larger group may entail that one's actions or statements have
a bearing on this larger group (or its social and political position) in
practice – in which case one inevitably (and perhaps unintentionally)
also ends up 'acting for' them. But drawing such conceptual distinctions may help to acquire a better understanding of how political
representation plays a role in various political practices, including
those of recent occupy movements. Upon closer inspection, it turns
out that certain forms of representation as 'standing for' may be
more elementary to our understanding of prefigurative democracy
than representation as 'acting for' (although some forms of the latter
may as well be implied here). In the next section I will briefly discuss
both in the context of recent occupy movements.

The Occupy Movements and Political Representation

At first sight, there may be good reasons to assume that recent occupy
movements were categorically opposed to any form of political representation. They often had a critique of electoral-representative
democracy in its current state – although the intensity and nature
of this critique may differ from case to case. Established political
parties often played no role in these movements, and there generally
was a strong distrust of elected representatives who claim to act in
the name or interest of the people. What is more, these movements
experimented with alternative forms of organisation and horizontalist decision-making procedures. This suggests that these movements dismissed some forms of representation as 'acting for' – at
least to the extent that this would require an exclusive mandate to
act on the behalf of others and preclude their participation in political decision-making. Such a conception of 'acting for' is implied in
electoral representation. But, as argued above, it may be too easy
to argue that these movements were against any form of political
representation – either as 'acting for' or 'standing for'. In fact, it
appears that they employed various forms of both within their own
prefigurative practices and discourses.

To begin with, and notwithstanding their critique of electoral-representative government, most recent occupy movements did not dismiss any form of representation as 'acting for'. They, for instance, employed forms of delegation. As we have seen in the previous chapter, a few months into the occupation of Zuccotti Park, OWS's General Assembly was gradually replaced as the most important organ of decision-making by a spokescouncil. Each working group or committee would delegate a spokesperson to participate on its behalf in these central spokescouncil meetings. In itself, this is by no means incompatible with the radical-democratic aspirations of these occupy movements. Most anarchists and radical democrats agree that a more decentralised or horizontalist form of democracy may nevertheless require some forms of recallable delegation or imperative mandate (Bookchin 2015: 26; Cohn 2006: 255–6; Teivainen 2016: 23; Tomba 2018; Wilson 2014: 147–8). It is also often suggested that there is a qualitative difference between delegation and political representation in the strict sense (Castoriadis 1993: 260). Unlike representatives, who have a formal mandate to act or decide on the basis of those represented, delegates would only be entitled to 'communicate the will of the smaller group' (Bray 2013: 88). But arguably, this is mostly a matter of semantics. It may be more accurate to say that delegation is a very minimal form of representation as 'acting for', as it requires a limited and closely circumscribed mandate, in which the representative is considered subordinate to the represented (Pitkin 1967: 134). It clearly is the case that delegates or spokespersons 'act for' a larger group – albeit perhaps in a very restricted sense.

Besides formal delegation, moreover, it is also questionable to what extent the prefigurative practices of recent occupy movements were indeed entirely devoid of more informal leadership relations. It is argued that the emergence of new, networked forms of communication and social media would cater to horizontalist forms of organisation and coordination that are entirely devoid of leadership. But these emerging technologies also seem to have given rise to new kinds of informal leadership in a social movement context (Gerbaudo 2012: 159; Nunes 2014; Smucker 2017: 184–6). As even the most self-proclaimed 'leaderless' movements often fail to live up to this self-image in practice, it may thus be counter-productive (or even dangerous) to ignore the many forms of informal leadership that tend to play a role in social movements. The risk, after all, is that de facto leaders could otherwise not be held accountable for their choices and performance (Freeman 1972). The real challenge for prefigurative movements thus may not be to abolish leadership or representation in its every kind, but instead to think of ways in which such roles can be rotated more frequently and distributed more equally (Nunes 2021: 180). Rather than wishing away forms of 'acting for', it would be more democratic to acknowledge and formalise at least some of them as an essential part of social movements politics.

What is more, it could be argued that recent occupy movements also fulfilled an important representative role in their own right. They surely did not have – or, for that matter, claimed to have – any mandate or legitimacy to act, negotiate or make decisions on behalf of a larger group of people. But nevertheless, OWS and similar occupy movements did claim to serve as its political representatives in at least some respects. As Jodi Dean rightly insists, OWS was never 'actually the movement of 99 percent of the population of the United States (or the world) against the top 1 percent. It [was] a movement mobilizing itself around an occupied Wall Street *in the name of* the 99 percent' (Dean 2012: 229; see also Žižek 2012: 88–9). It appears that many of the involved activists were very much aware of this. Whereas the established political parties represent the 1%, David Graeber writes, OWS sought to 'represent the 99% whose lives are essentially left out of the equation' (2013: 40).

This gives rise to the question of how these occupy movements could legitimately function as the representatives of a '99%' – or of 'the nation' or 'the people' in other contexts? After all, they did not receive any mandate to act or decide on its behalf. In order to appreciate this, we need to return to the second, more symbolic concept of 'representation' that I fleshed out above: namely, representation as a symbolic 'standing for'. A social movements politics without any form of symbolic representation is practically unimaginable. Logos, flags, slogans and banners evidently fulfil an important symbolic function. Not only do they communicate a message or demand to the public, but activists also derive a sense of identity and community from them. Even the most devoted anarchist, who may reject *any* form of institutional representation, would surely not deny that their own black flag or their Guy Fawkes mask 'stand for' something (Cohn 2006).

The occupy movements of the past decade were no exception to this. Let me once again return to OWS's statement quoted above. As established, the statement is critical of electoral-representative democracy in its current condition. But the text *also* adamantly states that 'we the people still know our power' (New York City General Assembly 2011: 1). And this 'we the people' – a loaded phrase in US political history – at least implies that the General Assembly issuing this statement claims to stand for a more encompassing 'people', and does not merely act in the name of those physically present in Zuccotti Park (Butler 2015: 177). More generally, many of these movements' most prominent slogans – such as 'We are the 99%' and 'They don't represent us!' – suggest that they claimed to stand for an 'us' that exceeded the amount of people assembled in the streets (Brito Vieira 2015: 506). Finally, the prefigurative practices of these movements arguably also implied a similar representative claim: the General Assembly, alternative decision-making procedures and organisational structures all 'stood for' a more encompassing view of what a more democratic society or its political institutions and procedures should be like. We can therefore recognise that a particular form of political representation as 'standing for' is presupposed in the practices, slogans and rhetoric of prefigurative democracy. Much like the various forms of 'acting for' discussed above, this symbolic form of political representation is compatible with the radical-democratic aspirations of these occupy movements. In fact, prefigurative democracy cannot be adequately conceptualised without it.

How, then, do prefigurative movements and practices fulfil this representative role? In his work on prefigurative politics, Benjamin Franks offers an interesting suggestion. What distinguishes prefiguration as a form of political action is that it already 'contains elements of the object it is representing. It stands both as a practical response to a given situation, but also as a symbol of the larger vision of societal change' (Franks 2003: 20). In consequence, prefiguration has a very distinctive symbolic form: it is synecdochal. As I will explain further below, the synecdoche is a figure of speech in which a constitutive part stands in for a larger whole. Whereas prefiguration entails the realisation of political alternatives in the here and now, Franks argues, such experimental practices do represent a broader image of the desired future (2003: 18–19; 2014: 63). One may think of squatting as a typically prefigurative form of protest. Whilst it is an effective way to provide those in need with affordable housing, squatting is also a form of protest against housing shortage and speculation with real estate. Squatting is prefigurative and synecdochal: it is a partial (and temporary) solution that offers immediate relief in the present, but at the same time it addresses a more fundamental social injustice (Cattaneo and Martínez 2014: 3).

However, one may add to Franks's account that prefigurative movements and practices not only symbolically stand for a more encompassing ideal of the future. Prefigurative democracy also, and perhaps more importantly, tends to take place in the name of a particular social group or support base (such as 'the 99%' or the homeless people in a local community). How can the figure of the synecdoche be employed to make sense of this representative aspect in prefigurative democracy? Ernesto Laclau's constructivist theory of representation helps us to understand why and how the synecdochal form is often implied in prefigurative democracy and the politics of contemporary social movements.

Neither Metaphor nor Metonymy: Synecdochal Representation

Although the term 'representation' is often associated with 'acting for', representation as 'standing for' is much more common. Works of art, symbols, protocols or even means of payment all represent something larger than themselves. However, this symbolic form of representation also fulfils a distinctively political role. It is of elementary importance for the construction of collective identities and discourses. Whereas representation as 'acting for' is a typically responsive process, where a representative seeks to adequately and accurately act or speak on behalf of the represented; representation as 'standing for' is a 'two-way process: a movement from represented to representative, and a correlative one from representative to represented' (Laclau 2005a: 158; see also Laclau 2007a: 98). As argued, this is also a distinctively political process since, in order to establish itself, any identity must seek hegemony and thus come at the expense of others (Laclau and Mouffe 2001: 141–5). When Ernesto Laclau speaks of 'political representation', he often implicitly refers to this much broader concept of representation as a symbolic 'standing for' (Arato 2013: 160).

As mentioned, an elementary aspect of Laclau's theory of representation is the synecdoche and its relation to the metaphor and the metonymy. By exploring the differences between these figures of speech Laclau hopes to better understand how hegemonic representations and discourses are being established (Laclau and Mouffe 2001: 110). But he nowhere gives a systematic account of the synecdoche: references to it are scattered throughout his oeuvre. Before this concept can be applied to the representative claims and practices of recent occupy movements, we therefore first need to reconstruct the specific (and often implicit) place of the synecdoche in his theory of representation.

But let me first qualify what exactly the synecdoche *is*, how it is distinguished from other figures of speech such as the metaphor and the metonymy, and why it is relevant in a discussion of political representation. As the synecdoche is generally regarded as a subcategory of the metonymy (Desiriis 2015: 60), we must start by distinguishing between the metonymy and the metaphor. Whereas the latter is based on analogy or association, the establishment of the metonymy requires a *contiguous* relation. For example, in the context of radical social movements it is common to refer to police officers as 'pigs'. This is a metaphor: after all, the officers in question probably do not bear greater physical resemblance to pigs than anyone else. The relation between 'pigs' and 'police officers' is merely based on *association* – the perceived brutishness or thoughtlessness of their behaviour reminds us of animals. Whether this association is justified or not is irrelevant (it is common knowledge that pigs are highly intelligent animals). In metonymy, on the other hand, the relation between the signifier and the signified must be warranted by a particular *contiguity*: that is, a more immediate relation between the signifier and its referent. Common examples are 'Wall Street' or 'the White House' as references to the financial industry or to a particular branch of the United States government, respectively. In both cases there is a direct and concrete relation between them (the stock market is perceived as the centre of financial power; the president lives in the White House), but the term used as a signifier is not exhaustive of this relation. Synecdoche, finally, implies a metonymic relation in that it is based on a similar contiguous relation. But there is one important, additional criterion: in a synecdochal relation the signifier is itself a constitutive part of the larger whole that it signifies. It requires a *pars pro toto* relation. Expressions such as 'we have hungry mouths to feed' or the use of 'wheels' as a reference to automobiles are famous examples of a synecdoche: 'mouths' and 'wheels' obviously are merely a part of their referent – albeit an elementary one.

Let me return to the distinction between metonymy and metaphor. As stated, metaphors are typically based on associations. But this also means that metaphorical representation can only be established as a more or less exclusive, closed relation (Laclau 2014d: 88). Precisely because it is based on mere association, many different metaphors can be constructed to describe a single referent. To return to the example given above: there is no particular reason why the contingent association between the police and 'pigs' has led to such an established metaphor in activist and youth culture (various species could have fulfilled the same metaphorical role, and arguably even better than that). But in order to succeed as a metaphor, 'pigs' had to exclude these other possible associations, and thus had to present itself as the *only* or most self-evident signifier for 'the police'. Precisely because it is contingent – and, thus, one among many options – a metaphor needs to be continuously reinforced in order to become effective.

This is different for the metonymy – which, as we have seen, is based on a contiguous relation. The part that serves as a signifier in a metonymic relation is more closely related to the whole that it embodies, and the contiguous relation between them thus 'speaks for itself'. Everyone with a rudimentary knowledge of US politics will immediately understand what 'the White House' or 'Washington' stand for – both terms, moreover, can readily be used in reference to the same referent. Thus, the success of metonymy depends less on its ability to exclude other possible symbolic relations: it remains more 'open'. As far as Laclau is concerned, however, this also means that the metonymy has only limited potential for the establishment of hegemonic discourses and representations. In a process of hegemonisation, a particular representation of society gradually takes upon itself the role of serving as a dominant representation of society as a whole. It must 'overflo[w] its own particularity' and become an 'incarnation' (Laclau 2007b: 72) – or, a complete and full embodiment of a social totality that always remains an impossibility (Laclau 1990b: 38–9). The problem with metonymies, however, is that they are loosely based on one of many possible contiguous relations. Unlike the metaphor, the effectiveness of a metonymy does not depend on its ability to make all other possible representations redundant. Metonymies thus lack the exclusionary potential that is required for the establishment of a hegemonic political representation (Torfing 1999: 112–13). In order to acquire discursive hegemony, a metonymy would first need to lose some of its contiguous openness (Laclau 2005a: 109; 2014b: 62).

This is where the figure of the synecdoche becomes relevant. Laclau ascribes a particular function to this rhetorical figure. He approvingly quotes Paul de Man, who describes the synecdoche as 'one of the borderline figures that creates an ambivalent zone between metaphor and metonymy' (De Man 1979: 63n8; see also Laclau 2014d: 87). Seen from this perspective, the synecdoche is not merely a subcategory of the metonymy: rather, it occupies a middle ground between these other figures, in that it constitutes a relation between signifier and signified that is neither contiguous nor analogous – and, therefore, neither open nor closed. The particular part that 'takes upon itself the task' (Miller 2004: 220) to embody or 'stand for' a larger whole is never the *only* part that could fulfill this role (Laclau 2000a: 57; Laclau et al. 1999: 135). Yet, its chance of succeeding as a synecdochal signifier does depend on its ability to be presented as the only (or, at least, the most obvious and self-evident) representation. The synecdochal representation creates the *illusion* of a closure (Laclau 2014d: 87–8).

As far as Laclau is concerned, this is exactly why the rhetorical figure of the synecdoche forms the ultimate basis for our understanding of political representation: it explains how one representative claim or relation can signify a larger whole – which, at the same time, must always exceed it (Laclau 2005a: 72; Desiriis 2015: 60–1, 216). The synecdochal form avoids both the Scylla of metonymic arbitrariness and the Charybdis of metaphoric closure. For Laclau it is therefore 'not simply one more rhetorical device, simply to be taxonomically added to other figures such as metaphor and metonymy, but [it] has a different ontological function' (Laclau 2005a: 72). And this function is to articulate hegemonic concepts of the social that will never be exhaustive, complete or even fully possible (Laclau 2014d: 97), but which will nevertheless present themselves as the embodiments of this social whole – and thus serve to constitute it.[1] Laclau's employment of these rhetorical figures thus should be taken literally, and not as mere analogies. Political representations are constructed *as* synecdoches – not merely *like* them.

Let me give two different examples of how this might work in practice. Imagine a local community whose members have a particular shared need or interest. It can be something rather mundane and seemingly unpolitical: in one of Laclau's own examples, citizens want a better bus connection to their neighbourhood (Laclau 2005b: 36). However, their request is turned down by the local authorities. As long as this remains an isolated case, Laclau argues, it will probably not give rise to a stronger counter-hegemonic mobilisation. But now let us imagine that this is only one among many different unsatisfied claims. It turns out that similar requests from other neighbourhood residents or surrounding communities have also been denied. Laclau describes how this may lead to the institution of a social frontier: their shared experience of neglect or their frustration with the authorities in question bring people together and constitute a sense of collectivity, which is counterpoised to a shared understanding or appreciation of the authorities that come to serve as its 'constitutive outside' (Laclau 1990b: 17; Marchart 2007: 139). The construction of a social frontier not only affects how these communities identify, but leads to a different articulation of their demands. It results in the establishment of a larger set of claims, 'one in which all the demands, in spite of their differential character, tend to reaggregate themselves, forming what we will call an *equivalential chain*' (Laclau 2005b: 37). Notwithstanding the initial differences between these people and their particular interests, needs or preferences, their shared experience of neglect and their positioning along the lines of a newly constituted social frontier leads them to see a seemingly 'logical' or 'natural' connection between these various claims and demands. This chain of equivalence, however, needs to be represented in a particular way: a mere summing up of these various demands will not be sufficient. The representation of an equivalential chain 'is only possible if a particular demand, without entirely abandoning its own particularity, starts also functioning as a signifier representing the chain as a totality' (Laclau 2005b: 39; see also Marchart 2019: 111–16). By virtue of its public appeal or its broad applicability, one particular demand (for instance for better public transport) comes to synecdochally represent the entire chain, thus 'standing for' a more encompassing series of demands or identities.[2]

Let us turn to a second example of synecdochal representation in the context of social movements. Imagine a trade union that seeks to organise in a working-class neighbourhood with strong racial and cultural diversity. Initially, the union's campaigns will focus on social-economic issues and working conditions. But it turns out that this community is also suffering from an increase in racist violence, and there are no other grassroots organisations focusing on such issues. It is likely that, through lack of an alternative, the union will gradually start to play a more significant role in this struggle as well. As Laclau (2005a: 109) argues, 'despite the differential particularism of the initial two kinds of struggles and demands, a certain equivalential homogeneity between them is being created'.

Consequently, the perceived meaning of the trade union might gradually change. Although there are obvious connections between these struggles, there is no particular reason why a trade union should necessarily be engaged in anti-racism. And yet, 'the union' comes to synecdochally stand for a larger chain of demands, struggles and identities, including racial equality and anti-racism. Neighbourhood residents and potential members may thus start to associate 'trade union' with 'anti-racism' and vice versa. The union eventually comes to represent a much larger group than its original rank and file or the workers in a particular trade or branch.

This example illustrates how an organisation gradually acquires a much broader representative role – but without losing its particularity at the same time (the trade union in Laclau's example may continue to advocate good working conditions). It is important to stress that this does not only affect the concrete demands, agenda or function of the organisation. It is also has a bearing on how the organisation comes to identify or understand itself: 'trade union' does not merely refer to its concrete function or mission, but also more broadly to a collective identity, a particular articulation of 'social justice', 'equality' or other values and ideals, and a strategic view of how these must be brought about.

The Occupy Camp as a Synechoche

How can Laclau's concept of synecdochal representation help to better understand the prefigurative practices and representative role of recent occupy movements?[3] Let me analyse three features of prefigurative democracy that have a significant synecdochal form. Prefigurative democracy often entails the articulation of representative claims, the creation or reappropriation of commons, and experimentation with participative democracy and decision-making. These aspects may obviously play out differently, depending on social, cultural and political context. But they are exemplary for how social movements seek to change society and its political form through the prefigurative realisation and representation of their ultimate goals, within their discourses as well as their activist and organisational practices. Moreover, these three features illustrate how the form and substance of prefigurative democracy are closely intertwined in practice.

A first feature of prefigurative democracy that has important synecdochal implications is that it always entails the articulation of a representative claim. Of course, this is by no means exceptional for prefigurative democracy: such claims are arguably made in any political context. What renders it particularly important in this context, however, is that this idea of the representative claim offers an alternative to electoral forms of representation as 'acting for', which many of these movements indeed rejected. Unlike parliamentary bodies or elected officials, social movements like OWS or the 15-M movement clearly did not act on the basis of a formal mandate. Saward's concept of the representative claim may help us to understand how they nevertheless fulfilled a representative function – in their experimental practices as much as through their slogans and rhetoric (Saward 2010: 16).

As argued above, representative claims are not 'responsive' to an already-existing subject or support base. They are made in anticipation of their approval or recognition by an audience. It is precisely for this reason that representative claims fulfil a constitutive role: they contribute to the gradual articulation of shared political discourses and collective identities. Take for example OWS's most famous rallying cry: 'We are the 99%'. This slogan was inspired by Joseph Stiglitz's (2011) article in *Vanity Fair*, in which he argued that a mere 1% of US Americans receives nearly a quarter of the nation's yearly income, and that it owns 40% of the nation's total wealth. A blog on Tumblr contributed to the popularisation of this idea that society could be divided between a 99% and a 1% (Graeber 2013: 41).[4] On this website, thousands of people, mostly from the United States, posted pictures of themselves, accompanied by a brief statement that described their individual situation: testimonies of debt, unemployment or systematic underemployment, poverty, chronic illness and war trauma. These were all undersigned with the slogan 'I am the 99%'. Although these were all individual accounts of many different situations and experiences, the slogan suggested that all these stories had something important in common. It seemed that, in a way, every single personal story could embody or encompass all the others – they all represented the entire '99%'. Whereas this idea of the '99%' suggests that they together constituted a majority, the *I* in 'I am the 99%' also suggested a synecdochal, representative claim: *my* story is representative of what we all are going through (in spite of the obvious differences between us). In this way, the slogan and the idea of a '99%' constructed what Laclau and Mouffe call an 'equivalential chain' between various stories and identities, on the basis of a relatively vague and undefined experience that they all seemed to have in common. This shared experience, which perhaps could best be described in terms of 'deprivation' or 'precarity', came to synecdochally represent a wide variety of concrete inequalities, instabilities and injustices – and thus gave rise to a newly articulated collective class identity (Dean 2014: 385).

Countless social movement slogans have fulfilled a similar synecdochal role. When OWS protesters claimed that 'This is what democracy looks like', they referred to their own experimental practices and forms of organisation as a synecdochal embodiment of the social and political conditions that they sought to bring about. When revolutionaries in Egypt chanted 'The people want the fall of this regime', they not only opened up the collective imagination to the possibility of a country without military dictatorship. They also gave rise to a new understanding of who these 'people' may be – thus inscribing the term with new meaning. Of course, this slogan was used well before a significant part (let alone a majority) of 'the people' was actually ready to subscribe to its message. It thus presupposed a popular desire that may not have existed at that moment. But it was precisely by treating the aspirations of a politicised minority as a synecdochal embodiment of the popular will as a whole that the revolutionaries would eventually be able to muster sufficient support for revolutionary change. This representative claim thus was prefigurative of 'a people' that would only emerge in response to it – much as OWS gave rise to the very '99%' that it claimed to represent.

Another feature of prefigurative democracy that has a significant synecdochal function is the production or reappropriation of commons. Originally associated with land and other natural recourses, today the term 'commons' is used in reference to a much broader range of spaces, infrastructures and means of production – as well as immaterial entities such as ideas, symbols, language and so forth (Hardt 2010: 350; Hardt and Negri 2009: viii). Commons belong to no one and to everyone: they defy the logic of (private as well as public) property. In a world dominated by neoliberal politics and a capitalist mode of production, commons thus both produce and symbolise what a radically different economy and political order might be like. They have an important prefigurative potential (Van de Sande 2017). At the same time, and in part because of this, commons are also continuously at risk of being appropriated or subsumed under a capitalist logic. The reappropriation of commons from capitalist control thus is both a political goal and a means or strategy for many contemporary radical-democratic movements.

One concrete example of how the production of commons played a role in the prefigurative politics of recent occupy movements is the fact that they all revolved around the occupation of squares, streets and other public spaces. In recent decades public space (both in the literal sense of a physical space, and in the more abstract sense of a public sphere) has become increasingly inaccessible. Neoliberal governments and policies all across the world have privatised such spaces – a development that in many ways corresponds with the establishment of an empty and watered-down concept of citizenship. For many recent occupy movements the occupation of public space thus was not merely a strategic instrument. The reappropriated public space *itself* was also often at stake (Butler 2015: 126). As Wendy Brown argues, many occupy movements around the world 'repossessed private space as public space, occupied what is owned, and above all, rejected the figure of citizenship reduced to sacrificial human capital and neoliberal capitalism as a life-sustaining sacred power' (Brown 2015: 220). For instance, Istanbul's Gezi Park was initially occupied in defiance of the city's plan to restructure it – and, more generally, to protest against the regime's attitude towards its citizens' right of assembly and freedom of press. New York's Zuccotti Park, to name another example, is not only conveniently located only a few blocks from Wall Street, but it is also a 'privately owned public space' (Foderaro 2011) that bears the name of its proprietor. Of course, occupying a single square will do very little to turn the tide against the privatisation of public space. But by focusing on the reappropriation of public space these various social movements embodied a broader protest – against the privatisation of public spaces, evidently, but also more generally against the ongoing enclosure of commons. The occupation of public space thus also synecdochally stood for a broader opposition against neoliberal appropriation, and arguably even for a more encompassing view of how a commons-based economy could replace the current capitalist one.

A third feature of prefigurative democracy that has important synecdochal implications is that it often entails experimentation with participatory forms of democratic organisation and decision-making. Ironically, it is precisely for this reason that prefigurative democracy is so often assumed to imply a rejection of political representation *tout court*. But especially in a context where 'democracy' is generally associated with electoral representation and parliamentarianism, experiments with participatory or 'direct' forms of democracy inevitably also do represent something in their own right. They synecdochally stand for a general (and continuously rearticulated) idea of what a more democratic society could look like.

A concrete realisation of this aspect can be found in the General Assemblies and consensus-oriented decision-making techniques of recent occupy movements. These experimental practices and procedures not only served an important organisational function. The continuous search for consensus at General Assemblies, for example, well exceeded their instrumental or strategic purposes. As Andy Cornell argues, '[i]n this case, the whole that consensus stands for is a participatory, egalitarian, self-determining movement, on the one hand, and, on the other, a society with the same characteristics' (Cornell 2012: 164). Graeber makes a similar point when he argues that OWS's direct-democratic decision-making procedures and horizontalist structures were understood to 'offer a *model*, or at the very least a glimpse of how free people might organize themselves, and therefore what a free society could be like' (Graeber 2013: 233; see also 43, 191–1). The synecdochal character of these democratic experiments was not limited to their procedural or organisational form. Habits, hand signals and other symbols – the 'jazz hands' signal to indicate agreement, the 'people's mic' as a way to communicate in a large group without using amplification – play an equally important role in this synecdochal enactment. This does not mean that these occupy movements always consistently used, or claimed to use, direct-democratic decision-making procedures. As we have seen above, their activist repertoire often also comprised various forms of representation as 'acting for', and many of these movements later turned to establish a more formal and vertically organised council system. But the point is that these experimental forms and practices, notwithstanding their limited and short-lived character, stood for a more encompassing view of what a more democratic society might look like. They also fulfilled a constitutive function: without its experimental enactment, both in procedures or organisational structures and in habits or rhetoric, these movements' ideal of a more democratic society would remain unarticulated and empty.

As the various features of prefigurative democracy in practice illustrate, it is impossible to even imagine it without any form of political representation. This is all the more so the case because, regardless of how they appreciate electoral-representative democracy in its current state, the practices of social movements must always be discursively mediated. How exactly their practices and organisational structures 'stand for' a more encompassing social ideal can only find expression through language, memes, images or symbols. The occupation of public space, the implementation of consensus-oriented decision-making procedures and the prefigurative realisation of new organisational structures could acquire a synecdochal meaning precisely *because* they were accompanied by – and, thus, mediated through – particular representative claims, demands, slogans and symbols. The point of the matter, in other words, is not simply that the synecdochal figure of speech serves as a helpful analogy for how these practices symbolically represent something larger than themselves: prefigurative action is not *like* a synecdoche. More accurately, these social movements show why political representation is essentially prefigurative in its own right. It is partially through their slogans, claims and statements that political agents give rise to a shared idea of who it is they symbolically stand for. In this way, as we have seen, representatives also play an elementary role in the constitution of their own support base or constituency. By claiming to stand for a larger whole – be it a particular goal or demand, an ideal of the future society, or indeed a particular social group or even 'the people' – representatives already presuppose the existence of a shared discourse or identity that must first be articulated through their own representative claims (Saward 2010: 67). A part or minority that claims to stand for a larger whole or majority thus partially co-constitutes the latter. Political representation is itself prefigurative in that it is always ahead of itself: it gives shape to a social and political reality that did not exist prior to its own articulation.

Conclusion: Participatory or Representative Democracy?

What is the role and relevance of political representation in the practices of recent occupy movements? Since their emergence in the course of the past decade, this has been a subject of debate among political theorists and social movement scholars. Many advocates as well as critics of these movements have argued that their horizontalist aspirations, their radical-democratic rhetoric and their prefigurative approach all evince a principled rejection of political representation. But although many of these movements indeed shared a critique of electoral-representative democracy in its current state, I argued, it is an exaggeration to state that their prefigurative practices evinced a 'presentist' (Lorey 2014) or 'post-representative' (Tormey 2015) view of democracy. In fact, it could be argued that prefigurative democracy requires a very specific – and, indeed, inherently prefigurative – form of political representation.

Drawing a conceptual distinction between representation as 'acting for' and representation as 'standing for' allows us to better understand its role in prefigurative democracy. As argued above, the prefigurative practices of recent occupy movements entailed various forms of both. Spokespersons, councils or working groups were delegated to 'act for' the movement as a whole – albeit on the basis of a limited mandate. But, more importantly, these movements also fulfilled an important representative function in their own right. By articulating representative claims, reappropriating public spaces and experimenting with participatory democracy and horizontal forms of organisation, they not only synecdochally stood for a larger 'people', but also articulated a more encompassing idea of what a future society and its political forms might look like. The part representing a larger whole thus also inscribed the latter with a particular meaning and association. Synecdochal representation is prefigurative in its own right, in the sense that it already presupposes the existence of a referent that must be co-constituted in the representative claim itself. It refers to a particular conception of 'the people' or 'the 99%' – or, more generally, to a social and political condition – before it can be recognised or acknowledged as a legitimate representative claim. In that sense, synecdochal representations like the ones that emerged in Zuccotti Park and other occupied spaces thus may also be interpreted as the representations of a not-yet-established future (Žižek 2012: 128).

Employing the synecdoche in the context of prefigurative democracy thus gives rise to an understanding of political representation that is not based on any formal mandate and does not restrict the ability of citizens to partake in democratic politics. Synecdochal claims can in principle be made by anyone, as their validity can only be recognised afterwards. Prefigurative democracy thus caters to a completely different conception of political representation than what is afforded by electoral-representative democracy. We may thus conclude that, rather than dismissing political representation per se, prefigurative democracy reconciles certain forms of representative politics with participatory democracy.

This idea has in fact become more widespread in the recent debate. Several studies suggest that occupy movements such as OWS and 15-M emerged from a contingent combination of representative as well as participatory forms of democracy. Paolo Gerbaudo argues that they comprised two different strands or tendencies. On the one hand, there was the obvious but limited influence of what he calls 'neo-anarchists', who insisted on prefigurative experimentation and horizontalist organisation as way to establish 'real democracy' in the here and now. Seen from this perspective, the activist tent camp and its bodies of decision-making were not merely the strategic means for political change, but also an end in itself. But another group of participants saw their movement or the activist tent camp as the expression of a demand for public sovereignty. For them, the occupied square was primarily a stage or mouthpiece by which to voice the discontent of a broader public. According to Gerbaudo (2017: 160), these neo-anarchist and populist tendencies 'clashed with one another in the everyday life of the camp, leading to different interpretations of the meaning of the occupations and of the movements they incubated'. OWS activist and political organiser Jonathan Smucker draws a similar distinction between two dominant tendencies within the movement. Whereas in his opinion the prefigurative tendency was more visibly present in the politics of OWS, there was also a strategic impulse of those who argued that a social movement must seek to acquire discursive hegemony and institutional power to be successful in the long term (Smucker 2017: 118–25). Although Smucker recognises the worth of prefigurative experimentation, he concludes that it can only be productive to the extent that it complements such a hegemony-oriented social movement strategy. In the practice of OWS, however, it often replaced or even undermined any strategic attempt to acquire political power (Smucker 2017: 122).

A slightly different position is taken by Cristina Flesher Fominaya in the context of the Spanish 15-M movement. Although 15-M initially comprised anarchist and autonomist groups as well as activists with stronger populist or neo-Gramscian inclinations, the movement eventually came 'close to successfully integrating these two positions' (Flesher Fominaya 2020: 15). Many 15-M activists ended up combining a prefigurative approach within their own movements with a strategic attempt to acquire discursive hegemony and institutional power outside of it (Flesher Fominaya 2020: 304). Flesher Fominaya's observation resonates with a recent development in the academic debate on social movement politics, as philosophers have also tried to overcome this binary distinction between 'horizontal' and 'vertical' logics of organisation at a theoretical level (Feenstra et al. 2017: 7–9). Rodrigo Nunes seeks to understand social movement politics as a diverse 'ecology' that comprises various, and potentially complementary, organisational forms and logics. Rather than trying to 'force a choice between self- and hetero-organisation, "purely" horizontal and "purely" vertical relations', Nunes (2021: 48) argues, we should start from the assumption that 'plurality is a given, which means that the question of organisation is never about the one organisational form or the one organisation' (Nunes 2021: 49). It follows that individual movements, organisations or activists within such a diverse ecology may not only employ a variety of tactics, but also pursue very different goals. Once social movements let go of the idea that they should always seek to be in control of the direction in which they are heading, Nunes suggests, it may become possible for movement actors with divergent aims or backgrounds to work towards the same horizon (Nunes 2021: 172). In a similar vein, Rahel Süß (2021) has sought to overcome the binary distinction between verticalism and horizontalism by focusing on the role of experimentation in a social movement politics. As both the means and goals of political action are continuously rearticulated throughout practice, there will always and inevitably be conflicting ideas on what goals should be pursued or on how to get there. Such conflicts, however, may as well be understood as an intrinsic part of a democratic social movement politics.

I am inclined to take a similar position. However, rather than it being a part of a diverse 'ecology' that comprises both prefigurative or horizontalist forms of organisation on the one hand, and a verticalist logic of representation on the other, I assert that prefigurative democracy precisely emerges from an encounter between them. Prefigurative democracy has typically horizontal features in that it accommodates participatory decision-making, direct-democratic organisation at a grassroots level, and decentralised 'bottom-up' forms of organisation. But it is also vertical in the sense that it requires the articulation of representative claims that do not appeal to an already-existing support base, but which instead are co-constitutive of their own referent. One thus has to take the initiative to stand for, and to speak or even act on behalf of, others – albeit without a formal mandate. Prefiguration and representation are by no means incompatible: the former presupposes the latter. In fact, symbolic political representation has a prefigurative element in that it anticipates a referent which must first be inscribed with a particular meaning. As contemporary social movements and their prefigurative practices combine aspects of verticalism and horizontalism, this suggests that we are 'not witnessing the end of representative politics but living through an era in which the ecology of representation is changing, becoming more complex and more dispersed' (Feenstra et al. 2017: 96).

Understanding how prefigurative democracy entails the articulation of representative claims also enables us to appreciate how prefigurative movements and practices continue to have an impact, long after the activist tent camps have been cleared out and the activists returned home. How to determine the measure of success that they have in the long term? Or is it at all possible to make such an assessment, based on the outcomes of a prefigurative practice or movement? This question will be addressed in the last chapter.

Chapter 5
Sedimentation and Crystallisation: Two Metaphors for Political Change

Arguably one of Occupy Wall Street's most characteristic features was 'the people's mic' – which, like many of its inventions, was 'mothered by necessity' (Gould-Wartofsky 2015: 67). The New York police would not permit the use of electronic amplification in Zuccotti Park, and so its occupiers resorted to another, more archaic means of mass communication. The idea is simple: anyone who wants to make an announcement shouts the words 'mic check'. Those within earshot will respond by repeating these words, and then those within a hearing distance from *them* again repeat the 'mic check' until a large crowd has become silent and is listening to the speaker – who then makes their statement in short intervals, which allows the people's microphone to repeat the message sentence by sentence. When Slavoj Žižek came to address the occupiers with a short speech, his message was thus amplified by repetition. Frequently interrupted (and visibly annoyed) by the people's mic, Žižek praised the movement for its ability to imagine alternatives to the failing, capitalist order. But he also warned the occupiers: 'There is a danger: Don't fall in love with yourselves. We have a nice time here. But remember: Carnivals come cheap. What matters is the day after when we will have to return to normal life. Will there be any changes then?' (Žižek 2011: 68).

How can prefigurative democracy lead to social and political change in the long term? In the course of the past decade prefigurative movements have often been dismissed as 'failures' because they did not immediately result in any durable and concrete changes at an institutional level. However, it is debatable to what extent the meaning of prefigurative democracy, or the value of the experiences that it entails, really depend on its concrete outcomes. It is precisely this instrumentalist understanding of political action that prefigurative democracy seeks to challenge (Van de Sande 2013). This does not mean, however, that prefigurative democracy does not or cannot lead to radical change in the long term. How may it a have a lasting impact, after the streets have been cleared out and the activists have returned home (or even ended up in prison)?

In this chapter I reconstruct two metaphors for political change that can be encountered in the political thought of Laclau and Arendt: sedimentation and crystallisation. Each offers a different perspective on how prefigurative democracy might continue to shape our understanding of the world, after its moment has passed. Laclau argues that systematic change requires the reactivation of our 'sedimented' social relations and practices. The originary acts and contingent divisions that lie at the origin of our social reality must be uncovered and reinscribed with a new political discourse. Radical change thus pertains to a simultaneous de-sedimentation (or dis-articulation) of our old social reality, and a sedimentation (or rearticulation) of a new one. A political movement will be successful if – and only if – it eventually manages to inscribe and consolidate a new discourse into our predominant conception of the social. But it is impossible to foretell in advance what discursive impact a political intervention might have in the long term.

Arendt may offer a very different understanding of political change and the impact of prefigurative democracy. One of her favourite quotes, which she took from the Roman poet Lucan and that she intended to use as an epigraph to the (unfinished) third part of *Life of the Mind*, well captures her view in this regard: 'The victorious cause pleased the gods, but the defeated one pleases Cato' (Arendt 1992: ii; see also Arendt 1978: 216; Beiner 1994). At the end of the day, what renders a political action meaningful is not the measure of 'success' that it had in the short or even the long term. Arendt employs the term 'crystallisation' to describe how political deeds and experiences of the past continue to have a bearing on the present. Even when they seem to have disappeared from our collective memory, she argues, such experiences may nevertheless continue to lead a subterranean life, and be resurfaced at a later stage in the form of story. They thus provide a testament to these experiences of the past and continue to inspire political deeds in the present. This is precisely why Arendt continues to return to the 'lost treasure' of council democracy – which was rediscovered and relived so many times in the course of the nineteenth and twentieth century. No matter how they ended or what their immediate outcomes turned out to be, these prefigurative experiences of the past continue to hold the promise of radical change in the present and future.

Laclau: Political Change as Sedimentation

Laclau uses the concept 'sedimentation' in a few places, most significantly his essay 'New Reflections on the Revolution of Our Time'. In order to appreciate his employment of this geological term, we must first reconstruct a few main aspects of his theoretical framework, in particular on his distinction between 'the social' and 'the political'. Laclau is a prominent exponent of what is sometimes called 'post-foundational' political philosophy. This means that, according to Laclau, our understanding of 'society' has no objective or essential foundation. What determines or characterises the social is radically open, and only this very openness is the 'constitutive ground or "negative essence" of the existing' (Laclau and Mouffe 2001: 95). As Oliver Marchart stresses, however, this does not mean that social relations are entirely groundless. After all, we do have a certain shared understanding of society, and one way or the other this understanding must have some sort of foundation (Marchart 2007: 12–13). The point of the matter is that this foundation is constructed and that, for this very reason, it can never be complete: precisely because the social is radically plural and lacks any objective ground, there will always be something that escapes its constructed self-understanding as a 'society' (Marchart 2018: 84). The social 'always exceeds the limits of the attempts to constitute society' (Laclau 1990a: 91).

To put it differently, a post-foundational ontology thus seeks to ground the social not in a bedrock foundation, but rather in a continuous practice of ground*ing* (Marchart 2007: 174). There always and inevitably remains a 'gap' or 'split' between a particular image of the society on the one hand, and the very process of its being constructed or articulated on the other. The very possibility of a continuous grounding, after all, presupposes precisely that no ground can ever be complete. This difference between *grounding* and *ground* corresponds with those 'between *ordering* and *order*, between *changing* and *change*, between the *ontological* and the *ontic* – oppositions which are only contingently articulated through the investment of the first of the terms into the second' (Laclau 2000a: 85). Were these two sides to coalesce with each other, then evidently no such gap would exist, and the *ground* for the social could not be differentiated from the practice of its *grounding*. In that case, no 'ontological difference would be possible: the ontic and the onto-logical would exactly overlap and we would simply have pure pres-ence' (Laclau and Zac 1994: 30). The social would fully coincide with itself and political change, or politics more generally, would not be imaginable (Marchart 2004). In other words, the social can-not have a ground that is completely closed in itself: it must always refer to a continuous process of *grounding* that reaches beyond it. And, the other way around, this grounding can only be made visible by reference to a particular, constructed ground, in which it has been invested.

What, then, *is* the social, according to Laclau? In order to answer this question, we first need to establish the distinction between 'the social' and 'the political'. Unlike classical Marxist theory, in which the political is generally understood to be part of a 'superstructure' that rests on a social or economic 'base', in Laclau's thought the political has 'the status of an *ontology of the social*' (Laclau and Mouffe 2001: xiv). It is impossible to conceive of a society that is completely free from the political, as this could only be 'a closed uni-verse merely reproducing itself through repetitive practice' (Laclau 1990b: 35). Laclau on this point agrees with Claude Lefort – who, as we have seen, argues that the social is always politically invested and that 'the very notion of society already contains within it a refer-ence to its political definition' (Lefort 1988b: 217). This is also why the social must always already have a particular institutional form (or, in Lefort's terms, a particular *mise en forme*).

Why, then, would it be necessary at all to distinguish between the social and the political, if the latter actively shapes and determines the former? This is so, because a social reality in which everything is immediately perceived as political is equally inconceivable. '[A] *total* political institution of the social can only be the result of an absolute omnipotent will, in which case the contingency of what has been instituted – and hence its political nature – would disap-pear' (Laclau 1990b: 35). As much as the social requires a distinctive political form, this form in turn loses its meaning if it is understood to encompass everything (Rancière 1999: 32). We must try to under-stand how the social – which is politically determined and thus potentially political in its every aspect – nevertheless 'overflows' the political and presents itself to us as the social.

This is where Laclau's concept of 'sedimentation' comes into play. He derives this metaphor from Edmund Husserl's phenomenological critique of science. Husserl argues that a scientific discipline becomes a constitutive part of our 'lifeworld' – the horizon on whose background we experience the world – only by virtue of its ability to forget or routinise its own history. The contingent choices, presuppositions and intuitions from which this discipline originated must be 'closed off through sedimentation or traditionalization' (Husserl 1970: 52). Thus perceived, scientific knowledge implies a forgetfulness for the contingencies that lie at its origins (Critchley 1999: 129). Smaller particles consolidate into larger particles, and eventually solidify. New layers of sediment cover the old ones, stratum upon stratum. The process of sedimentation is contingent, yet it may have a significant influence on the course of a stream or river, the composition of its water, or the vegetation in its beds. Sedimented particles may continue to have significant effects, even when they have long been covered under layers of dirt or debris. In a similar way, Husserl suggests, a scientific discipline gradually sediments, so that the contingencies and conventions at its origin can no longer be distinguished.

Laclau employs this metaphor in a slightly different context, when he claims that 'we live in a world of sedimented social practices' (Laclau et al. 1999: 146). Much like the scientific disciplines in Husserl's example, however, the institution of our social reality in general may also be understood to require a certain measure of 'forgetfulness'. The contingent actions and choices that lie at its origin – and the political divisions that originally invested our understanding of the social – are gradually concealed. The social could have been instituted in many different ways, but one of the effects of sedimentation is that 'the system of possible alternatives tends to vanish and the traces of the original contingency to fade' (Laclau 1990b: 34). Although the social has no 'objective' origins, the process of sedimentation gives rise to particular 'forms of "objectivity"' that underpin our understanding of the social (Lalcau 1990b: 35; Mouffe 2005b: 17).

Thus, whereas according to Husserl the task of philosophers is to reveal or 'reactivate' the sedimented origins of scientific traditions (Critchley 1999: 130–1), Laclau argues that the task of political actors is to disclose the antagonism and contingency that lie at the origins of sedimented social practices and relations (1990b: 34). 'It is only through this confrontation,' he holds, 'that the specifically political moment emerges, for it shows the contingent nature of articulations' (Laclau 2014b: 68). This, then, is what Laclau defines as 'the political': the 'instituting moment of society' (Laclau 1996: 49). Mouffe stresses that this is in fact a 'double moment . . . of dis-articulation and re-articulation' (Mouffe 2013: 74). The moment of 'the political' emerges whenever a sedimented conception of the social is confronted by a counter-hegemonic discourse that reactivates its contingent origins and inscribes it with a new understanding of the social.

How can Laclau's concept of sedimentation help us to better understand prefigurative democracy and its ability to change our understanding of the world – and, in consequence, the world itself? It seems evident that the occupations of Tahrir Square, Zuccotti Park and Gezi Park had a certain reactivating potential. They effectively disclosed a range of sedimented social relations and practices. The dictatorial regimes, democratic deficits, economic inequalities or severe austerity policies that these various occupy movements contested were generally held to be unquestionable or unchangeable. But as Žižek put it in his speech to OWS, when these movements emerged a taboo was broken (Žižek 2011: 68). Through their rhetoric and demands, as much as in their prefigurative practices, they showed that another world is indeed possible.

OWS, for instance, has clearly had a significant influence on the dominant political discourse – both in the United States and abroad. Arguably its chief accomplishment 'was changing the national conversation by giving Americans a new language – the 99 percent and the 1 percent – to frame the dual crises of income inequality and the corrupting influence of money in politics' (Levitin 2015). In the aftermath of these protests, many people in the US and abroad have continued to discuss economic issues in terms of class distinctions. And, though eventually unsuccessful, it is unlikely that Bernie Sanders's bid for the presidential nomination would have garnered so much popular support without this discursive shift (Stewart 2019).

Does this mean that Žižek's question, which was raised at the beginning of this chapter, can be answered in the positive? Have there been any significant societal changes on the 'day after', when the activist tent camps had been dismantled? In the next section I argue why, for Laclau, it will never be sufficient to temporarily challenge or reactivate a hegemonic discourse and its sedimented conception of the social. In order to establish durable political change in the long term, such discursive shifts must also be accompanied by structural change at an institutional level.

Politics, the Political, and the Need for Institutional Change

In one of the last texts he wrote before his death in 2014, Laclau critically reflects on the political impact of occupy movements and their prefigurative practices. Of course, he acknowledges, movements such as OWS and 15-M had been successful in establishing a mass mobilisation at a civil society level. They also significantly contributed to the establishment of new equivalential chains and forged new political alliances between various social groups and minorities. But they would never lead to substantial political change in the long term as long as their experiments with horizontalist and decentralised forms of organisation were not 'complemented by the vertical dimension of "hegemony" – that is, a radical transformation of the state' (Laclau 2014c: 9). Real political change, in other words, also requires institutional reform. Any reactivation or re-sedimentation of our social 'objectivity' needs to translate itself at the institutional level. Alternatively, one may argue that change at the level of 'the political' must be accompanied by change at the level of 'politics'. This formulation, however, hints at a conceptual distinction that is often made in contemporary political theory, but which largely remains implicit in Laclau's work: the distinction between 'the political' and 'politics' (Marchart 2007: 142; Torfing 1999: 294). If we are to understand Laclau's conception of political change and his critique of recent occupy movements, we may first need to reconstruct this implicit conceptual distinction.

The distinction between 'the political' and 'politics' is generally considered to originate in Carl Schmitt's seminal *The Concept of the Political*. Schmitt seeks to establish a clear criterion by which to distinguish the political from other modes of human thought and action, such as morality, aesthetics and economics. The criterion that he ends up with is that in any political action or relation there is (at least potentially) a conflict at play between friends and enemies. 'Politics', then, refers to a plurality of ways in which this conflict is accommodated – both at the level of the state and outside of it (Schmitt 2007: 26). Whereas Laclau seems more reluctant to uncritically endorse this Schmittian distinction, Mouffe has employed it more explicitly to show why a certain measure of conflict is vital for our understanding of democracy. However, she does seek to 'domesticate' Schmitt's conception of politics. Rather than the ontic level on which the antagonism between friends and enemies comes to the surface, she reads politics as an institutional sphere in which the animosity or conflict between these camps can be staged in a non-violent and democratically legitimate fashion. Politics thus comes to be understood as 'the ensemble of practices, discourses and institutions which seek to establish a certain order and organize human coexistence in conditions that are always potentially conflictual because they are affected by the dimension of "the political"' (Mouffe 2005a: 101).

If a similar distinction between the political and politics can be found at all in Laclau's thought, it does significantly deviate from Schmitt's and Mouffe's conception in at least one respect. Laclau's differentiation between the social and the political suggests that the ordering and organising function (which Mouffe ascribes to the level of politics) should instead be located on the plane of the political itself. After all, as Laclau and Mouffe state in *Hegemony and Socialist Strategy*, 'the problem of the political is the problem of the institution of the social, that is, of the definition and articulation of social relations in a field criss-crossed with antagonisms' (2001: 153). In this respect, then, Laclau is much closer to Lefort than to Schmitt and Mouffe. If the political pertains to the moment when sedimented social practices and relations are reactivated and rearticulated, then the question how the social is to be instituted must already be at stake at this level. And the other way around: if the social is defined as a sedimentation of such relations and practices, then this always already implies a particular understanding of political order, democratic legitimacy and social organisation. The question by which kinds of institutions and procedures the social comes to be informed, in other words, cannot exclusively belong to a secondary, ontic level – this is already immediately at stake at the ontological moment of reactivation and articulation.

How, then, does Laclau implicitly distinguish between politics and the political? Since the latter is defined as the ontological moment of political institution, this suggests that politics could be understood as its 'enactment' (Marchart 2007: 142) or 'actualisation' (Dyrberg 2004: 243) on an everyday, institutional, discursive and organisational level (Laclau 1996: 62). This enactment takes place against the background of sedimented relations and practices that we have called 'the social'. As we have seen, the political cannot be accessed or known as such, since its moment of investment in the social is always sedimented. We thus need to imagine 'politics' as a distinctive sphere of institutions, practices, discourses and strategies that embody or actualise this particular investment in our everyday interactions. If the political entails the articulation of the kind of 'order' or 'structure' that must be inscribed into the social, then politics refers to the structuring of these articulations in practice (Dyrberg 2004: 241).

This does not mean, however, that this political moment of reactivation and rearticulation must be a rare or once-in-a-lifetime event. Unlike, for instance, Alain Badiou, Laclau does not regard the political as a 'Truth-Event' that emerges out of nothing and thus reveals the singular Truth of the situation in which it intervenes (Badiou 2003: 14; 2012: 81; see also Žižek 2008: 147–55). Seen from a Laclauian point of view, after all, the political is enacted at the most everyday level of our social and political reality (Laclau 2014a: 205n18). We thus 'always already enact, in the most diverse and "shattered" ways, the political within the realm of the social' (Marchart 2007: 174). This has two further consequences. First, the reactivation and rearticulation of our understanding of the social may occur at any moment, any time, and in any context. Even 'the most minor forms of acting' can be of political significance 'as long as they recall the original political moment of foundation' (Marchart 2018: 153). Second, it follows that no grand or small political act can ever have any revelatory or universal meaning in and of itself. After all, the political is only accessible at the ontic level of everyday politics. Its enactment at this ontic level is a gradual process, which requires the establishment of new political institutions and discourses that can inscribe the political with a particular meaning.

In consequence, if the politics of a social movement – its forms and strategies of mass mobilisation, its street protests and democratic experiments – is prefigurative, then as far as Laclau is concerned, the 'pre' should be taken rather literally here. As we have seen, social movements and their prefigurative practices can make a significant difference. They can serve to reactivate the sedimented relations and practices that constitute our social reality. They can, moreover, articulate significant, synecdochal representative claims ('We are the 99%') that prefigure a particular concept of collectivity or political agency. But, Laclau holds, these protesters will eventually return home. Others will have to take upon themselves the task of mediating, reformulating, claiming and exploiting these movements' message as theirs. In that respect, what happens on 'the day after' matters a great deal. The prefigurative will be refigured, so to speak. A particular, figural unity will be inscribed in the various experiences and perspectives that the political moment comprised, so that a new, limited set of relations and practices will start to sediment. In this way, prefigurative democracy may indeed give rise to significant social and political change in the long term – although a longer process of gradual refiguration, using different institutional and procedural means, will be required to effectuate it. Prefigurative democracy must then be followed by an attempt to acquire hegemony at an institutional level.

I will return to this relation between prefiguration and its figural unity further below, when I reconstruct Arendt's concept of crystallisation. At this point, however, I will conclude my discussion of Laclau with a brief, critical note. As argued, Laclau's synecdochal concept of representation requires that a particular part of a 'people' takes upon itself the role of embodying or representing it as a whole. Political representation, he argues, is a 'vehicle of universalization', as the particular comes to signify the universal (Laclau 2000b: 212). Radical change thus pertains to the gradual sedimentation of *one truth* – one compatible set of demands and identities – which is understood to fully and exhaustively signify the many different positions and experiences that originally comprised a social movement and its discourses and practices.

If we are to understand how the prefigurative practices of social movements may lead to radical change in the long term, Laclau's approach has one important shortcoming. At the end of the day, his concept of sedimentation only allows us to scrutinise the particular ideas, demands, experiences and identities that eventually come to comprise the centre of a counter-hegemonic discourse – or its 'nodal points', as Laclau and Mouffe call it (2001: 112). The eventual political impact of a singular demand, claim or practice wholly depends on its ability to inscribe a hegemonic discourse and its key signifiers with a new meaning. In other words, all that really matters are the ideas and concepts that eventually come to sediment and consolidate in our dominant understanding of the social. The rest can and will most likely be forgotten.

But, one may object, is this the only way in which prefigurative democracy may have political impact in the long run? Is a discourse, or sedimented social practice, all that remains after the political moment has passed? Is it really only the core demand or the predominant identity and discourse of a social movement that may be of relevance in the long term – alongside its ability to acquire or reform institutional power? Surely, OWS will primarily be remembered for its '99%' slogan, and the Egyptian revolution of 2011 for forcing Mubarak's resignation. But it is neither impossible nor unlikely that other experiences or minor aspects of these recent occupy movements will, eventually, turn out to have a lasting effect or impact on our world as well. Some of these experiences – or the stories that result from them – may presently not fulfil any significant articulatory role whatsoever. They may not even 'fit in', or correspond with, the dominant representation that a social movement has of itself. But perhaps, to stick with Laclau's own geological metaphor, a single political event or movement might as well result in a variety of sedimentations and thus have a plurality of outcomes.

For another perspective on the meaning or impact of political action on the 'day after', I return to Arendt. Like Laclau, Arendt uses a metaphor to explain how the deeds of political actors may persist after their moment has passed: she compares it with the process of 'crystallisation'. This idea of crystallisation not only resonates with her open-ended conception of political action, but explains her fascination with the history of revolutionary councils. More importantly, it provides us with an answer to the question formulated above: how can prefigurative democracy be understood to have a plurality of outcomes? And how can some of these outcomes continue to have a political relevance?

Arendt: Political Change as Crystallisation

Throughout her oeuvre, Arendt tends to use the term 'crystallisation' in two different ways. First, she regularly employs it in her earlier work to describe the emergence of particular political tendencies, movements or ideas (such as totalitarianism or antisemitism). In one of her later essays on Walter Benjamin she establishes it as an analogy for his philosophical method. Thinking, she argues, could be compared with pearl diving, in the sense that the theorist searches for crystallised or ossified fragments of the past, in order to retrieve them from oblivion. Nevertheless, I argue that these two concepts of crystallisation are more similar than they appear to be at first sight.

Before we turn to Arendt's reading of Benjamin, let me first reconstruct her earlier references to crystallisation, which appear most frequently in *Origins of Totalitarianism*.[1] Arendt deliberately employs the term here. In fact, she later suggests that it more accurately grasps what is at stake in her book, which 'does not really deal with the "origins" of totalitarianism – as its title unfortunately claims – but gives a historical account of the elements which crystallized into totalitarianism' (Arendt 1994a: 403). She elsewhere notes that '[t]he elements of totalitarianism comprise its origins, if by origins we do not understand "causes." Elements by themselves never cause anything. They become origins of events if and when they suddenly crystallize into fixed and definite forms' (Arendt 1994c: 325n12). It is not entirely clear where Arendt first picked up this metaphor. Lisa Disch (1994: 147) retraces it to Immanuel Kant's *Kritik der Urteilskraft*. In his Third Critique, which largely deals with questions of aesthetics, Kant discusses the beauty that we encounter in nature. He refers to crystals as an example of this natural beauty, which has no purpose outside itself (Kant 2000: 224). What is distinctive about crystalline formations, Kant claims, is that they take shape 'through a sudden solidification, not through a gradual transition from the fluid to the solid state, but as it were through a leap' (Kant 2000: 222).[2] This, then, is what Kant calls crystallisation: the abrupt moment when – under specific conditions – different elements suddenly join together, and thus bring about new formations that have entirely different qualities than these constituent elements.

Arendt describes the emergence of totalitarianism in similar terms. It was the product of various contingent circumstances: a range of racist and antisemitic traditions, imperialist tendencies and European pan-movements; various organisational principles, propaganda techniques and methods of domination. Many of the constituent elements of totalitarianism had been subterraneously present in European culture for decades or even centuries. It was only when these simmering movements, ideas and principles met each other that the totalitarian form of government could come into being. '[N]early all elements that later crystallized in the novel totalitarian phenomenon,' Arendt stresses, 'had hardly been noticed by either learned or public opinion' before they surfaced in the form of a totalitarian politics (Arendt 1968f: xv). It was only 'the final crystallizing catastrophe [that] brought these subterranean trends into the open and to public notice' (Arendt 1968f: xv). Much like in Kant's description of crystallisation, there was something immediate about the emergence of totalitarianism, which may have been perceived as a sudden 'leap'.

Another striking point of commonality between the formation of crystalline structures and that of totalitarianism is that, in both cases, the constituent elements tend to crystallise into something that is not merely a sum of its constituent parts. In the case of totalitarianism, several movements and tendencies 'crystallized into a new form of government and domination' (Arendt 2006c: 26). Moreover, Arendt strongly opposes the idea that the crystallisation of totalitarianism was historically inevitable given its conditions of emergence (Bernstein 1996: 52). These conditions are always contingent: they do not follow any predefined plan or order, and thus can only be reconstructed from a retrospective point of view. However, in one of her earlier discussions of antisemitism Arendt also suggests that at various historical stages, the 'most disparate elements crystallised, joining together to form a unified structure again and again, despite the numerous occasions when its political core split apart' (Arendt 2007: 101). The conditions of crystallisation may be contingent, but they are by no means arbitrary, and thus can always reappear. Crystallisation, thus perceived, is a process that has no single, identifiable 'root' or 'origin', and no clear, predefined end. It pertains to a sudden fusion – under particular, contingent conditions – of different elements, some of which have been subterraneously present for a long time.

Although Arendt uses the term 'crystallisation' most frequently in her earlier writings on totalitarianism and antisemitism, it also appears in other places throughout her oeuvre. In *On Revolution*, for instance, she employs it in reference to the French and Russian revolutions (2006a: 47, 220). But the most elaborate discussion of the metaphor is given in her 1968 essay on Walter Benjamin. It does appear, however, that Arendt here uses it in a slightly different way. Whereas in her earlier work crystallisation is presented as a relatively sudden moment of fusion between different elements (or a 'leap', as Kant puts it), in her reading of Benjamin it precisely refers to a gradual process of ossification or transformation.

The overall objective of Arendt's essay is to reconstruct a typical philosophical methodology that Benjamin applies throughout his writings. Benjamin, Arendt claims, was a philosopher who 'without being a poet . . . thought poetically' (1968e: 166). He also made extensive use of metaphors, text fragments and quotations. His unfinished *Passagenwerk*, for example, largely consists of quotations from other writings that he collaged together and then complemented with brief comments of his own (Benjamin 1999). Arendt claims that, for Benjamin, 'to quote is to name, and naming rather than speaking, the word rather than the sentence, brings truth to light' (Arendt 1968e: 203). What necessitates this 'poetic' approach, moreover, is an end to the philosophical tradition and the decline of authority that both Arendt and Benjamin claimed to witness in their lifetime. A past that does not bear the authority of a tradition cannot be transmitted. It cannot simply be passed on by one generation, and accepted by the next. Benjamin's work could therefore be read as an attempt to invent a new form of writing history, which tries to break with the historical 'continuum' (Benjamin 1968b: 262) or the 'homogeneous, empty time' (Benjamin 1968b: 261) that most historians seek to reconstruct. Benjamin's solution was to use a different historiographic methodology. His aim was not to give an exhaustive and consistent representation of the past, but rather to trace its fragments – the bits and pieces of passed ages that could be restored and re-examined. It is through these particular shards or fragments that we can acquire an understanding of our history (Arendt 1968e: 193).

One of Benjamin's central premises, therefore, is that no causal relation or moment can be deemed 'historical' in its own right. Any event, any act or experience, might eventually be singled out as a turning point in history, but this is always done retrospectively, from the position of the historian (Benjamin 1968b: 263). It is key, therefore, not to distinguish between 'minor' and 'major' historical events, as their relevance or significance is never given. 'Nothing that has ever happened,' Benjamin states, 'should be regarded as lost for history', as these fragments could always be retrieved (Benjamin 1968b: 254). It is one thing to say that a particular event or act has no place in our current tradition or dominant discourse. What does not follow, however, is that the act or event in question therefore is irrelevant. In fact, Benjamin states, one could 'speak of an unforgettable life or moment even if all men [sic] had forgotten it' (1968a: 70).

Seen from this perspective, historiography is first and foremost the work of collectors, who search among the debris of history for experiences that are worth being recalled, or memories that must be retold (Arendt 1968e: 199–200). Such historical 'monads', as Benjamin calls them, must be treated as if they could encompass the whole of history in their own right. Rather than 'digging' for forgotten origins or uncovering subterraneous layers of sediment, historiography thus is more comparable to making a 'snapshot' – to use a more contemporary metaphor. The historian should always try to 'arrest' the historical event or moment: 'Thinking involves not only the flow of thoughts, but their arrest as well. Where thinking suddenly stops in a configuration pregnant with tensions, it gives

that configuration a shock, by which it crystallizes into a monad'
(Benjamin 1968b: 262–3).

According to Seyla Benhabib, it is precisely this 'method of
fragmentary historiography' that Arendt adopted from Benjamin.
Arendt too sought a methodology that could 'shatter chronology
as the natural structure of narrative', and that would instead focus
on the forgotten fragments of history – its 'dead ends, failures, and
ruptures' (Benhabib 1996: 88). One example is Arendt's biograph-
ical writings, in which she gives an account of an historical epoch
through the lens of a particular individual and their life story (see for
instance Arendt 1974). Another example is her engagement with the
short-lived revolutionary councils that emerged in various moments
and contexts throughout the past two centuries. Finally, Arendt's
historiographic methodology also becomes apparent in her use of
etymological analysis. It is through theoretical concepts as well as
more mundane terms that we can encounter the shards of a time
long gone, which nevertheless – through their very presence in our
everyday language – continue to shape our world and our understanding of it. The Greek *polis*, for example, 'will continue to exist
on the bottom of our political existence . . . for as long as we use
the word "politics"' (Arendt 1968e: 204). One important task of
theorists is to retrieve these fragments from oblivion.

It is not hard to imagine why the Benjaminian metaphor of
'crystallisation' applies so well here. Arendt compares his 'historical fragments' to bones or other organic remains that sink to
the bottom of the ocean and whose form and substance gradually
change there over time. '[A]lthough the living is subject to the ruin
of the time,' she claims, this 'process of decay is at the same time a
process of crystallization' (Arendt 1968e: 206). In the depth of the
sea these fragments 'survive in new crystallized forms and shapes
that remain immune to the elements' (Arendt 1968e: 206). Sooner
or later, they may be found and brought back to the surface. But
by that time, these fragments may not even remotely resemble their
original, constitutive elements. Paraphrasing Shakespeare, Arendt
claims that they will have 'suffered . . . the sea-change from living
eyes to pearls, from living bones to coral' (Arendt 1968e: 203).[3]
People will have forgotten about them, and perhaps one may not
even be able to recognise their original shape or texture. But the
'pearls' or 'crystals' that are eventually found on the bottom of the
ocean will be no less valuable or interesting than the remains that
once sank down. The purpose of pearl diving, then, is neither to

restore these remains in their original form, nor to investigate or appreciate the environment in which they ossified and crystallised over time. The point is to retrieve them and bring them to the surface, where they can be admired in their new, crystallised form. This, Arendt concludes in her reading of Benjamin, is the task of the theorist:

> Like a pearl diver who descends to the bottom of the sea, not to excavate the bottom and bring it to light but to pry loose the rich and the strange, the pearls and the coral in the depths and to carry them to the surface, . . . *thinking* delves into the depths of the past – but not in order to resuscitate it the way it was and to contribute to the renewal of extinct ages. (Arendt 1968e: 205)

Thus, two different concepts of crystallisation that can be found throughout Arendt's oeuvre. The first, which appears frequently in her earlier work, is derived from Kant's aesthetics. Arendt uses it 'to resist making a causal explanation of totalitarianism, describing it as an amalgam of fragments that are only contingently related' (Disch 1994: 147). Rather than attempting to uncover the origins or causes of totalitarianism's emergence, she seeks to disentangle and reconstruct its various, constituent elements, and the conditions of their encounter. In Arendt's later essay on Benjamin, however, crystallisation is presented as a gradual process rather than as a sudden moment or eruption. It should be noted that both, indeed, are natural processes of crystallisation – but they nevertheless are different processes, which have different implications as analogies of political change. The difference between her Kantian and her Benjaminian concept of crystallisation is that in the latter case, crystalline formations do not 'spring forth' from a fusion of various subterraneous elements. Instead, crystallisation here is understood as a gradual process.

However, these two conceptions of crystallisation also seem to have something essential in common (Disch 1997: 147n12). Both teach us that political experiences, ideas, memories or tendencies from the past may disappear from the public eye, but they can continue to lead a subterraneous life. They may resurface whenever they meet other subterraneous elements, thus constituting a new crystalline formation. Or they undergo a gradual transformation. The conditions under which these forgotten fragments may resurface are contingent. But when they do make it back to the surface, in a new form and context, these forgotten fragments of the past can have a significant impact.

What does this mean concretely? How exactly can the experiences, memories or ideas of political actors be preserved – and, eventually, retrieved – in order to make a difference in the long term? Arguably the greatest weakness of Arendt's metaphor is that it implies (much like Laclau's sedimentation, for that matter) that such processes tend to take their own, natural course. It suggests that all political theorists need to do is to '[dig] under the rubble of history so as to recover those "pearls" of past experience' (Benhabib 1996: 87). But the concept of crystallisation only makes for a useful metaphor if it helps us to understand the role of the theorist or storyteller in this process of transformation. In that respect, the metaphor indeed falls short. This weakness becomes most notable in Arendt's discussion of Benjamin, where she discusses crystallisation as a gradual process. Ultimately, an additional metaphor is required to explain how past ideas and experiences may continue to play a political role long after their moment has passed: that of the pearl diver, who retrieves these crystalline formations from the bottom of the ocean. One may argue that this is the real political metaphor: without the work of theorists, historians and storytellers we would never learn of the existence of these past ideas and experiences. Before I continue to compare Arendt's metaphor of crystallisation with Laclau's notion of sedimentation, I will therefore briefly reconstruct the political role that she ascribes to stories and storytelling in the next section.

The Political Role of the Storyteller

One essential trait of prefigurative democracy is its open-endedness. Those involved in a prefigurative politics thus often seek to prolong their practices as much as possible. It is for this reason that Arendt's concept of action corresponds so well with the self-perception of prefigurative social movements, which often do not seem to pursue any clear, predefined end. This also explains why the council may be the most suitable institutional form for a prefigurative democracy in the long term, as it best caters to a radically open-ended politics.

Yet, it nevertheless seems to be the case that political action often does, sooner or later, come to its end – even if, in many cases, this end is not wanted, anticipated or projected by the actors in question. The occupy movements of the previous decade, such as OWS, 15-M, the Gezi Park protests or Nuit Debout, clearly were no exception to this rule: eventually, the squares cleared out, the activist tent camps were dismantled, and their temporary inhabitants were either arrested or returned home. Of course, such social movements may always come back and try again, or instead resolve to different tactics next time. But even from Arendt's point of view, there is a certain truth to the idea that, eventually, 'people always go home' (Errejón and Mouffe 2016: 72). What, then, is supposed to happen on the 'day after'?

In some respects, Arendt's answer to this question seems to resonate with that of Laclau. Even if political actions come to an end – eventually, and often in spite of themselves – it does not follow that they cease to have political significance. The experiences and memories of the political moment may continue to shape our world and our understanding of it, long after the actors have left the scene. For Arendt, the end of political action is by no means the end of politics. Once the moment has passed and the actors returned home, there is another political role to be played by the storyteller or the historian who will narrate their story (Beiner 1994: 374).

Throughout her work, Arendt presents a number of arguments to distinguish between the political role of actors and of storytellers. Although the former 'may in rare cases give an entirely trustworthy statement of intentions, aims, and motives' (Arendt 1958: 192), they usually do not offer a very accurate account of their own deeds. What exactly was at stake in a moment of political action, Arendt claims, 'reveals itself fully only to the storyteller, that is, to the backward glance of the historian, who indeed always knows better what it was all about than the participants' (Arendt 1968e: 192; see also Arendt 1968c: 21). Arendt hence is rather critical of actors who seek to 'make' their own life story (1968b: 106). How one's acts will be remembered and one's stories retold, she holds, is not in the hands of the actor themselves. In the end, 'the stories, the results of action and speech, reveal an agent, but this agent is not an author or producer' (Arendt 1958: 184; see also Cavarero 2000: 28). The storyteller, in turn, is dependent on the actions that others began since nobody – neither the actor nor the storyteller – can legitimately claim to have authored this story on their own. Rather, it is precisely in the interaction between actor and storyteller that a story takes shape (Pirro 2001: 77–8).

A second, related, reason to distinguish between the role of the actor and that of the storyteller is that political action is often too complex and messy. The anarchist author and independent diplomat Carne Ross offers an interesting metaphor that helps to better appreciate this complexity. In popular culture, politics is often imagined to resemble a game of chess: 'it is complicated, it involves two clearly defined opponents, and, . . . although a very difficult game, it is ultimately comprehensible' (Ross 2011: 130). But rather than an orderly chessboard, Ross argues, politics is more comparable to a Jackson Pollock painting: 'a swirling miasma of billions upon billions of interactions, not on a fixed pattern, or a net, but an ever-changing mesh of connections, some significant but temporary, some long-lasting but inconsequential' (Ross 2011: 132; see also Scott 2012: 141). Hence, to grasp the meaning of a particular political act or moment, we need to differentiate between the innumerable experiences, ideals, motivations and impressions that it comprises.

Arendt also holds that, in itself, such a 'totality of facts and event . . . is unascertainable' (2006d: 257). Truth is never revealed simply by summing up facts. They must first lose some of their eventual contingency, and instead 'acquire some humanly comprehensible meaning' (Arendt 2006d: 257). This is the task of the storyteller – be it an artist, a historian, a philosopher or a political theorist. By constructing relations between different events or acts; by amplifying and emphasising certain aspects whilst concealing or omitting others; by drawing patterns, and inscribing metaphors or comparisons, the storyteller creates a certain unity that was present – but not immediately apparent – in the bare facts themselves. Storytellers thus add something to the narrated story. They provide a structure, consistency or focus without which the facts would remain incomprehensible. As Adriana Cavarero argues, '[t]he significance of the story lies precisely in the figural *unity* of the design'. But it is only through storytelling that this design can be retrospectively inscribed in it. Political action 'does not follow from any projected plan' (Cavarero 2000: 1). If it at all acquires a figural unity, this 'only comes afterwards' (Cavarero 2000: 144). Storytellers preserve our experiences by abstracting a certain figural unity or structure from them (Cavarero 2000: 25). This articulatory process is precisely what Arendt elsewhere describes as crystallisation: a gradual transformation or a sudden 'springing together' of past memories and experiences into a new formation. Such a crystalline formation may show us its constituent elements in an entirely different structure and composition.

What, then, does this teach us about political change? For Arendt, change is never established in the moment of action per se. Although many of her more radical, contemporary commentators tend to focus on her analysis of the extraordinary or constitutive political moments itself, what happens in its aftermath is of no less significance. Arendt's concept of political action pertains first and foremost to the prefigurative and experimental moment in which actors gather to act and organise without any predefined end. But in order to become a constitutive part of our lifeworld, their deeds and words 'must first be seen, heard and remembered and then transformed' (Arendt 1958: 95). Through storytelling, the prefigurative moment may lose some of its initial, 'messy' or 'swirly' characteristics (to stick with Ross's metaphor of the Pollock painting), and retrospectively acquire a more concrete and figurative form. Moreover, such stories not only have an important, articulatory function, but they also serve to 'provoke and inspire others to act' (Kateb 1987: 14).

Take, for example, David Graeber's book *The Democracy Project*, from which I have quoted extensively throughout the past chapters. OWS has been widely dismissed as an utter failure, as it allegedly did not establish anything of significance. But in his account, Graeber instead seeks to explain why this movement in fact *did* 'work' (Graeber 2013: 59; Van de Sande 2014). 'In one year,' he asserts, '*Occupy* managed to both identify the problem – a system of class power that has effectively fused together finance and government – and to propose a solution: the creation of a genuinely democratic culture' (Graeber 2013: 149). Seen from this perspective, then, OWS indeed was very successful: it introduced a new popular identity ('the 99%'), and established a new political discourse that allows Americans to speak of their society in terms of a class distinction (Graeber 2013: 109). By occupying public space, it created or reappropriated a commons. OWS also experimentally gave rise to new experiences with, and notions of, political organisation, decision-making and mass mobilisation. And, Graeber holds, it 'broke the spell' of a hegemonic, neoliberal discourse, and proved to its participants that another world *is* possible (Graeber 2013: 295). Of course, one could give many other – and much less favourable – accounts of these experiences. Graeber's story is undeniably incomplete and selective. But, with Arendt, we may conclude that this is precisely what renders storytelling a political practice. From the vast amount of experiences and memories that comprised OWS's prefigurative practices, Graeber has carved out a story that follows a concrete pattern and inscribes the moment with a particular meaning. It thus presents OWS experiences in a new, crystalline form. Through such accounts, OWS and similar prefigurative movements may continue

to inform the political practices and discourses of future generations
of activists.

Conclusion: 'In the Beginning' and 'Once Upon a Time'

Two metaphors may help us to understand how prefigurative practices continue to shape our social and political reality, long after the
street or the occupied square has been evacuated and the protesters
have returned home (or have been arrested): Laclau's notion of sedimentation and Arendt's concept of crystallisation. Both imply that,
in order to have significant impact in the long term, political experiences must be translated in one way or the other. Arendt and Laclau
also seem to agree that whatever happens in the political moment
itself by no means determines how it will be perceived or appreciated
in the future. Whether a prefigurative action can be deemed (un)suc-
cessful, (in)significant or historically (ir)relevant largely depends on
the meaning that is retrospectively inscribed in it. Sedimentation and
crystallisation could both be considered as figurative processes that
succeed the prefigurative moment of political action. In this respect,
there appears to be a strong similarity between these two metaphors.

Yet, these two metaphors also serve very different purposes.
Laclau's sedimentation refers to the establishment of a political
discourse and its inscription in a sedimented concept of the social.
Arendt's crystallisation, on the other hand, is closely related to the
practice of storytelling. Discourses and stories differ from each other
in a number of respects. To begin with, discourses have no 'outside',
so to speak. We continuously reproduce a hegemonic discourse in
our everyday relations and communication – often without being
aware of it. Stories, on the other hand, 'are designed and deliberate,
at least broadly scripted . . . and deployed in pursuit of particular
objectives' (Selbin 2010: 48). They tend to have a concrete form,
which distinguishes them from other discursive elements. Or, as
Francesca Polletta (2006: 7) puts it, 'most people know when they
are telling a story'. From this follows, second, that different stories
or divergent accounts of the same event are not mutually exclusive.
The very particularity of stories – the fact that they are always told
from a particular position or perspective, with a specific intention,
and that they have a deliberate structure – precisely implies that
there will always be other stories that may shed an entirely different
light on the matter. Any act or moment can be narrated or explained
in innumerable different ways. In fact, for Arendt this is precisely

the purpose of storytelling: it is by hearing many different stories, each told from their own perspective, that we learn to 'think with an enlarged mentality' and that 'one trains one's imagination to go visiting' (Arendt 1992: 43). Stories have a pedagogic function: they stimulate and develop the critical faculties of the audience (Disch 1993: 681), precisely because they are always told from a singular and particular perspective. This also implies that, unlike discourses, stories do not necessarily seek hegemony. A story can well exist in the periphery of a dominant discourse without losing any of its critical potential. Even if it goes largely forgotten, it always remains to hold the promise of rediscovery. Sooner or later, Benjamin's 'pearl diver' may retrieve it from oblivion and bring it back to the surface.

A political discourse, on the other hand, typically seeks to 'dominate the field of discursivity' (Laclau and Mouffe 2001: 112). As we have seen in the previous chapter, this means that it must take upon itself the role to represent or embody the social in its entirely – even though this always remains an impossibility. A discourse must at least pretend to be totalising and exhaustive. Its success precisely depends on its ability to dominate the public debate and institutions and to sediment in our common understanding of the social. Of course, there are always different discourses competing for hegemony, but they merely coexist to the extent that they are each other's constitutive outside – an outside that, paradoxically, is inevitably implied in any attempt to represent the social in its totality.

It is here that we arrive at the heart of the matter. The difference between discourses and stories is precisely that the former must sediment into our dominant understanding of the social, whilst stories may crystallise independently of each other, and thus continue to live subterraneously. The question is to what extent these two perspectives are compatible. Can sedimentation and crystallisation be understood to exist alongside, or even presuppose, each other? The latter most certainly seems to be the case if we approach it from Laclau's perspective. What he describes as a process of articulation pertains precisely to the continuous incorporation – and, as a consequence, the reinscription – of demands, identities, stories and experiences into a new, counter-hegemonic discourse. The construction of equivalential chains, in other words, could well be compared with a 'springing together' of old discursive elements into new formations and compositions. In fact, Laclau uses the term 'crystallisation' rather frequently to describe precisely this process. He argues, for instance, that a chain of equivalence 'would not go beyond a vague feeling of solidarity if [it] did not crystallize in a certain discursive identity' (Laclau 2005a: 93). When demands and identities acquire hegemony, he states elsewhere, they thus come to be 'crystallised in sedimented social practices' (Laclau 2005a: 224). As much as stories are among the constituent part of a discourse, crystalline formations can indeed be seen to settle into a more encompassing sediment bed. But all that matters for Laclau, ultimately, is what crystalline formations end up constituting the 'top layer' of social sediment. This is where his account of crystallisation differs significantly from that of Arendt, for whom any crystalline formation will retain its potential relevance and promise for the future, no matter what role it may eventually come to play in the establishment of a new counter-hegemonic discourse.

Perhaps the best way to illustrate the difference between these two logics is to compare them with two fundamentally different narrative forms. In *On Human Conduct*, Michael Oakeshott makes a distinction between stories that typically start with 'In the beginning . . .' and the ones that commence with 'Once upon a time . . .' Stories of the first category serve to construct a myth. They seek to unearth one particular origin or create a single grand narrative that may 'serve as an authority for future conduct' (Oakeshott 1975: 105). This is why most foundational myths of cultural and/or political communities start with 'In the beginning there was . . .' It appears that the sedimentation of social relations and practices requires such foundational myths. But Oakeshott – who is arguably a rare case of a non-foundationalist conservative (Marchart 2007: 3) – also distinguishes another narrative form. 'Such a story does not open with the unconditional, "In the beginning . . ." but with a conditional, "Once upon a time . . ." And it has no unconditional conclusion; its end is the beginning of another story' (Oakeshott 1975: 105).

Rather than fixating on the supposed origin or outcomes of a narrated act or event, these 'Once upon a time . . .' stories allow us to look for its own meaning. And, Bonnie Honig (2009: 36) adds, they 'invite entry into another time and postulate many temporalities. (That they imagine *a* time suggests there are others as well)'. Their narrative form implies that there are in fact many 'times' existing alongside each other – and, thus, that there are many different stories to be told. Whereas an 'In the beginning . . .' story testifies to a sedimentary logic, the 'Once upon a time . . .' form implies that stories can also continue to lead their own, subterraneous life in the peripheries of our hegemonic, political discourses.

Arendt's and Laclau's concepts of political change thus seem to correspond with these two different narrative forms. Nevertheless, what these philosophers seem to have in common is that both shed a different light on the question whether, or how, prefigurative democracy can be rendered a 'success' or a 'failure'. Seen from both perspectives, Žižek's appeal to the OWS activists – 'What matters is the day after . . . Will there be any changes then?' – cannot immediately be answered. From a Laclauian point of view this is impossible because prefigurative democracy must eventually contribute to the articulation of a counter-hegemonic discourse. But this is often a long and gradual process, the course of which is contingent on many factors and influences. And although prefigurative practices and the representative claims that accompany them may thus have a significant impact, it is impossible to pinpoint the exact contribution of singular political events or interventions.

Arendt, on the other hand, criticises the very notion that political action can be 'successful' to a greater or lesser extent. She enables us to understand how prefigurative democracy questions this criterion at a much more fundamental level. Seen from an Arendtian perspective, prefigurative democracy is first and foremost a meaningful experience to those engaged in it. Its eventual outcomes do not affect the immediate experience of freedom that it entails. This does not mean, of course, that such experiences cannot be a source of inspiration, hope or empowerment to others in the future. What remains are the stories and accounts of political deeds in the past. They may be forgotten, or suppressed. But eventually they can always be retrieved and retold. This is precisely why Arendt repeatedly returns to the past experiences of revolutionary councils throughout the nineteenth and twentieth century. No matter how these previous experiments with radical self-organisation and spaces of *isonomia* eventually came to an end, the accounts of these short-lived council systems also continued to inspire others and testified to the possibility that freedom be realised in the 'here and now'. Thus, as much as 'success' is never a sufficient criterion by which to assess such prefigurative practices, they can also never 'fail' since the stories based on them will retain their promise for the future. Sooner or later these stories may re-emerge in a new form and continue to play their part in the political institution of society.

Conclusion
What Is Prefigurative Democracy?

The concept of 'prefiguration' or 'prefigurative politics' has a complex and diverse history. As a term, it has been employed in a variety of contexts since the 1970s and thus has acquired a range of different uses and meanings over time. However, it refers to a particular logic of social and political change that has informed, or even shaped, various radical tendencies and practices since the nineteenth century. In the wake of recent 'occupy movements' such as Occupy Wall Street (OWS), the Spanish 15-M movement, Nuit Debout or the Gezi Park protests this concept has received increased attention in academic debates. But it often remains unclear what 'prefiguration' exactly is. Some take it to be a revolutionary strategy that is employed in the pursuit of radical change. Others see it as a way to experience political liberation within their everyday lives and environment. My aim is to conceptualise prefigurative democracy as an attempt to change the political institution of society. This yields an understanding of the radical potential of protest and social movements today. In the remaining pages, let me summarise my theory of prefigurative democracy in five theses.

1: Prefigurative Democracy Is Neither Revolutionary Nor Reformist

The purpose of prefigurative democracy is to politically re-institute society – and to do this now, not merely in a distant future. In this sense, it poses an alternative to both reform and revolution as traditional conceptions of radical change. Prefigurative democracy derives from the originally anarchist conception of prefiguration to some degree, and breaks with it in a number of other respects.

On the one hand, it aligns with the anarchist notion insofar as it maintains that meaningful change can and must be realised in the 'here and now' – and not merely in a distant future. But on the other hand, the anarchist idea of prefiguration as a process of 'building a new society in the shell of the old' no longer applies in a discussion of contemporary social movements. The image of a 'new society' – which, like a sterile embryo, gradually grows in the womb of the 'old' one – evinces the implicit ideal of an organic or post-political society that is essentially devoid of social conflict or antagonism. Even if this is perceived as the ultimate aim rather than a feasible objective of prefigurative democracy, the ideal of a post-political society detracts from its true radical potential.

More importantly, the ultimate aim of a post-political society is not only unattainable but also undesirable. It is here that radical-democratic theory offers an important insight, which is often referred to as the 'autonomy of the political'. This means that the social is always and inevitably politically instituted (Marchart 2007: 48). There is no such thing as a 'society' that ontologically precedes, or exists in isolation of, its political institutions or procedures. Of course, political conflict may be understood to have its proper or legitimate place within a distinctively political sphere. But the ability to imagine such a political sphere already presupposes a particular shared understanding of who or what a well-ordered 'society' is, and what kind of institutions or procedures it deems legitimate to begin with. To put it in the words of Claude Lefort, our 'very notion of society already contains within it a reference to its political definition' (1988b: 217). This definition can be given in a myriad of different ways and from a variety of perspectives. It thus follows that the meaning and structure of 'society' will always and inevitably be subject to political conflict and contestation. Consequently, the ideal of a post-political society is essentially anti-democratic, since any attempt to establish a society devoid of conflict or division will render such political differences invisible. This is one of the key insights of radical democracy as a theoretical tendency: that our understanding of 'society' is politically constituted – and that, in a pluralistic society, its meaning thus will always be subject to political debate, revision and rearticulation. The task of democratic institutions or procedures is precisely to accommodate and stage such a pluralistic and continuous debate.

It is for this reason that I have proposed an alternative, radical-democratic conception of prefiguration. If society is always already politically constituted, then it is primarily at the level of its political form or institutions that change must be pursued. Rather than an attempt to foreshadow an organic or harmonious society in the here and now, prefigurative democracy is a way to experimentally change its political institution. Critics may argue that by insisting on the autonomy of the political, I risk neglecting the social or economic implications and potentials of prefigurative democracy. Most prefigurative movements tend to be strongly anti-capitalist: they not only seek political or institutional change, but also aim to restructure social relations at an economic level. Indeed, prefigurative experimentation often takes place at the most everyday level of social and economic life. The purpose of prefigurative democracy is precisely to politicise social relations or contexts that were hitherto not perceived as legitimately political. As Arendt has argued in the context of revolutionary councils, such radical forms of participatory democracy can emerge in any 'accidental proximity' (2006a: 259). The point, therefore, is not to deny that social and economic relations will often be at stake in prefigurative democracy – and that, in consequence, prefigurative democracy must indeed be anti-capitalist. But this entails challenging the supposedly a-political nature of these social and economic relations, which starts by questioning the (often invisible and implicit) way in which they are politically instituted, and by proposing a different form in which they can be organised.

One may nevertheless ask if, by conceptualising prefiguration from a radical-democratic perspective, I have not effectively given up on its revolutionary aspirations? After all, what is the point of pursuing radical change if it is not at least informed by the ultimate goal of a just society that is devoid of any social division or conflict? Indeed, prefigurative democracy is not revolutionary in the traditional sense. Its success or failure also does not depend on its ability to establish complete and definitive systemic change in the long term or to change society in its every aspect. Prefigurative democracy may as well occur on a smaller scale or temporary basis, and nevertheless be of great significance to its participants (and thus continue to hold a promise for the future). What is more, many participants in recent prefigurative movements (such as OWS and 15-M) were rather ambivalent about their revolutionary inclinations (Flesher Fominaya 2020: 80). Although most of them sought radical change, they did not necessarily dismiss representative democracy per se – or even all of its existing procedures and institutions. At the same time, prefigurative democracy clearly is also not reformist, if this means that social and political change must be piecemeal, gradual, and based on the implementation of a predefined model or plan. And it is certainly a radical form of politics in that it intervenes in society's institution at the most fundamental level. It questions and seeks to reconstitute its political form (*mise en forme*), staging (*mise en scène*) and meaning (*mise en sens*).

2: Prefigurative Democracy Is Both Formal and Substantive

Although it is often suggested that prefigurative politics implies an equivalence of (or full consistency between) means and ends, I assert that prefigurative democracy is a radically open-ended practice. In fact, it is underpinned by a critique of instrumentalism and the very logic of means and ends in politics. Rather than the pursuit of a clearly defined and distant end, prefigurative democracy has a distinctively *experimental* form, in that the rearticulation of its abstract goals is continuously at stake in prefigurative democracy itself. It also has an important *experiential* value, in that it entails the immediate experience of freedom in practice. It thus appears that those engaged in a prefigurative movement or practice often seek to maintain their practices as long as possible – rather than to bring it to a close. A good illustration of this is the attempt of various occupy movements to set up durable networks of neighbourhood councils or local assemblies after their occupy camps had been evacuated (Flesher Fominaya 2020: 120; Roos 2013; Sánchez 2012).

This gives rise to the question if prefigurative democracy may acquire a more durable institutional form, whilst retaining precisely its radical open-endedness. Many recent occupy movements typically employed the public assembly as its most important body of collective decision-making. Although the assembly clearly has a number of important prefigurative features, it also tends to have a temporary and fleeting character. Butler (2015: 75) describes the assembly as an 'anarchist moment' or 'anarchist passage' that only briefly emerges to make an intervention in the political status quo. Is there a specific institutional form that may accommodate prefigurative democracy in the long term? Following Arendt, we have seen that the council – or, to be more precise, a federated system of democratic councils in various forms and capacities – best serves to reconcile the open-ended nature of prefigurative democracy with the need to give it a durable institutional form. More than any other form of government, council democracy is subject to constant augmentation and rearticulation. In fact, radical self-reform may well be considered the primary political matter at stake in any institutionalised form of prefigurative democracy.

This also leads us to ask whether prefigurative democracy pertains to a formal view of social movement strategy and organisation, or to a more substantive idea of democracy. In most theoretical accounts prefiguration is first and foremost understood to prescribe a particular formal relation between the means and ends, or the present and the future, in activist practices. For others, however, it rather connotes direct-democratic or consensus-oriented decision-making, horizontal and decentralised organisational structures, or an attempt to immediately establish greater gender and racial equality within one's social movement or everyday life. It is also often associated with attempts to establish alternative economic structures and relations of property. However, I assert that there is a more immediate connection between the institutional or organisational form of prefigurative democracy on the one hand, and the substantive ideal of democracy that is implied in it, on the other. Its preference for participatory decision-making and decentralised organisation clearly corresponds with its experimental and open-ended character. If prefigurative democracy typically seeks its own continuation, rather than pursuing a predefined end, then it arguably requires a durable institutional form that is always open to alteration and reconstitution. Whereas there is a constant – and, to some degree, irresolvable – tension between political action and its institutionalisation, this tension at the same time manifests a close interconnection between the form and content of prefigurative democracy. Much like a conceptual distinction between means and ends, which is often projected on political practices from an external and abstract point of view, form and content may not be as easily distinguishable as political theorists often seem to assume.

3: Prefigurative Democracy Is Horizontal as Well as Vertical

The slogans and prefigurative practices of recent occupy movements have been widely understood to celebrate participatory democracy and manifest a principled rejection of political representation in its every kind. Many of these movements indeed were rather critical of electoral-representative democracy in its current state. At the same time, as is evinced by slogans such as 'We are the 99%', these practices have never been entirely devoid of representative claims. I argue that contemporary social movements are prefigurative not *in spite of* their representative role, but precisely *by virtue of* these aspects. Whereas prefigurative democracy often entails experimentation with participatory or horizontal forms of organisation and decision-making, such practices also symbolically 'stand for' something or someone that exceeds them. Rather than a dismissal of political representation per se, prefigurative democracy thus presupposes a very specific form of representation, which is not based on a formal mandate and thus does not limit citizens in their ability to take the initiative and participate in democratic politics. Laclau suggests that political representation typically has a synecdochal form, in which the whole is represented by one of its constitutive parts. This form of the *pars pro toto* may indeed be recognised in various aspects of recent occupy movements: the way they articulated representative claims (such as 'We are the 99%'), their laying claim to public space and its reappropriation as a commons, and their experiments with more horizontal and participatory forms of organisation.

This means that neither a purely participatory view of democracy nor a theory that largely equates political action with representation can offer a sufficient basis for our understanding of prefigurative democracy. The experiences of the past decade urge us to include both perspectives in our analysis of prefigurative movements and practices. As we saw in the introductory chapter, prefigurative politics was originally associated with a relatively limited range of radical or revolutionary social movements on the Left. It might be an exaggeration to state that today, with the emergence of the politically more diverse occupy movements, prefiguration has entered the mainstream of contentious politics. But it clearly has come to play a much more important role in the repertoire and rhetoric of contemporary social movements. At the same time, many of these movements no longer fit into the binary opposition between participatory democracy or 'horizontalism' on the one hand, and representative democracy or 'verticalism' on the other (Nunes 2021; Süß 2021). If we are to make sense of recent developments, it thus is necessary to reconcile these various strands of the radical-democratic tradition. A theory of 'prefigurative democracy' that combines key insights of these various tendencies can help us to acquire a better understanding of these movements and their democratic relevance and potential today.

Of course, such combinations between participatory and representative forms of democracy may take very different shapes and directions. One way would be to create new representative institutions, alongside the liberal-democratic state (Teivainen 2016: 31–3). As we saw in Chapter 3, this is precisely what some recent occupy movements set out to do. The public assemblies, neighbourhood councils and networks of local 'communes' that continue to emerge in various places around the world offer a space for democratic participation and collective deliberation. At the same time, these alternative institutions of participatory democracy also fulfil an important representative role. They symbolically 'stand for' – and, in consequence, give rise to – a broader constituency or support base.

4: Prefigurative Democracy Is In, Against, Beyond and In Engagement With the State

By challenging this binary opposition between horizontalism and verticalism, my conception of prefigurative democracy arguably also opens up new avenues for rethinking its relation with the liberal-democratic state and its electoral-representative institutions. Prefiguration is traditionally understood as 'the ideal strategy for the construction of an alternative world without engaging with the state or other powers that be' (Maeckelbergh 2009: 95). But even if its ultimate goal is to radically change the political form of society – in other words: even if it deliberately seeks to oppose or reach beyond liberal democracy as we know it today – it remains questionable if it is always desirable, or even feasible, for a prefigurative movement or practice to eschew any engagement with established electoral-representative governments (at a local or national level).

There are a number of reasons to suggest that prefigurative democracy may not always be incompatible with a more strategic approach at various levels of the state. For one, by refusing to engage with such platforms, activists and social movements arguably deny themselves a valuable opportunity to use them for their own purposes. Rather than a cohesive set of institutions and procedures that all serve a common purpose, the modern liberal-democratic state may as well be understood as a more 'complex set of relations, dynamic and traversed by contradictions' (Mouffe 2013: 119). There may often be a potential to exploit the many tensions, conflicts and differences that exist between its various levels of governance and decision-making. Why should one not try to 'use the state, to secure new universal rights . . . of the type that have been prefigured in the occupied squares of 2011?' (Gerbaudo 2013). Perhaps the most important question, then, is not how any form of contact or engagement with the state may be avoided, but instead how a prefigurative movement could explore these possibilities whilst retaining its radical-democratic, experimental and open-ended character.

One evident objection to engagement with the liberal-democratic state is that such an approach would not be consistent with the aim of establishing a more participatory form of democracy – in short, that it would not be prefigurative. This is indeed how prefiguration has traditionally been defined: as an attempt to establish a perfect consistency between the means and ends of one's political practice. However, as we saw in Chapter 2, it may be impossible to maintain consistency as one of the defining features of prefigurative democracy. Many recent prefigurative movements or practices do not appear to have had a clearly defined end in the first place. The criterion of consistency between means and ends arguably also feeds into a rather puritan and self-limiting understanding of social movement politics. This is also implied in the idea that a 'new society' can and must be 'built within the shell of the old'. To what extent is it at all possible to create a sterile, embryonic new society in a time when the modern state has permeated nearly every aspect of our social and everyday life?

For these reasons, and notwithstanding their previous critique of electoral-representative government, some activists and social movements have indeed continued to pursue an electoral strategy, after their prefigurative experiments in occupied public spaces had come to an end (Flesher Fominaya 2020: 304; Tormey 2015: 113). Probably the most prominent example is the Spanish left-populist party Podemos, which emerged in the aftermath of the 15-M movement and initially had considerable success in national and European elections (Errejón and Mouffe 2016: 70–1). For its founder and former leader Pablo Iglesias, the turn to an electoral strategy was simply a logical next step (Iglesias 2015: 11–15). For others, it was arguably a much more unexpected and innovative turn towards a different political repertoire. In the Spanish city of Castellón de la Plana, for example, 15-M activists have taken part in the formation of a new public platform named Castelló en Moviment, which ran in the local elections of 2014 (Ordóñez et al. 2017). Their aim was to 'change traditional mechanisms of political intermediation to create channels of citizen participation and thus transform local government into a radical, direct municipalist structure' (Ordóñez et al. 2017: 10). Several political parties, some of which emerged from the occupy movements of the past decade, have sought to integrate online forms of participatory decision-making within a more vertical party structure. By establishing digital voting mechanisms and online platforms, they hoped to take advantage of the renewed enthusiasm for participatory democracy that the occupy movements had aroused (Gerbaudo 2019: 35–6).

It remains to be seen how, or to what extent, engagement with electoral-representative institutions and procedures can be made compatible with basic principles and aspirations of prefigurative democracy. There obviously is a danger of co-optation: not least because these electoral-representative institutions are based on an entirely different conception of democracy. It may be difficult for a prefigurative movement to maintain its open-ended and spontaneous character, its horizontal and decentralised structure, and its constitutive and synecdochal representative function once it engages with the inegalitarian and restricted forms of representation that are implied in electoral-representative democracy. But these experiences suggest that prefigurative democracy may not necessarily preclude any form of engagement with some of the existing electoral-democratic institutions and procedures.

Another option for some prefigurative movements or practices may be to put pressure on the liberal-democratic state and its institutions from the outside. Prefigurative democracy thus can have an important 'counter-democratic' function – albeit, perhaps, in spite of itself. This conception of 'counter-democracy' is derived from the work of Pierre Rosanvallon, who defines it as 'a democracy of indirect powers disseminated throughout society – in other words, a durable democracy of distrust, which complements the episodic democracy of the usual electoral-representative system' (Rosanvallon 2008: 8). 'Counter-democracy' thus refers to a broad range of institutions and organisations, action groups and NGOs, parties, cooperatives, campaigns and other citizens' initiatives, which each serve different goals and functions. Whilst these various counter-democratic actors tend to have very different goals and purposes, seen from a distant point of view it may nevertheless be possible to ascribe a shared democratic role to them. They all serve to critically monitor and assess the policies and legislation of governments at various levels. And, if necessary, they often mobilise against it in an attempt to influence, frustrate or prevent the process of its implementation. A similar conception is developed by John Keane, who uses the term 'monitory democracy' to describe 'a host of non-party, extra-parliamentary, and often unelected bodies' that together serve to monitor and scrutinise 'all fields of social and political life' (Keane 2011: 216). In the age of digitisation, Keane argues, monitoring has become the most important form of democratic engagement for most citizens – much more, for instance, than voting.

These concepts of 'counter-democracy' and 'monitory democracy' originally serve a different purpose in that their aim is to understand the democratic role of protest and social movements *within* the liberal-democratic order. Prefigurative movements and practices often seek to imagine a radically different future *beyond* liberal democracy in its current electoral-representative state. But I nevertheless assert that these two concepts may still be fruitfully employed in the context of prefigurative democracy. Even if they do not manage to establish radical change in the long term, prefigurative movements may still serve to give a democratic impulse to electoral-representative governments – or at least force them to live up to their own democratic pretensions. This conception of 'counter-democracy' may thus be used to understand how prefigurative movements or practices serve to democratise electoral-representative democracy, even though their original intention (and their eventual potential) may at the same time be much more radical. It helps one to obtain a more nuanced or complex understanding of how prefigurative democracy can relate to the state at its various governmental and political levels.

5: Prefigurative Democracy Is Only the Beginning

Finally, this gives rise to the question of what remains after prefigurative practices have come to an end. As argued in Chapter 2, prefigurative democracy often seeks its own continuation and thus does not pursue a predefined end. At the same time, and as is illustrated by the experiences of recent occupy movements, it often does eventually come to a close: the occupied square or squat gets evacuated, protesters are sent home or even arrested and detained, movements gradually disintegrate or lose momentum. Does this mean that prefigurative democracy is only meaningful while it lasts? Or is there a way to imagine how prefigurative democracy may retain some of its relevance or significance, long after its moment has passed and the protesters have gone?

There are at least two ways in which prefigurative experiences from the past continue to hold radical potential in the present as well as the future. As Laclau argues, first, radical change requires that 'the social' – the seemingly 'objective' or 'neutral' understanding of society that has sedimented in our shared discourse and social reality – be rearticulated and reinscribed with a different meaning and content. Change may thus gradually occur after our established idea of society has been disrupted through a political intervention. The recent experiences of occupy movements serve to illustrate this. Although the activist tent camps in Zuccotti Park and Puerta del Sol have indeed disappeared, these movements did eventually contribute to a new political discourse in which economic inequality and class distinctions have come to play a more central role. The relative success of politicians such as Bernie Sanders and Alexandria Ocasio-Cortez, parties such as Podemos, and movements such as Black Lives Matter arguably would not have been imaginable without these occupy movements.

But even if prefigurative practices may not lead to such significant, re-sedimentations in our dominant political discourse, they nevertheless continue to hold promise for the future. This brings us to a second perspective on the lasting impact of prefigurative democracy. Arendt shows how experiences and memories from the past may continue to lead a subterranean life. They gradually acquire a new form and content, but precisely in doing so preserve some of this past experience. Such 'crystalline formations', as she calls them, may sooner or later be rediscovered and returned to the surface, where they continue to inspire or motivate new generations. Any moment of prefiguration (no matter how long it lasts) must eventually be accompanied by a process of refiguration, during which it is inscribed with new meaning. Prefigurative practices and movements thus cannot simply be assessed by means of their immediate outcomes. Nor can they evidently be appreciated as either a 'success' or a 'failure' (Van de Sande 2013). They instead retain their political relevance or potential for the future, long after their momentum has passed.

In short, prefigurative democracy is always only the beginning. As is already implied in the very word 'prefiguration', it can never be complete. It would thus be impossible to give a definitive account or a comprehensive definition of what prefigurative democracy essentially *is* or what it *should* be. It can have a variety of different outcomes and its effects may be wide-ranging. The various occupy movements that have emerged in the course of the past decade were only the most recent chapter in a long history of prefigurative politics. They have significantly contributed to its popularisation, and given new use and meaning to this idea of radical, political change. Prefiguration is likely to acquire many new forms, applications and articulations in the future. In that respect, prefigurative democracy inevitably is also prefigurative of itself.

Notes

Introduction

1. Many different terms have been used in reference to these movements –
   some more astute or accurate than others. In my opinion, the term
   'assembly movements' (Butler 2015) is insufficient as it emphasises a
   specific aspect that was shared by many, but definitely not all, of these
   movements (i.e. the General Assembly as a platform of organisation and
   decision-making), and the often-used reference to 'global movements'
   (Sitrin and Azzelini 2014) is both too generic and tends to exaggerate
   the international or 'global' character of these movements. I will instead
   use the term 'occupy movements' in reference to a broad range of movements – from the so-called 'Arab Spring' to the 15-M movement and
   from Occupy Wall Street and Occupy London Stock Exchange to the
   Gezi Park protests, Nuit Debout and the Sudanese revolution of 2018,
   to name but a few examples. One of the most distinctive features shared
   by all of them, after all, is the occupation of public space as a shared
   technique and symbolic expression.
2. 'Les conseils étaient regardés comme une préfiguration de la société
   socialiste' (Guérin 1965: 129). Guérin arguably used the term 'prefiguration' more loosely than (for instance) Carl Boggs. For instance, he
   elsewhere describes the repression of the Kronstadt rebellion by the
   Bolshevists in 1921 as a 'préfiguration de Budapest' in 1956 (Guérin
   1965: 121).

Chapter 1

1. It may be debatable if the various organisations and unions named
   below should be qualified as syndicalist, revolutionary syndicalist or
   anarcho-syndicalist. Whereas some sources stress the strategic and
   ideological differences between various syndicalist unions such as CGT,
   CNT and IWW (Damier 2009; Marshall 1993: 500–1), and others focus

on intersections and mutual influence between anarchist and syndicalist tendencies (Solidarity Federation 2012), still other sources stress that the difference between these various tendencies must not be exaggerated, as they all stem from the same syndicalist tradition that found its origin in the anti-authoritarian wing of the First International (Schmitt and Van der Walt 2009: 159–60).

2. It must be stressed, however, that the feminist credo 'the personal is political' often goes misinterpreted. As Keeanga-Yamahtta Taylor (2017: 9) argues, '[t]his slogan was not just about "lifestyle" issues, as it came to be popularly understood, rather it was initially about how the experiences within the lives of Black women shaped their political outlook'.

3. Engels was by no means the first author to use this phrase, yet in his political thought it arguably did acquire a particular meaning. For a genealogy of the idea that politics must be replaced with 'the administration of things', see Kafka (2012).

Chapter 3

1. It must be stressed that the terms 'assembly' and 'council' are used in very different ways – and in reference to various kinds of institutions. First, the term 'assembly' is also used in reference to formal parliamentary bodies representing popular sovereignty (e.g. the 'National Assembly' in France). It must be clear that this is something rather different from the temporary public assemblies discussed in the previous sections. However, in other accounts (e.g. Bookchin 2015), the public or popular assembly is presented as a durable institution, where members of a community (for instance, a neighbourhood) meet on a regular basis to discuss political matters. The assembly then delegates some of its members to councils at a higher or more central level to represent its position and/or interests, on the basis of an imperative mandate. This particular concept of the assembly is not necessarily incompatible with Arendt's idea of a council system. In this chapter I use the term 'public assembly' in reference to the temporary (and often spontaneous) gatherings of bodies in public space (as we have seen in the context of recent prefigurative social movements). 'Council' stands for a more durable and formal institution (and may include some of the grassroots institutions that Bookchin and others refer to as popular or neighbourhood assemblies).

2. Arendt stresses that our contemporary concept of 'principle' is derived from the Latin *principium*, which also means 'beginning'. Any new beginning or foundation must carry 'its own principle within itself' (Arendt 2006a: 205). In other words: by beginning something new one inevitably postulates a set of principles or values that embodies the

spirit of this beginning. This explains why, in the Roman perception, a political order always had to refer back to its original beginning, and to the principles or binding promises that were implied in it.

3. These self-selecting councils at the 'lower' or decentralised level arguably are rather similar to what other radical-democratic theorists, such as Murray Bookchin, describe as 'popular assemblies' or 'neighbourhood assemblies' (Bookchin 2015: 30).

4. Note that in the German original, Luxemburg formulates this last sentence as follows: 'Sie werden geschult indem sie zur Tat greifen' (Luxemburg 1974a: 512).

5. Again, a strikingly similar point is made by Castoriadis, who argues that the Hungarian councils of 1956 both sought to alter the 'institution of society' and at the same time provided themselves with 'some of the means for doing it' (Castoriadis 1993: 254; see Popp-Madsen 2021 for an elaborate comparison between Arendt and Castoriadis).

Chapter 4

1. It should be stressed, however, that at this point the interpretations of Laclau's position tend to diverge. Stefan Rummens and Mark Wenman, for example, have a significantly different reading of the synecdochal moment in Laclau – which, according to them, defines the very distinction between Laclau's populist defence of hegemony on the one hand, and Mouffe's advocacy for an 'agonistic pluralism' on the other. Rummens argues that 'in a democratic regime, the collectivity of the temporary majority simply cannot and should not be identified with the collectivity of the people-as-a-whole, encompassing both the majority *and* the minority'. But, he asserts, 'in the synecdochal movement in which a particular claims to represent the universal, the distinction between these two collectivities is suppressed' (Rummens 2009: 382–3). Rummens therefore concludes that in a hegemonic embodiment of the whole by one of its parts, 'the losers are delegitimised as representatives of the people' (Rummens 2009: 381). In a similar vein, Wenman argues that 'the monism implied in the (post-)Marxist notion of synecdoche' is incompatible with a pluralist, radical democracy (Wenman 2003: 592) and that Laclau's 'conscription of particularistic struggles into the ontologically necessary role of forever attempting to impersonate the universal is a violation of personal freedom' (Wenman 2003: 601). I suspect, however, that both Rummens and Wenman read Laclau's concept of hegemony too much in terms of a 'regime', rather than an ongoing movement. It is precisely on *this* plane that a distinction between Laclau and Mouffe could be drawn. Whereas for Mouffe 'hegemony' first and foremost implies a 'stabilization of power' (Mouffe 2005a: 104), Laclau presents it as a *process*, in which 'a contingent group within a given

society . . . "takes upon itself the task"' to embody or 'stand for' this society as a whole (Miller 2004: 218). In this respect, Laclau's theory of hegemonisation and synecdochal representation indeed is more helpful if we want to understand the prefigurative politics of contemporary protest movements.

2. A literal example of this is the Estallido Social: a wave of civic protests that emerged Chile in 2019. Whereas it originally started as a fare evasion campaign to protest against the raising price of public transport, demonstrators would soon contest a broader set of policies, police brutality and social inequality more generally (Johanson 2019).

3. It might seem counter-intuitive to draw on Laclau's thought in this context. Both Laclau (2014c: 9) and his co-author Chantal Mouffe (2013) have strongly criticised these movements for their perceived refusal to engage with representative politics. My claim, however, is that their work could nevertheless be employed in an analysis of these very movements and their prefigurative practices (Decreus et al. 2014: 138; Van de Sande 2019).

4. wearethe99percent.tumblr.com (accessed 11 April 2022).

Chapter 5

1. In the third edition of *The Origins of Totalitarianism*, the term appears eight times, either as a verb or a noun. See Arendt (1968f: xv (twice), 53, 55, 94, 222, 365, 440).

2. Kant uses the word *Anschießen*, which could best be translated as 'shooting together'. See Kant (1995: 241 §58).

3. Arendt gives a full quotation from Shakespeare (1934: 1140) earlier on in the essay (1968e: 193):

> Full fathom five thy father lies,
> Of his bones are coral made,
> Those are pearls that were his eyes,
> Nothing of him that doth fade,
> But doth suffer a sea-change
> Into something rich and strange.

Bibliography

Abensour, Miguel. 2011. *Democracy Against the State: Marx and the Machiavellian Moment*. Translated by Max Blechman and Martin Breaugh. Cambridge: Polity Press.

Abul-Magd, Zeinab. 2012. 'Occupying Tahrir Square: The Myths and the Realities of the Egyptian Revolution'. *The South-Atlantic Quarterly* 111 (3): 565–72.

Agamben, Giorgio. 2000. *Means Without End: Notes On Politics*. Translated by Vincenzo Binetti and Cesare Casarino. Minneapolis: University of Minnesota Press.

Ahmed, Sara. 2017. *Living a Feminist Life*. Durham, NC: Duke University Press.

Akuno, Kali and Ajamu Nangwaya (eds). 2017. *Jackson Rising. The Struggle for Economic Democracy and Black Self-Determination in Jackson, Mississippi*. Ottawa: Daraja Press.

Althusser, Louis. 2014. 'Ideology and Ideological State Apparatuses'. In *On the Reproduction of Capitalism*, edited by G. M. Goshgarian, 232–72. London: Verso.

Anderson, Benedict. 2006. *Imagined Communities: Reflections on the Origin and Spread of Nationalism* (revised edition). London: Verso.

Angaut, Jean-Christophe. 2007. *Bakounine jeune hégélien: La philosophie et son dehors*. Lyons: ENS Éditions.

Anweiler, Oskar. 1974. *The Russian Workers, Peasants, and Soldiers Councils 1905–1921*. Translated by Ruth Hein. New York: Pantheon.

Apter, Emily. 2018. *Unexceptional Politics: On Obstruction, Impasse, and the Impolitic*. London: Verso.

Arato, Andrew. 2013. 'Political Theology and Populism'. *Social Research* 80 (1): 143–72.

Arendt, Hannah. 1958. *The Human Condition*. Chicago: University of Chicago Press.

Arendt, Hannah. 1968a. 'Hermann Broch: 1886–1951'. In *Men in Dark Times*, 111–51. San Diego: Harcourt Brace.

Arendt, Hannah. 1968b. 'Isak Dinesen: 1885–1963'. In *Men in Dark Times*, 95–109. New York: Harcourt Brace.

Arendt, Hannah. 1968c. 'On Humanity in Dark Times: Thoughts About Lessing'. In *Men in Dark Times*, 3–31. New York: Harcourt Brace.

Arendt, Hannah. 1968d. 'Rosa Luxemburg: 1871–1919'. In *Men in Dark Times*, 33–56. San Diego: Harcourt Brace.

Arendt, Hannah. 1968e. 'Walter Benjamin: 1892–1940'. In *Men in Dark Times*, 153–206. New York: Harcourt Brace.

Arendt, Hannah. 1968f. *The Origins of Totalitarianism*. New York: Harcourt.

Arendt, Hannah. 1972a. 'On Violence'. In *Crises of the Republic*, 103–98. New York: Harcourt Brace.

Arendt, Hannah. 1972b. 'Thoughts on Politics and Revolutions'. In *Crises of the Republic*, 199–233. New York: Harcourt Brace.

Arendt, Hannah. 1974. *Rahel Varnhagen: The Life of a Jewish Woman*. Translated by Richard and Clara Winston. New York: Harcourt Brace Jovanovich.

Arendt, Hannah. 1978. *The Life of the Mind*. San Diego and New York: Harcourt.

Arendt, Hannah. 1992. *Lectures on Kant's Political Philosophy*, edited by Ronald Beiner. Chicago: Chicago University Press.

Arendt, Hannah. 1993. *Was ist Politik? Fragmente aus dem Nachlaß*. Munich: Piper Verlag.

Arendt, Hannah. 1994a. 'A Reply to Eric Voegelin'. In *Essays in Understanding*, edited by Jerome Kohn, 401–8. New York: Schocken Books.

Arendt, Hannah. 1994b. 'The Eggs Speak Up'. In *Essays in Understanding*, edited by Jerome Kohn, 270–84. New York: Schocken Books.

Arendt, Hannah. 1994c. 'Understanding and Politics (The Difficulties of Understanding)'. In *Essays in Understanding*, edited by Jerome Kohn, 307–27. New York: Schocken Books.

Arendt, Hannah. 1996. *Love and Saint Augustine*. Chicago: University of Chicago Press.

Arendt, Hannah. 2005a. 'Introduction into Politics'. In *The Promise of Politics*, edited by Jerome Kohn, 93–200. New York: Schocken Books.

Arendt, Hannah. 2005b. 'The Tradition of Political Thought'. In *The Promise of Politics*, edited by Jerome Kohn, 40–62. New York: Schocken Books.

Arendt, Hannah. 2006a. *On Revolution*. London: Penguin.

Arendt, Hannah. 2006b. 'The Concept of History: Ancient and Modern'. In *Between Past and Future: Eight Exercises in Political Thought*, 41–90. London: Penguin.

Arendt, Hannah. 2006c. 'Tradition and the Modern Age'. In *Between Past and Future: Eight Exercises in Political Thought*, 17–40. London: Penguin.

Arendt, Hannah. 2006d. 'Truth and Politics'. In *Between Past and Future: Eight Exercises in Political Thought*, 223–59. London: Penguin.

Arendt, Hannah. 2006e. 'What is Authority?' In *Between Past and Future: Eight Exercises in Political Thought*, 91–141. London: Penguin.

Arendt, Hannah. 2006f. 'What is Freedom?' In *Between Past and Future: Eight Exercises in Political Thought*, 142–69. London: Penguin.

Arendt, Hannah. 2007. 'Antisemitism'. Translated by John E. Woods. In *The Jewish Writings*, edited by Jerome Kohn and Ron H. Feldman, 46–121. New York: Schocken Books.

Arendt, Hannah. 2018a. 'The Great Tradition'. In *Thinking Without a Bannister: Essays in Understanding 1953–1975*, edited by Jerome Kohn, 43–68. New York: Schocken Books.

Arendt, Hannah. 2018b. 'Hannah Arendt on Hannah Arendt'. In *Thinking Without a Bannister: Essays in Understanding 1953–1975*, edited by Jerome Kohn, 433–75. New York: Schocken Books.

Arendt, Hannah. 2018c. 'The Hungarian Revolution and Totalitarian Imperialism'. In *Thinking Without a Bannister: Essays in Understanding 1953–1975*, edited by Jerome Kohn, 105–56. New York: Schocken Books.

Arendt, Hannah. 2018d. 'Labor, Work, Action'. In *Thinking Without a Bannister: Essays in Understanding 1953–1975*, edited by Jerome Kohn, 291–307. New York: Schocken Books.

Auerbach, Erich. 1984. *Scenes from the Drama of European Literature*. Manchester: Manchester University Press.

Auerbach, Erich. 1946. *Mimesis: Dargestellte Wirklichkeit in der Abendländischen Literatur*. Berne: A. Francke AG. Verlag.

Avrich, Paul. 2005. *The Russian Anarchists*. Oakland, CA and Edinburgh: AK Press.

Aziz, Omar. 2013. 'A Discussion Paper on Local Councils in Syria'. *The Anarchist Library*. Available at https://tahriricn.wordpress.com/2013/09/22/syria-translated-a-discussion-paper-on-local-councils-in-syria-by-the-martyr-and-anarchist-comrade-omar-aziz/ (last accessed 13 April 2022).

Badiou, Alain. 2003. *Saint Paul: The Foundation of Universalism*. Translated by Ray Brassier. Stanford: Stanford University Press.

Badiou, Alain. 2012. *The Rebirth of History*. Translated by Gregory Elliot. London: Verso.

Bakunin, Michael. 1971a. 'The Policy of the International'. In *Bakunin on Anarchy*, edited by Sam Dolgoff, 160–74. London: George Allen & Unwin.

Bakunin, Michael. 1971b. 'The Program of the Alliance'. In *Bakunin on Anarchy*, edited by Sam Dolgoff, 243–58. London: George Allen & Unwin.

Bakunin, Michael. 1971c. 'The International and Karl Marx'. In *Bakunin on Anarchy*, edited by Sam Dolgoff, 286–320. London: George Allen & Unwin.

Bakunin, Michael. 1974a. 'God and the State'. In *Michael Bakunin, Selected Writings*, edited by Arthur Lehning, 111–35. New York: Grove Press.

Bakunin, Michael. 1974b. 'The Paris Commune and the Idea of the State'. In *Michael Bakunin, Selected Writings*, edited by Arthur Lehning, 195–213. New York: Grove Press.

Bakunin, Michael. 1974c. 'The Reaction in Germany'. In *Michael Bakunin, Selected Writings*, edited by Arthur Lehning, 37–58. New York: Grove Press.

Bakunin, Michael. 1990. *Statism and Anarchy*. Translated by Marshall Schatz. Cambridge: Cambridge University Press.

Bakunin, Mikhail. 1992. 'The Report of the Committee on the Question of Inheritance'. In *The Basic Bakunin: Writings 1869–1871*. Translated and edited by Robert M. Cutler, 126–30. Amherst, NY: Prometheus Books.

Balibar, Étienne. 2014. 'Hannah Arendt: The Right to Have Rights, and Civic Disobedience'. In *Equaliberty*. Translated by James Ingram, 165–86. Durham, NC: Duke University Press.

Bargu, Banu. 2013. 'The Politics of Commensality'. In Jacob Blumenfeld, Chiara Bottici and Simon Critchley (eds), *The Anarchist Turn*, 35–58. London: Pluto Press.

Beiner, Ronald. 1994. 'Judging in a World of Appearances: A Commentary on Hannah Arendt's Unwritten Finale'. In Lewis P. Hinchman and Sarah K. Hinchman (eds), *Hannah Arendt: Critical Essays* 365–88. Albany: State University of New York Press.

Benhabib, Seyla. 1996. *The Reluctant Modernism of Hannah Arendt*. Thousand Oaks, CA: Sage.

Benjamin, Walter. 1968a. 'The Task of the Translator'. In *Illuminations*, edited by Hannah Arendt and translated by Harry Zohn, 69–82. New York: Schocken Books.

Benjamin, Walter. 1968b. 'Theses on the Philosophy of History'. In *Illuminations*, edited by Hannah Arendt and translated by Harry Zohn, 253–64. New York: Schocken Books.

Benjamin, Walter. 1999. *The Arcades Project*. Translated by Howard Eiland and Kevin McLaughlin. Cambridge, MA: The Belknap Press of Harvard University Press.

Bernstein, Richard J. 1986. 'Rethinking the Social and the Political'. *Graduate Faculty Philosophy Journal* 11: 111–30.

Bernstein, Richard J. 1996. *Hannah Arendt and the Jewish Question*. Cambridge, MA: MIT Press.

Bey, Hakim. 2003. *T.A.Z. The Temporary Autonomous Zone, Ontological Anarchy, Poetic Terrorism*. Brooklyn, NY: Autonomedia.

Blätter, Sidonia and Irene M. Marti. 2005. 'Rosa Luxemburg and Hannah Arendt: Against the Destruction of Political Spheres of Freedom'. *Hypathia* 20 (2): 88–101.

Boggs, Carl. 1977a. 'Marxism, Prefigurative Communism, and the Problem of Workers' Control'. *Radical America* 11 (6): 99–122.

Boggs, Carl. 1977b. 'Revolutionary Process, Political Strategy, and the Dilemma of Power'. *Theory and Society* 4 (3): 359–93.

Bookchin, Murray. 1995a. *From Urbanization to Cities: Toward a New Politics of Citizenship*. London: Cassell.

Bookchin, Murray. 1995b. *Social Anarchism or Lifestyle Anarchism: An Unbridgeable Chasm*. San Francisco, CA and Edinburgh: AK Press.

Bookchin, Murray. 2003. *Post-Scarcity Anarchism*. Oakland, CA and Edinburgh: AK Press.

Bookchin, Murray. 2015. 'The Communalist Project'. In *The Next Revolution: Popular Assemblies & The Promise of Direct Democracy*, edited by Debbie Bookchin and Blair Taylor, 1–30. London: Verso.

Bowen-Moore, Patricia. 1989. *Hannah Arendt's Philosophy of Natality*. New York: St. Martin's Press.

Bray, Mark. 2013. *Translating Anarchy: The Anarchism of Occupy Wall Street*. Winchester and Washington: Zero Books.

Breaugh, Martin. 2013. *The Plebeian Experience: A Discontinuous History of Political Freedom*. Translated by Lazer Lederhendler. New York: Columbia University Press.

Breckman, Warren. 2013. *Adventures of the Symbolic: Post-Marxism and Radical Democracy*. New York: Columbia University Press.

Breines, Wini. 1980. 'Community and Organization: The New Left and Michels' "Iron Law"'. *Social Problems* 27 (4): 419–29.

Breines, Wini. 1989. *Community and Organisation and the New Left 1962–1968: The Great Refusal*. South Hadley: J. F. Bergin; New York: Praeger.

Brito Vieira, Monica. 2015. 'Founders and Re-Founders: Struggles of Self-Authorized Representation'. *Constellations* 22 (4): 500–13.

Brown, Wendy. 2015. *Undoing the Demos: Neoliberalism's Stealth Revolution*. New York: Zone Books.

Butler, Judith. 1990. *Gender Trouble: Feminism and the Subversion of Identity*, 2nd edition. New York and London: Routledge.

Butler, Judith. 2011a. 'Bodies in Public'. In Astra Taylor, Keith Gessen, and editors from N+1, Dissent, Triple Canopy and The New Inquiry (eds), *Occupy! Scenes From Occupied America*, 192–3. London: Verso.

Butler, Judith. 2011b. 'For and Against Precarity'. *Tidal: Occupy Theory, Occupy Strategy* 1: 12–13. Available at http://www.e-flux.com/wp-content/uploads/2013/05/TIDAL_occupytheory.pdf?b8c429 (last accessed 13 April 2022).

Butler, Judith. 2015. *Notes Toward a Performative Theory of Assembly*. Cambridge, MA: Harvard University Press.

Butler, Judith and Athena Anthanasiou. 2013. *Disposession: The Performative in the Political*. Cambridge: Polity Press.

Canovan, Margaret. 1992. *Hannah Arendt: A Reinterpretation of Her Political Thought*. Cambridge: Cambridge University Press.

Castells, Manuel. 2015. *Networks of Outrage and Hope: Social Movements in the Internet Age*. Cambridge: Polity Press.

Castoriadis, Cornelius. 1993. 'The Hungarian Source'. In *Political and Social Writings, Vol. 3, 1961–1979*, edited and translated by David Ames Curtis. Minneapolis: University of Minnesota Press.

Castoriadis, Cornelius. 1997. 'Democracy as Procedure and Democracy as Regime'. *Constellations* 4 (1): 1–18.

Cattaneo, Claudio and Miguel A. Martínez. 2014. 'Squatting as an Alternative to Capitalism: An Introduction'. In Claudio Cattaneo and Miguel A. Martínez (eds), *The Squatters' Movement in Europe: Commons and Autonomy as Alternatives to Capitalism*, 1–25. London: Pluto Press.

Cavarero, Adriana. 2000. *Relating Narratives: Storytelling and Selfhood*. Translated by Paul A. Kottman. London: Routledge.

CGT (Confédération Générale du Travail). 2012. 'The Charter of Amiens'. *Libcom.org*. Available at https://libcom.org/library/charter-amiens (last accessed 13 April 2022).

Cohn, Jesse. 2006. *Anarchism and the Crisis of Representation: Hermeneutics, Aesthetics, Politics*. Selinsgrove, PA: Susquehanna University Press.

Cole, Peter, David Struthers and Kenyon Zimmer. 2017. 'Introduction'. In Peter Cole, David Struthers and Kenyon Zimmer (eds), *Wobblies of the World: A Global History of the IWW*, 1–25. London: Pluto Press.

Cooper, Davina. 2014. *Everyday Utopias: The Conceptual Life of Promising Spaces*. Durham, NC: Duke University Press.

Cooper, Davina. 2017. 'Prefiguring the State'. *Antipode* 49 (2): 335–56.

Cooper, Davina. 2019. *Feeling Like a State: Desire, Denial, and the Recasting of Authority*. Durham, NC: Duke University Press.

Cooper, Davina. 2020. 'Towards an Adventurous Institutional Politics: The Prefigurative "As If" and the Reposing of What's Real'. *Sociological Review* 68 (5): 893–916.

Cornell, Andy. 2011. *Oppose and Propose: Lessons From Movement for a New Society*. Oakland, CA and Edinburgh: AK Press.

Cornell, Andy. 2012. 'Consensus: What It Is, What It Is Not, Where It Came From, and Where It Must Go'. In Kate Khatib, Margaret Killjoy and Mike McGuire (eds), *We Are Many: Reflections on Movement Strategy From Occupation to Liberation*, 163–73. Oakland, CA and Edinburgh: AK Press.

Cornell, Andy. 2016. *Unruly Equality: U.S. Anarchism in the 20th Century*. Oakland, CA: University of California Press.

Coulthard, Glen Sean. 2014. *Red Skin, White Masks: Rejecting the Colonial Politics of Recognition*. Minneapolis: University of Minnesota Press.

Crass, Chris. 2013. *Towards Collective Liberation: Anti-Racist Organizing, Feminist Praxis, and Movement Building Strategy*. Oakland, CA: PM Press.

Critchley, Simon. 1999. *Ethics-Politics-Subjectivity. Essays on Derrida, Levinas, and Contemporary French Thought*. London: Verso.

Critchley, Simon. 2007. *Infinitely Demanding: Ethics of Commitment, Politics of Resistance*. London: Verso.

Crow, Scott. 2011. *Black Flags and Windmills: Hope, Anarchy, and the Common Ground Collective*. Oakland, CA: PM Press.

Damier, Vadim. 2009. *Anarcho-Syndicalism in the 20th Century*. Translated by Malcolm Archibald. Edmonton: Black Cat Press.

Dau, Elisabeth. 2020. *A contre-courant. Un bilan des dynamiques de lestes participatives aux élections municipales françaises en 2020*. Available at https://commonspolis.org/wp-content/uploads/2020/08/BilanMunicipales_V10-compress%C3%A9.pdf (last accessed 13 April 2022).

Däumig, Ernst. 2012. 'The National Assembly Means the Councils' Death'. In Gabriel Kuhn (ed.), *All Power to the People! A Documentary History of the German Revolution of 1918–1919*, 51–8. Oakland, CA: PM Press.

Day, Richard. 2005. *Gramsci is Dead: Anarchist Currents in the Newest Social Movements*. London: Pluto Press; Toronto: Between the Lines.

Dean, Jodi. 2012. *The Communist Horizon*. London: Verso.

Dean, Jodi. 2014. 'Occupy Wall Street: Forcing Division'. *Constellations* 21 (3): 382–9.

Decreus, Thomas, Matthias Lievens and Antoon Braeckman. 2014. 'Building Collective Identities: How New Social Movements Try to Overcome Post-politics'. *Parralax* 20 (2): 136–48.

Dee, E. T. C. 2016. 'Squatted Social Centres in London: Temporary Nodes of Resistance to Capitalism'. *Contention* 4 (1–2): 109–27.

De Ligt, Bart. 1989. *The Conquest of Violence: An Essay on War and Revolution*. London: Pluto Press.

De Man, Paul. 1979. *Allegories of Reading: Figural Language in Rousseau, Nietzsche, Rilke, and Proust*. New Haven, CT: Yale University Press.

De Paepe, César. 2018. 'The Present Institutions of the International in Relation to the Future'. Available at https://robertgraham.wordpress.com/2018/03/24/the-present-institutions-of-the-international-in-relation-to-the-future-1869/ (last accessed 13 April 2022).

Deseriis, Marco. 2015. *Improper Names: Collective Pseudonyms From the Luddites to Anonymous*. Minneapolis: University of Minnesota Press.

De Smet, Brecht. 2015. *A Dialectical Pedagogy of Revolt: Gramsci, Vygotsky, and the Egyptian Revolution*. Leiden: Brill.

De Smet, Brecht. 2016. *Gramsci on Tahrir: Revolution and Counter-Revolution in Egypt*. London: Pluto Press.

De Smet, Brecht. 2020. 'The Prince and the Minotaur. Egypt in the Labyrinth of Counter-Revolution'. *LSE Middle East Centre Paper Series* 36.

Dewey, John. 1973. 'Means and Ends'. In Leon Trotsky, *Their Morals and Ours*, 73–9. New York: Pathfinder Press.

Dietz, Mary G. 1994. '"The Slow Boring of Hard Boards": Methodical Thinking and the Work of Politics'. *The American Political Science Review* 88 (4): 873–86.

Dinerstein, Ana Cecilia. 2015. *The Politics of Autonomy in Latin America: The Art of Organizing Hope*. Basingstoke: Palgrave Macmillan.

Disch, Lisa. 1993. 'More Truth Than Fact: Storytelling as Critical Understanding in the Writings of Hannah Arendt'. *Political Theory* 21: 665–94.

Disch, Lisa. 1994. *Hannah Arendt and the Limits of Philosophy*. Ithaca, NY and London: Cornell University Press.

Disch, Lisa. 1997. '"Please Sit Down, But Don't Make Yourself at Home": Arendtian "Visiting" and the Prefigurative Politics of Consciousness-Raising'. In Craig Calhoun and John McGowan (eds), *Hannah Arendt and the Meaning of Politics*, 132–65. Minneapolis: University of Minnesota Press.

Disch, Lisa. 2011a. 'How Could Hannah Arendt Glorify the American Revolution and Revile the French? Placing *On Revolution* in the Historiography of the French and American Revolutions'. *European Journal of Political Theory* 10 (3): 350–71.

Disch, Lisa. 2011b. 'Toward a Mobilization Concept of Democratic Representation'. *American Political Science Review* 105 (1): 100–14.

Disch, Lisa. 2019. 'Introduction: The End of Representative Politics?' In Lisa Disch, Mathijs van de Sande and Nadia Urbinati (eds), *The Constructivist Turn in Political Representation*, 1–18. Edinburgh: Edinburgh University Press.

Dixon, Chris. 2014. *Another Politics: Talking Across Today's Transformative Movements*. Oakland: University of California Press.

Douzinas, Costas. 2013. *Philosophy and Resistance in the Crisis: Greece and the Future of Europe*. Cambridge: Polity Press.

Dyrberg, Torben Bech. 2004. 'The Political and Politics in Discourse Analysis'. In Simon Critchley and Oliver Marchart (eds), *Laclau: A Critical Reader*, 241–55. Abingdon: Routledge.

Eckhardt, Wolfgang. 2016. *The First Socialist Schism: Bakunin vs. Marx in the International Working Men's Association*. Translated by Robert M. Homsi, Jesse Cohn, Cian Lawless, Nestor McNab and Bas Moreel. Oakland, CA: PM Press.

Engels, Friedrich. 1987. 'Anti-Dühring'. In *Karl Marx, Friedrich Engels Collected Works Vol 25*. New York: International Publishers.

Epstein, Barbara. 1991. *Political Protest and Cultural Revolution: Nonviolent Direct Action in the 1970s and 1980s*. Berkeley: University of California Press.

Errejón, Íñigo and Chantal Mouffe. 2016. *Podemos: In the Name of the People*. Translated by Sirio Canós Donnay. London: Lawrence & Wishart.

Estes, Nick. 2019. *Our History is the Future: Standing Rock versus the Dakota Access Pipeline, and the Long Tradition of Indigenous Resistance*. London: Verso.

Feenstra, Ramón A., Simon Tormey, Andreu Caséro-Ripollés and John Keane. 2017. *Re-Figuring Democracy: The Spanish Political Laboratory*. Abingdon: Routledge.

Flesher Fominaya, Cristina. 2020. *Democracy Reloaded: Inside Spain's Political Laboratory from 15-M to Podemos*. Oxford: Oxford University Press.

Foderaro, Lisa W. 2011. 'Privately Owned Park, Open to the Public, May Make its Own Rules'. *New York Times*, 13 October 2011. Available at http://www.nytimes.com/2011/10/14/nyregion/zuccotti-park-is-privately-owned-but-open-to-the-public.html.

Frank, Jason. 2021. *The Democratic Sublime: On Aesthetics and Popular Assembly*. New York: Oxford University Press.

Frank, Thomas. 2013. 'Yes, But What Are You For?' *Monde Diplomatique*, January. Available at http://mondediplo.com/2013/01/06occupy (last accessed 13 April 2022).

Franks, Benjamin. 2003. 'The Direct Action Ethic from 59 Upwards'. *Anarchist Studies* 11 (1): 13–41.

Franks, Benjamin. 2006. *Rebel Alliances: The Means and Ends of Contemporary British Anarchisms*. Oakland, CA and Edinburgh: AK Press.

Franks, Benjamin. 2007. 'Postanarchism: a Critical Assessment'. *Journal of Political Ideologies* 12 (2): 127–45.

Franks, Benjamin. 2008. 'Postanarchism and Meta-Ethics'. *Anarchist Studies* 16 (2): 135–53.

Franks, Benjamin. 2010. 'Anarchism and the Virtues'. In Benjamin Franks and Matthew Wilson (eds), *Anarchism and Moral Philosophy*, 135–60. Basingstoke: Palgrave Macmillan.

Franks, Benjamin. 2014. 'Anti-Fascism and the Ethics of Prefiguration'. *Affinities: a Journal of Radical Theory* 8 (1): 44–72.

Franks, Benjamin. 2018. 'Prefiguration'. In Benjamin Franks, Nathan Jun and Leonard Williams (eds), *Anarchism: A Conceptual Approach*, 28–43. New York: Routledge.

Freeman, Jo. 1972. 'The Tyranny of Structurelessness'. *Journal of Sociology* 17: 151–64.

Futrell, Robert and Pete Simi. 2004. 'Free Spaces, Collective Identity, and the Persistence of U.S. White Power Activism'. *Social Problems* 51 (1): 16–42.

Gago, Verónica. 2020. *Feminist International: How to Change Everything*. London: Verso.

Gelderloos, Peter. 2007. *How Nonviolence Protects the State*. Cambridge, MA: South End Press.

Gelderloos, Peter. 2016. *Worshipping Power: An Anarchist View of Early State Formation*. Chicago and Edinburgh: AK Press.

Gerbaudo, Paolo. 2012. *Tweets and the Streets: Social Media and Contemporary Activism*. London: Pluto Press.

Gerbaudo, Paolo. 2013. 'Why It's Time to Occupy the State'. *The Guardian*, 10 December. Available at https://www.theguardian.com/comment-isfree/2013/dec/10/occupy-protesters-electoral-politics (last accessed 13 April 2022).

Gerbaudo, Paolo. 2017. *The Mask and the Flag: Populism, Citizenism and Global Protest*. London: Hurst.

Gerbaudo, Paolo. 2019. *The Digital Party: Political Organisation and Online Democracy*. London: Pluto Press.

Gessen, Keith. 2011. 'Laundry Day'. In Astra Taylor, Keith Gessen, and editors from *N+1*, *Dissent*, *Triple Canopy* and *The New Inquiry* (eds), *Occupy! Scenes From Occupied America*, 195–212. London: Verso.

Gluckstein, Donny. 2011. 'Workers' Councils in Europe: A Century of Experience'. In Immanuel Ness and Dario Azzellini (eds), *Ours to Master and to Own: Workers' Control from the Commune to the Present*, 32–47. Chicago: Haymarket Books.

Goldman, Emma. 1969. 'Anarchism: What it Really Stands For'. In *Anarchism and Other Essays*, 47–67. New York: Dover.

Goldman, Emma. 2003. *My Disillusionment in Russia*. Mineola, NY: Dover.

Gordinier, Jeff. 2011. 'Want to get Fat on Wall Street? Try Protesting'. *New York Times*, 11 October. Available at https://www.nytimes.com/2011/10/12/dining/protesters-at-occupy-wall-street-eat-well.html.

Gordon, Uri. 2008. *Anarchy Alive! Anti-authoritarian Politics from Practice to Theory*. London: Pluto Press.

Gordon, Uri. 2018. 'Prefigurative Politics between Ethical Practice and Absent Promise'. *Political Studies* 66 (2): 521–37.

Gorz, André. 1968. 'The Way Forward'. *New Left Review* 1 (52): 47–66.

Gould-Wartofsky, Michael. 2015. *The Occupiers: The Making of the 99 Percent Movement*. Oxford: Oxford University Press.

Graeber, David. 2002. 'The New Anarchists'. *New Left Review* 13 (1): 61–73.

Graeber, David. 2009. *Direct Action, an Ethnography*. Oakland, CA and Edinburgh: AK Press.

Graeber, David. 2011. *Debt: The First 5000 Years*. New York: Melville House Publishing.

Graeber, David. 2013. *The Democracy Project: A History, a Crisis, a Movement*. London: Allen Lane.

Graham, Robert. 2015. *We Do Not Fear Anarchy – We Invoke It. The First International and the Origins of the Anarchist Movement*. Oakland, CA and Edinburgh: AK Press.

Gray, Rosie. 2011. 'Occupy Wall Street Debuts the New Spokescouncil'. *The Village Voice*, 8 Novermber. Available at https://www.villagevoice.com/2011/11/08/occupy-wall-street-debuts-the-new-spokes-council/ (last accessed 13 April 2022).

Guérin, Daniel. 1965. *L'anarchisme. De la doctrine à l'action*. Paris: Éditions Gallimard.

Gündoğdu, Ayten. 2015. *Rightlessness in an Age of Rights: Hannah Arendt and the Contemporary Struggles of Migrants*. Oxford: Oxford University Press.

Habermas, Jürgen. 1996. *Between Facts and Norms: Contributions to a Discourse Theory of Law and Democracy*. Translated by William Rehg. Cambridge: Polity Press.

Hammond, John L. 2013. 'The Significance of Space in Occupy Wall Street'. *Interface: A Journal For and About Social Movements* 5 (2): 499–524.

Hammond, John L. 2015. 'The Anarchism of Occupy Wall Street'. *Science & Society* 79 (2): 288–313.

Hardt, Michael. 2010. 'The Common in Communism'. *Rethinking Marxism* 22 (3): 346–56.

Hardt, Michael and Antonio Negri. 2000. *Empire*. London: Harvard University Press.

Hardt, Michael and Antonio Negri. 2004. *Multitude: War and Democracy in the Age of Empire*. London: Penguin.

Hardt, Michael and Antonio Negri. 2009. *Commonwealth*. Cambridge, MA: The Belknap Press of Harvard University Press.

Hardt, Michael and Antonio Negri. 2012. *Declaration*. Argo Navis Author Services.

Hardt, Michael and Antonio Negri. 2017. *Assembly*. Oxford: Oxford University Press.

Harvey, David. 2012. *Rebel Cities: From the Right to the City to the Urban Revolutions*. London: Verso.

Hobsbawm, Eric. 2007a. 'Bolshevism and the Anarchists'. In *Revolutionaries*, 81–97. London: Abacus.

Hobsbawm, Eric. 2007b. 'Reflections on Anarchism'. In *Revolutionaries*, 111–22. London: Abacus.

Hofmann, Hasso. 1974. *Repräsentation. Studien zur Wort- und Begriffsgeschichte von der Antike bis ins 19. Jahrhundert*. Berlin: Duncker & Humblot.

Holloway, John. 2010a. *Change the World Without Taking Power*. London: Pluto Press.

Holloway, John. 2010b. *Crack Capitalism*. London: Pluto Press.

Honig, Bonnie. 1993. *Political Theory and the Displacement of Politics*. Ithaca, NY: Cornell University Press.

Honig, Bonnie. 1995. 'Toward an Agonistic Feminism: Hannah Arendt and the Politics of Identity'. In Bonnie Honig (ed.), *Feminist Interpretations of Hannah Arendt*, 135–66. University Park: Pennsylvania State University Press.

Honig, Bonnie. 2009. *Emergency Politics: Paradox, Law, Democracy*. Princeton, NJ: Princeton University Press.

Howard, Neil and Keira Pratt-Boyden. 2013. 'Occupy London as Pre-Figurative Action'. *Development in Practice* 23: 729–41.

Husserl, Edmund. 1970. *The Crisis of European Sciences and Transcendental Phenomenology*. Translated by David Carr. Evanston, IL: Northwestern University Press.

Iglesias, Pablo. 2015. *Politics in a Time of Crisis: Podemos and the Future of a Democratic Europe*. London: Verso.

Ingram. James. 2006. 'The Politics of Claude Lefort: Between Liberalism and Radical Democracy'. *Thesis Eleven* 87: 33–50.

Isaac, Jeffrey. 2002. 'Ends, Means, and Politics'. *Dissent* 49 (4): 32–7.

IWW (Industrial Workers of the World). 2021. 'Preamble, Constitution, & General Bylaws of the Industrial Workers of the World'. Available at https://towardfreedom.org/wp-content/uploads/2016/04/CurrentIWW Constitution.pdf (last accessed 13 April 2022).

Johanson, Mark. 2019. 'How a $0.04 Metro Fare Price Hike Sparked Massive Unrest in Chile'. *Vox.com*, 29 October. Available at https://www.vox.com/world/2019/10/29/20938402/santiago-chile-protests-2019-riots-metro-fare-pinera (last accessed 13 April 2022).

Jun, Nathan. 2012. *Anarchism and Political Modernity*. New York and London: Continuum.

Jura Federation. 2015. 'Sonvillier Circular'. In Robert Graham (ed.), *Anarchism: A Documentary History of Libertarian Ideas. Vol. I: From Anarchy to Anarchism (300 CE to 1939)*, 96–8. Montreal: Black Rose Books.

Juris, Jeffrey. 2008. *Networking Futures: The Movements Against Corporate Globalisation*. Durham, NC and London: Duke University Press.

Juris, Jeffrey. 2012. 'Reflections on Occupy Everywhere'. *American Ethnologist* 39 (2): 259–79.

Kafka, Ben. 2012. 'The Administration of Things: A Genealogy'. *86th West*. Available at https://www.west86th.bgc.bard.edu/articles/the-administration-of-things-a-genealogy/ (last accessed 15 May 2022).

Kalyvas, Andreas. 2008. *Democracy and the Politics of the Extraordinary: Max Weber, Carl Schmitt, and Hannah Arendt*. Cambridge: Cambridge University Press.

Kalyvas, Andreas. 2018. 'Constituent Power'. In J. M. Bernstein, Adi Ophir and Ann Laura Stoler (eds), *Political Concepts: A Critical Lexicon*, 87–117. New York: Fordham University Press.

Kant, Immanuel. 2000. *Critique of the Power of Judgment*. Translated by Paul Guyer and Eric Matthews. Cambridge: Cambridge University Press.

Kant, Immanuel. 1995. *Kritik der Urteilskraft (Werke 4)*. Cologne: Könemann.

Kateb, George. 1987. *Hannah Arendt: Politics, Conscience, Evil*. Oxford: Rowman & Allenheld.

Kauffman, L.A. 2017. *Direct Action: Protest and the Reinvention of American Radicalism*. London: Verso.

Keane, John. 2011. 'Monitory Democracy?' In Sonia Alonso, John Keane, and Wolfgang Merkel (eds), *The Future of Representative Democracy*, 212–35. Cambridge: Cambridge University Press.

Khalil, Ashraf. 2011. *Liberation Square: Inside the Egyptian Revolution and the Rebirth of a Nation*. New York: St. Martin's Press.

Kinna, Ruth. 2016a. *Kropotkin: Reviewing the Classical Anarchist Tradition*. Edinburgh: Edinburgh University Press.

Kinna, Ruth. 2016b. 'Utopianism and Prefiguration'. In S. D. Chrostowska and James D. Ingram (eds), *Political Uses of Utopia: New Marxist, Anarchist, and Radical Democratic Perspectives*, 198–215. New York: Columbia University Press.

Klein, Ezra. 2011. 'You're Creating a Vision of the Sort of Society You Want to Have in Miniature'. *The Washington Post*, 3 October. Available at https://www.washingtonpost.com/blogs/wonkblog/post/youre-creating-a-vision-of-the-sort-of-society-you-want-to-have-in-miniature/2011/08/25/gIQAXVg7HL_blog.html (last accessed 13 April 2022).

Knapp, Michael, Anja Flach and Ercan Ayboga. 2016. *Revolution in Rojava: Democratic Autonomy and Women's Liberation in Syrian Kurdistan*. London: Pluto Press.

Koch, Andrew M. 1993. 'Post-structuralism and the Epistemological Basis of Anarchism'. *Philosophy of the Social Sciences* 23 (3): 327–51.

Kotsev, Victor. 2013. 'How the Protests Will Impact Turkey at Home and Abroad'. *The Atlantic*, 2 June. Available at http://www.theatlantic.com/international/archive/2013/06/how-the-protests-will-impact-turkey-at-home-and-abroad/276456/ (last accessed 13 April 2022).

Kropotkin, Peter. 1899. *Memoirs of a Revolutionist, Vol. II*. London: Smith, Elder, & Co.

Kropotkin, Peter. 1970a. 'Anarchism – Encyclopedia Britannica Article'. In *Kropotkin's Revolutionary Pamphlets*, edited by Roger N. Baldwin, 283–300. New York: Dover.

Kropotkin, Peter. 1970b. 'Anarchist Morality'. In *Kropotkin's Revolutionary Pamphlets*, edited by Roger N. Baldwin, 79–113. New York: Dover.

Kropotkin, Peter. 1970c. 'Modern Science and Anarchism'. In *Kropotkin's Revolutionary Pamphlets*, edited by Roger N. Baldwin, 145–94. New York: Dover.

Kropotkin, Peter. 1985. *Fields, Factories and Workshops*, edited by Colin Ward. London: Freedom Press.

Kropotkin, Peter. 1992. 'The Commune'. In *Words of a Rebel*. Translated by George Woodcock, 81–9. Montreal: Black Rose Books.

Kropotkin, Peter. 2006. *Mutual Aid: A Factor of Evolution*. Mineola, NY: Dover.

Kropotkin, Peter. 2015. *The Conquest of Bread*. London: Penguin.

Kuhn, Gabriel. 2010. *Sober Living for the Revolution: Hardcore Punt, Straight Edge, and Radical Politics*. Oakland, CA: PM Press.

Laclau, Ernesto. 1990a. 'The Impossibility of Society'. In *New Reflections on the Revolution of Our Time*, 89–92. London: Verso.

Laclau, Ernesto. 1990b. 'New Reflections on the Revolutions of Our Time'. In *New Reflections on the Revolution of Our Time*, 3–85. London: Verso.

Laclau, Ernesto. 1996. 'Deconstruction, Pragmatism, Hegemony'. In *Deconstruction and Pragmatism*, edited by Chantal Mouffe, 49–70. London: Routledge.

Laclau, Ernesto. 2000a. 'Identity and Hegemony: The Role of Universality in the Constitution of Political Logics'. In Judith Butler, Ernesto Laclau and Slavoj Žižek, *Contingency, Hegemony, Universality: Contemporary Dialogues on the Left*, 44–89. London: Verso.

Laclau, Ernesto. 2000b. 'Structure, History, and the Political'. In Judith Butler, Ernesto Laclau and Slavoj Žižek, *Contingency, Hegemony, Universality: Contemporary Dialogues on the Left*, 182–212. London: Verso.

Laclau, Ernesto. 2005a. *On Populist Reason*. London: Verso.

Laclau, Ernesto. 2005b. 'Populism: What's in a Name?' In Francisco Panizza (ed.), *Populism and the Mirror of Democracy*, 32–49. London: Verso.

Laclau, Ernesto. 2007a. 'Power and Representation'. In *Emancipation(s)*, 84–104. London: Verso.

Laclau, Ernesto. 2007b. 'The Time is Out of Joint'. In *Emancipation(s)*, 66–83. London: Verso.

Laclau, Ernesto. 2014a. 'An Ethics of Militant Engagement'. In *The Rhetorical Foundations of Society*, 181–206. London: Verso.

Laclau, Ernesto. 2014b. 'Articulation and the Limits of Metaphor'. In *The Rhetorical Foundations of Society*, 53–78. London: Verso.

Laclau, Ernesto. 2014c. 'Introduction'. In *The Rhetorical Foundations of Society*, 1–9. London: Verso.

Laclau, Ernesto. 2014d. 'The Politics of Rhetoric'. In *The Rhetorical Foundations of Society*, 79–99. London: Verso.

Laclau, Ernesto and Chantal Mouffe. 2001. *Hegemony and Socialist Strategy: Towards a Radical Democratic Politics*. London: Verso.

Laclau, Ernesto, Gary Olson and Lynn Worsham. 1999. 'Hegemony and the Future of Democracy: Ernesto Laclau's Political Philosophy'. In Gary Olson and Lynn Worsham (eds), *Race, Rhetoric, and the Postcolonial*, 129–64. Albany: State University of New York Press.

Laclau, Ernesto and Lilian Zac. 1994. 'Minding the Gap: The Subject of Politics'. In Ernesto Laclau (ed.), *The Making of Political Identities*, 11–39. London: Verso.

Lakey, George. 1987. *Powerful Peacemaking: A Strategy for a Living Revolution*. Philadelphia: New Society Publishers.

Lederman, Shmuel. 2019. *Hannah Arendt and Participatory Democracy: A People's Utopia*. Cham: Palgrave Macmillan.

Lefort, Claude. 1986. 'Politics and Human Rights'. In *The Political Forms of Modern Society: Bureaucracy, Democracy, Totalitarianism*, edited by John B. Thompson, 239–72. Cambridge, MA: MIT Press.

Lefort, Claude. 1988a. 'Human Rights and the Welfare State'. In *Democracy and Political Theory*. Translated by David Macey, 21–44. Cambridge: Polity Press.

Lefort, Claude. 1988b. 'The Permanence of the Theologico-Political?' In *Democracy and Political Theory*. Translated by David Macey, 213–55. Cambridge: Polity Press.

Lefort, Claude. 1988c. 'The Question of Democracy'. In *Democracy and Political Theory*. Translated by David Macey, 9–20. Cambridge: Polity Press.

Lefort, Claude. 2007. 'Utopia and Tragedy'. In *Complications: Communism and the Dilemmas of Democracy*. Translated by Julian Bourg, 109–12. New York: Columbia University Press.

Legros, Claire. 2020. 'Le Municipalisme ou la Commune au Pouvoir'. *Le Monde*, 7 February. Available at https://www.lemonde.fr/idees/article/2020/02/07/le-municipalisme-ou-la-commune-au-pouvoir_6028746_3232.html (last accessed 13 April 2022).

Le Guin, Ursula. 1974. *The Dispossessed. An Ambiguous Utopia*. New York: Harper & Row.

Leier, Mark. 2006. *Bakunin: The Creative Passion*. New York: St. Martin's Press.

Lenin, Vladimir Ilyich. 1987. 'The State and Revolution'. In *Essential Works of Lenin*, edited by Henry Christman, 271–364. New York: Dover.

Levitin, Michael. 2015. 'The Triumph of Occupy Wall Street'. *The Atlantic*, 10 June. Available at https://www.theatlantic.com/politics/archive/2015/06/the-triumph-of-occupy-wall-street/395408/ (last accessed 13 April 2022).

Lorde, Audre. 1984. *Sister Outsider. Essays and Speeches by Audre Lorde*. Berkeley, CA: Crossing Press.

Lorey, Isabell. 2014. 'The 2011 Occupy Movements: Rancière and the Crisis of Democracy'. *Theory, Culture & Society* 31 (7/8): 43–65.

Lorey, Isabell. 2015. *State of Insecurity: Government of the Precarious*. Translated by Aileen Derieg. London: Verso.

Lorey, Isabell. 2020. *Demokratie im Präsens: Eine Theorie der politischen Gegenwart*. Berlin: Suhrkamp.

Löwy, Michael. 2016. *Fire Alarm: Reading Walter Benjamin's 'On the Concept of History'*. Translated by Chris Turner. London: Verso.

Luxemburg, Rosa. 1961a. 'Leninism or Marxism?' In *The Russian Revolution and Leninism or Marxism?*, 81–108. Ann Arbor: University of Michigan Press.

Luxemburg, Rosa. 1961b. 'The Russian Revolution'. In *The Russian Revolution and Leninism or Marxism?*, 25–80. Ann Arbor: University of Michigan Press.

Luxemburg, Rosa. 1971. 'Our Program and the Political Situation'. In *Selected Political Writings of Rosa Luxemburg*, edited by Dick Howard, 377–408. New York: Monthly Review Press.

Luxemburg, Rosa. 1974a. 'Gründungsparteitag der Kommunistischen Partei Deutschlands vom 30 Dezember 1918 bis 1 Januar 1919 in Berlin'. In *Versammelte Werke Bd4*, 481–513. Berlin: Dietz.

Luxemburg, Rosa. 1974b. 'Versäumte Pflichten'. In *Versammelte Werke Bd4*, 521–4. Berlin: Dietz.

Luxemburg, Rosa. 2012. "'What Does the Spartacus League Want?' In Gabriel Kuhn (ed.), *All Power to the People! A Documentary History of the German Revolution of 1918–1919*, 999–106. Oakland, CA: PM Press.

MacIntyre, Alisdair. 1985. *After Virtue: A Study in Moral Theory*. London: Duckworth.

Mac Laughlin, Jim. 2016. *Kropotkin and the Anarchist Intellectual Tradition*. London: Pluto Press.

Maeckelbergh, Marianne. 2009. *The Will of the Many: How the Alterglobalisation Movement is Changing the Face of Democracy*. London: Pluto Press.

Maeckelbergh, Marianne. 2011a. 'Doing Is Believing: Prefiguration as Strategic Practice in the Alterglobalisation Movement'. *Social Movement Studies* 10 (1): 1–20.

Maeckelbergh, Marianne. 2011b. 'The Road to Democracy: The Political Legacy of "1968"'. *International Review of Social History* 56: 301–32.

Manilov, Marianne. 2013. 'Occupy at One Year: Growing the Roots of a Movement'. *The Sociological Quarterly* 54: 159–228.

Manin, Bernard. 1997. *The Principles of Representative Government*. Cambridge: Cambridge University Press.

Mansbridge, Jane. 1999. 'Should Blacks Represent Blacks and Women Represent Women? A Contingent "Yes"'. *The Journal of Politics* 61 (3): 628–57.

Mansbridge, Jane. 2003. 'Rethinking Representation'. *American Political Science Review* 97 (4): 515–28.

Marchart, Oliver. 2004. 'Politics and the Ontological Difference'. In Simon Critchley and Oliver Marchart (eds), *Laclau: A Critical Reader*, 54–72. Abingdon: Routledge.

Marchart, Oliver. 2005. *Neu Beginnen: Hannah Arendt, die Revolution und die Globalisierung*. Vienna: Verlag Turia + Kant.

Marchart, Oliver. 2007. *Post-Foundational Political Thought: Political Difference in Nancy, Lefort, Badiou, and Laclau*. Edinburgh: Edinburgh University Press.

Marchart, Oliver. 2018. *Thinking Antagonism: Political Ontology After Laclau*. Edinburgh: Edinburgh University Press.

Marchart, Oliver. 2019. *Conflictual Aesthetics. Artistic Activism and the Public Sphere*. London: Sternberg Press.

Markell, Patchen. 2006. 'The Rule of the People: Arendt, *Archê*, and Democracy'. *American Political Science Review* 100 (1): 1–14.

Markell, Patchen. 2011. 'Arendt's Work: On the Architecture of The Human Condition'. *College Literature* 38 (1): 15–44.

Marshall, Peter. 1993. *Demanding the Impossible: A History of Anarchism*. London: Fontana.

Marx, Karl. 2010a. 'The Civil War in France'. In *The First International and After (Political Writings Volume 3)*, edited by David Fernbach, 187–236. London: Verso.

Marx, Karl. 2010b. 'Conspectus of Bakunin's *Statism and Anarchy*'. In *The First International and After (Political Writings Volume 3)*, edited by David Fernbach, 333–8. London: Verso.

Marx, Karl. 2010c. 'Critique of the Gotha Programme'. In *The First International and After (Political Writings Volume 3)*, edited by David Fernbach, 339–59. London: Verso.

Mason, Paul. 2012. *Why It's Kicking Off Everywhere: The New Global Revolutions*. London: Verso.

May, Todd. 1994. *The Political Philosophy of Poststructuralist Anarchism*. University Park: Pennsylvania State University Press.

McLaughlin, Paul. 2002. *Mikhail Bakunin: The Philosophical Basis of his Anarchism*. New York: Algora Publishing.

McNay, Lois. 2014. *The Misguided Search for the Political: Social Weightlessness in Radical Democratic Theory*. Cambridge: Polity Press.

Meade, Elizabeth. 1997. 'The Commodification of Values'. In Larry May and Jerome Kohn (eds), *Hannah Arendt, Twenty Years Later*, 107–26. Cambridge, MA: MIT Press.

Mensahawy, Mustafa. 2020. *Leaving the Muslim Brotherhood. Self, Society, and the State*. Cham: Palgrave Macmillan.

Miller, J. Hillis. 2004. '"Taking up a Task": Moments of Decision in Ernesto Laclau's Thought'. In Simon Critchley and Oliver Marchart (eds), *Laclau: A Critical Reader*, 217–25. Abingdon: Routledge.

Milstein, Cindy. 2010. *Anarchism and its Aspirations*. Oakland, CA and Edinburgh: AK Press.

Milstein, Cindy. 2012. 'Occupy Anarchism'. In Kate Khatib, Margaret Killjoy and Mike McGuire (eds), *We Are Many: Reflections on Movement Strategy from Occupation to Liberation*, 291–305. Oakland, CA and Edinburgh: AK Press.

Mintz, Frank. 2013. *Anarchism and Workers' Self-Management in Revolutionary Spain*. Translated by Paul Sharkey. Oakland, CA and Edinburgh: AK Press.

Mirowski, Philip. 2013. *Never Let a Serious Crisis Go to Waste: How Neoliberalism Survived the Financial Meltdown*. London: Verso.

Morris, Brian. 2018. *Kropotkin: The Politics of Community*. Oakland, CA: PM Press.

Mouffe, Chantal. 2005a. 'For an Agonistic Model of Democracy'. In *The Democratic Paradox*, 80–107. London: Verso.

Mouffe, Chantal. 2005b. *On the Political*. Abingdon: Routledge.

Mouffe, Chantal. 2013. *Agonistics: Thinking the World Politically*. London: Verso.

Mouffe, Chantal. 2018. *For a Left Populism*. London: Verso.

Muldoon, James. 2011. 'The Lost Treasure of Arendt's Council System'. *Critical Horizons* 12 (3): 396–417.

Muldoon, James. 2016. 'The Origins of Hannah Arendt's Council System'. *History of Political Thought* 37 (4): 761–89.

Muldoon, James. 2020. *Building Power to Change the World: The Political Thought of The German Council Movemements*. Oxford: Oxford University Press.

Mulieri, Alessandro. 2019. 'Exploring the Semantics of Constructivist Representation'. In Lisa Disch, Mathijs van de Sande and Nadia Urbinati (eds), *The Constructivist Turn in Political Representation*, 205–23. Edinburgh: Edinburgh University Press.

Negri, Antonio. 1999. *Insurgencies: Constituent Power and the Modern State*. Translated by Maurizia Boscagli. Minneapolis: University of Minnesota Press.

Nettl, J. P. 2019. *Rosa Luxemburg*. London: Verso.

Nettlau, Max. 1996. *A Short History of Anarchism*. Translated by Ida Pilat Isca. London: Freedom Press.

Newman, Saul. 2001. *From Bakunin to Lacan: Anti-Authoritarianism and the Dislocation of Power*. Lanham, MD: Lexington Books.

Newman, Saul. 2016. *Post-Anarchism*. Cambridge: Polity Press.

Newman, Saul. 2020. 'Gustav Landauer's Anarcho-Mysticism and the Critique of Political Theology'. *Political Theology* 21 (5): 434–51.

New York City General Assembly. 2011. 'Occupy Wall Street: Frequently Asked Questions'. Available at https://www.scribd.com/document/68299558/OWS-FAQs-10-10-11 (last accessed 13 April 2022).

New York City General Assembly. 2012. 'Declaration of the Occupation of New York City'. In Kate Khatib, Margaret Killjoy and Mike McGuire (eds), *We Are Many: Reflections on Movement Strategy from Occupy to Liberation*. Oakland, CA and Edinburgh: AK Press.

Ngwane, Trevor. 2021. *Amakomiti: Grassroots Democracy in South-African Shack Settlements*. London: Pluto Press.

Nixon, Jon. 2018. *Rosa Luxemburg and the Struggle for Democratic Renewal*. London: Pluto Press.

Nunes, Rodrigo. 2014. *Organisation of the Organisationless: Collective Action After Networks*. Lüneburg: Mute Books and Post-Media Lab.

Nunes, Rodrigo. 2021. *Neither Vertical Nor Horizontal: A Theory of Political Organization*. London: Verso.

Oakeshott, Michael. 1975. *On Human Conduct*. Oxford: Clarendon Press.

Oikonomakis, Leonidas. 2019. *Political Strategies and Social Movements in Latin America. The Zapatistas and Bolivian Cocaleros*. Cham: Palgrave Macmillan.

Ordóñez, Vincente, Ramón Feenstra and Benjamin Franks. 2018. 'Spanish Anarchist Engagements in Electoralism: From Street to Party Politics'. *Social Movement Studies* 17 (1): 85–98.

Pataud, Émile and Émile Pouget. 1990. *How We Shall Bring About the Revolution: Syndicalism and the Cooperative Commonwealth*. London: Pluto Press.

Pickerill, Jenny and John Krinsky. 2012. 'Why Does Occupy Matter?' *Social Movement Studies* 11 (3–4): 279–87.

Pirro, Robert C. 2001. *Hannah Arendt and the Politics of Tragedy*. Dekalb: Northern Illinois University Press.

Pitkin, Hannah. 1967. *The Concept of Representation*. Berkeley: University of California Press.

Pitkin, Hannah. 1998. *The Attack of the Blob: Hannah Arendt's Concept of the Social*. Chicago: University of Chicago Press.

Polletta, Francesca. 2002. *Freedom is an Endless Meeting: Democracy in American Social Movements*. Chicago: University of Chicago Press.

Polletta, Francesca. 2006. *It Was Like a Fever: Storytelling in Protest and Politics*. Chicago: University of Chicago Press.

Polletta, Francesca and Katt Hoban. 2016. 'Why Consensus? Prefiguration in Three Activist Eras'. *Journal of Social and Political Psychology* 4 (1): 286–301.

Popp-Madsen, Benjamin Ask. 2021. *Visions of Council Democracy: Castoriadis, Lefort, Arendt*. Edinburgh: Edinburgh University Press.

Popp-Madsen, Benjamin Ask and Gaard Kets. 2021. 'Workers' Councils and Radical Democracy. Toward a Conceptual History of Council Democracy from Marx to Occupy'. *Polity* 53 (1): 160–88.

Portwood-Stacer, Laura. 2013. *Lifestyle Politics and Radical Activism*. New York and London: Bloomsbury.

Pouget, Émile. 2005. 'What is the Trade Union?' In *No Gods, No Masters: An Ontology of Anarchism*, edited by Daniel Guérin and translated by Paul Sharkey, 427–35. Oakland, CA and Edinburgh: AK Press.

Pouget, Émile. 2010. 'L'action directe'. In *L'action directe et autres écrits syndicalistes*, edited by Miguel Chueca, 153–83. Marseilles: Agone.

Proudhon, Pierre-Joseph. 1994. *What is Property?* Translated by Donald Kelly and Bonnie Smith. Cambridge: Cambridge University Press.

Raekstad, Paul. 2018. 'Revolutionary Practice and Prefigurative Politics: A Clarification and Defence'. *Constellations* 25 (3): 359–72.

Raekstad, Paul and Sofa Sajo Gradin. 2020. *Prefigurative Politics: Building Tomorrow Today*. Cambridge: Polity Press.

Rancière, Jacques. 1999. *Dis-agreement: Politics and Philosophy*. Translated by Julie Rose. Minneapolis: University of Minnesota Press.

Rancière, Jacques. 2006. *Hatred of Democracy*. Translated by Steve Corcoran. London: Verso.

Rocker, Rudolf. 2004. *Anarcho-Syndicalism: Theory and Practice*. Oakland, CA and Edinburgh: AK Press.

Roos, Jerome. 2013. 'Assemblies Emerging in Turkey: A Lesson in Democracy'. *Roarmag.org*, 19 June. Available at https://roarmag.org/essays/assemblies-emerging-in-turkey-a-lesson-in-democracy/ (last accessed 13 April 2022).

Rosanvallon, Pierre. 2008. *Counter-Democracy: Politics in an Age of Distrust*. Translated by Arthur Goldhammer. Cambridge: Cambridge University Press.

Ross, Carne. 2011. *The Leaderless Revolution: How Ordinary People Will Take Power and Change Politics in the 21st Century*. London: Simon & Schuster.

Rowbotham, Sheila. 1979. 'The Women's Movement & Organizing for Socialism'. In Sheila Rowbotham, Lynne Segal and Hilary Wainwright, *Beyond the Fragments: Feminism and the Making of Socialism*, 21–155. London: Merlin Press.

Rühle, Otto. 2021. 'The Revolution is Not a Party Affair'. In Paul Mattick Jr (ed.), *The Council Communist Reader*, 91–8. Pattern Books.

Rummens, Stefan. 2009. 'Democracy as a Non-Hegemonic Struggle? Disambiguating Chantal Mouffe's Agonistic Model of Politics'. *Constellations* 16 (3): 377–91.

Sánchez, Marta. 2012. 'Losing Strength? An Alternative View of the Indignados'. *Roarmag.org*, 23 June. Available at https://roarmag.org/essays/losing-strength-an-alternative-vision-of-the-indignados/ (last accessed 13 April 2022).

Saward, Michael. 2010. *The Representative Claim*. Oxford: Oxford University Press.

Schaap, Andrew. 2021. 'Inequality, Loneliness, and Political Appearance: Picturing Radical Democracy with Hannah Arendt and Jacques Rancière'. *Political Theory* 49 (1): 28–53.

Schmidt, Michael and Lucien van der Walt. 2009. *Black Flame: The Revolutionary Class Politics of Anarchism and Syndicalism*. Oakland, CA and Edinburgh: AK Press.

Schmitt, Carl. 1985. *Political Theology: Four Chapters on the Concept of Sovereignty*. Translated by George Schwab. Cambridge, MA: MIT Press.

Schmitt, Carl. 2007. *The Concept of the Political*. Translated by George Schwab. Chicago: University of Chicago Press.

Schürmann, Reiner. 1987. *Heidegger on Being and Acting: From Principles to Anarchy*. Translated by Christine-Marie Gros. Bloomington: Indiana University Press.

Scott, James C. 2012. *Two Cheers for Anarchism*. Princeton, NJ: Princeton University Press.

Scott, James C. 2017. *Against the Grain: A Deep History of the Earliest States,* New Haven, CT and London: Yale University Press.

Segal, Lynne. 2017. *Radical Happiness: Moments of Collective Joy*. London: Verso.

Selbin, Eric. 2010. *Revolution, Rebellion, Resistance: The Power of Story*. London: Zed Books.

Shakespeare, William. 1934. 'The Tempest'. In *The Works Of William Shakespeare*, 1135–59. Oxford: Blackwell.

Sintomer, Yves. 2013. 'Les sens de la représentation politique: usages et mesusages d'une notion'. *Raisons Politiques* 50: 13–34.

Sitrin, Marina. 2012. 'Horizontalism and the Occupy Movements'. *Dissent* 59: 74–5.

Sitrin Marina and Dario Azzelini. 2014. *They Can't Represent Us! Reinventing Democracy From Greece to Occupy*. London: Verso.

Sitton, John. 1987. 'Hannah Arendt's Argument for Council Democracy'. *Polity* 20 (1): 80–100.

Smucker, Jonathan. 2017. *Hegemony How-To: A Roadmap for Radicals*. Oakland, CA and Edinburgh: AK Press.

Solidarity Federation. 2012. *Fighting for Ourselves: Anarcho-Syndicalism and the Class Struggle*. London: Freedom Press.

Solnit, Rebecca. 2009. *A Paradise Built in Hell: The Extraordinary Communities that Arise in Disaster*. London: Penguin.

Spivak, Gayatri Chakravorty. 1988. 'Can the Subaltern Speak?' In Cary Nelson and Lawrence Grossberg (eds), *Marxism and the Interpretation of Culture*, 217–313. Basingstoke and London: Macmillan Education.

Springer, Simon. 2016. *The Anarchist Roots of Geography: Toward Spatial Emancipation*. Minneapolis: University of Minnesota Press.

Srnicek, Nick and Alex Williams. 2015. *Inventing the Future: Postcapitalism and a World Wiithout Work*. London: Verso.

Stahler-Sholk, Richard. 2019. 'Zapatistas and the New Ways of Doing Politics'. *Oxford Research Encyclopedias, Politics*. Available at https://oxfordre.com/politics/view/10.1093/acrefore/9780190228637.001.0001/acrefore-9780190228637-e-1724 (last accessed 13 April 2022).

Stewart, Emily. 2019. 'We are (still) the 99 Percent'. *Vox*, 30 April. Available at https://www.vox.com/the-highlight/2019/4/23/18284303/occupy-wall-street-bernie-sanders-dsa-socialism (last accessed 13 April 2022).

Stiglitz, Joseph E. 2011. 'Of the 1%, By the 1%, For the 1%'. *Vanity Fair*, 31 March, 2017. Available at http://www.vanityfair.com/news/2011/05/top-one-percent-201105 (last accessed 13 April 2022).

Süß, Rahel. 2021. 'Horizontal Experimentalism: Rethinking Democratic Resistance'. *Philosophy and Social Criticism* 1–17. doi: 10.1177/01914537211033016.

Swain, Dan. 2019. 'Not Not but Not Yet: Present and Future in Prefigurative Politics'. *Political Studies* 67b (1): 47–62.

Swann, Thomas. 2018. 'Towards an Anarchist Cybernetics: Stafford Beer, Self-Organisation and Radical Social Movements'. *Ephemera: Theory & Politics in Organisation* 18 (3): 427–56.

Tarì, Marcello. 2011. *Autonomie! Italie, les années 1970*. Translated by Étienne Dobenesque. Paris: La Fabrique éditions.

TATORT Kurdistan. 2013. *Democratic Autonomy in North Kurdistan*. Translated by Janet Biehl. Porsgrunn: New Compass Press.

Taylor, Astra. 2019. *Democracy May Not Exist, But We'll Miss It When It's Gone*. London: Verso.

Taylor, Keeanga-Yamahtta. 2017. 'Introduction'. In Keeanga-Yamahtta Taylor (ed.), *How We Get Free: Black Feminism and the Combahee River Collective*, 1–14. Chicago: Haymarket Books.

Teivainen, Teivo. 2016. 'Occupy Representation and Democratise Prefiguration: Speaking for Others in Global Justice Movements'. *Capital & Class* 40 (1): 19–36.

Thaler, Matthias. 2019. 'Peace as a Minor, Grounded Utopia: On Prefigurative and Testimonial Pacifism'. *Pespectives on Politics* 17 (4): 1003–18.

Tomba, Massimiliano. 2018. 'Who is Afraid of the Imperative Mandate?' *Critical Times* 1 (1): 108–19.

Topolski, Anya. 2015. *Arendt, Levinas, and a Politics of Relationality*. London and New York: Rowman & Littlefield.

Torfing, Jacob. 1999. *New Theories of Discourse: Laclau, Mouffe, and Žižek*. Oxford: Blackwell.

Tormey, Simon. 2015. *The End of Representative Politics*. Cambridge: Polity Press.

Trautman, William E. 2014. 'Direct Action and Sabotage'. In Salvatore Salerno (ed.), *Direct Action & Sabotage: Three Classic IWW Pamphlets From the 1910s*, 27–56. Oakland, CA: PM Press.

Trotsky, Leon. 1973. 'Their Morals and Ours'. In Leon Trotsky, *Their Morals and Ours*, 17–58. New York: Pathfinder Press.

Van de Sande, Mathijs. 2013. 'The Prefigurative Politics of Tahrir Square – An Alternative Perspective on the 2011 Revolutions'. *Res Publica*, 19 (3): 223–239.

Van de Sande, Mathijs. 2014. 'Why Did It Work This Time? David Graeber on Occupy Wall Street. Review of *The Democracy Project*, by David Graeber'. *Ephemera* 14 (4): 1041–7.

Van de Sande, Mathijs. 2015. 'Fighting With Tools: Prefiguration and Radical Politics in the Twenty-First Century'. *Rethinking Marxism* 27 (2): 177–94.

Van de Sande, Mathijs. 2017. 'The Prefigurative Power of the Common(s)'. In Guido Ruivenkamp and Andy Hilton (eds), *Perspectives on Commoning: Autonomist Principles and Practices*, 25–63. London: Zed Books.

Van de Sande, Mathijs. 2019. 'The Constructivist Paradox: Contemporary Protest Movements and (Their) Representation'. In Lisa Disch, Mathijs van de Sande and Nadia Urbinati (eds), *The Constructivist Turn in Political Representation*, 239–56. Edinburgh: Edinburgh University Press.

Van de Sande, Mathijs. 2020. 'They Don't Represent Us? Synecdochal Representation and the Politics of Occupy Movements'. *Constellations* 27 (3): 397–411.

Van Outryve d'Ydewalle, Sixtine. 2019. 'Becoming Mayor to Abolish the Position of Mayor? Thinking the Line Between Reform and Revolution in a Communalist Perspective'. *Unbound: Harvard Journal of the Legal Left* 12: 55–100.

Vatter, Miguel. 2007. 'Legality and Resistance: Arendt and Negri on Constituent Power'. In Timothy S. Murphy and Abdul-Karim Mustapha (eds), *The Philosophy of Antonio Negri. Vol. 2, Revolution in Theory*, 52–83. London: Pluto Press.

Vergara, Camila. 2020. *Systemic Corruption: Constitutional Ideas for an Anti-Oligarchic Republic*. Princeton, NJ: Princeton University Press.

Vinthagen, Stellan. 2015. *A Theory of Nonviolent Action: How Civil Resistance Works*. London: Zed Books.

Virno, Paolo. 1996. 'Virtuosity and Revolution: The Political Theory of Exodus'. In Michael Hardt and Paolo Virno (eds), *Radical Thought in Italy: A Potential Politics*, 189–209. Minneapolis: University of Minnesota Press.

Ward, Colin. 2008. *Anarchy in Action*. London: Freedom Press.

Weisman, Tama. 2014. *Hannah Arendt and Karl Marx: On Totalitarianism and the Tradition of Western Political Thought*. Plymouth: Lexington Books.

Wenman, Mark Anthony. 2003. 'Laclau or Mouffe? Splitting the Difference'. *Philosophy and Social Criticism* 29 (5): 581–606.

Wilson, Matthew. 2014. *Rules Without Rulers: The Possibilities and Limits of Anarchism*. Winchester and Washington DC: Zero Books.

Wolin, Sheldon. 2016. 'Hannah Arendt: Democracy and the Political'. In *Fugitive Democracy and Other Essays*, edited by Nicholas Xenos, 237–49. Princeton, NJ: Princeton University Press.

Woodcock, George. 1963. *Anarchism: A History of Libertarian Ideas and Movements*. Harmondsworth: Pelican.

Wright, Steve. 2002. *Storming Heaven: Class Composition and Struggle in Italian Autonomist Marxism*. London: Pluto Press.

Yassin-Kassab, Robin and Leila Al-Shami. 2016. *Burning Country: Syrians in Revolution and War*. London: Pluto Press.

Yates, Luke. 2015. 'Rethinking Prefiguration: Alternatives, Micropolitics and Goals in Social Movements'. *Social Movement Studies* 14 (1): 1–21.

Yates, Luke. 2020. 'Prefigurative Politics and Social Movement Strategy: The Roles of Prefiguration in the Reproduction, Mobilisation and Coordination of Movements'. *Political Studies*. doi: 10.1177/0032321720936046.

Young-Bruehl, Elisabeth. 2004. *Hannah Arendt, For Love of the World*. New Haven, CT and London: Yale University Press.

Zerilli, Linda. 2004. 'The Universalism Which is Not One'. In Simon Critchley and Oliver Marchart (eds), *Laclau: A Critical Reader*, 88–109. Abingdon: Routledge.

Žižek, Slavoj. 2008. *The Ticklish Subject: The Absent Centre of Political Ontology*. London: Verso.

Žižek, Slavoj. 2011. 'Don't Fall In Love With Yourselves'. In Astra Taylor, Keith Gessen, and editors from *N+1*, *Dissent*, *Triple Canopy* and *The New Inquiry* (eds), *Occupy! Scenes From Occupied America*, 66–9. London: Verso.

Žižek, Slavoj. 2012. *The Year of Dreaming Dangerously*. London: Verso.

Index

EU representative:
Easy Access System Europe
Mustamäe tee 50, 10621 Tallinn, Estonia
Gpsr.requests@easproject.com

www.ingramcontent.com/pod-product-compliance
Lightning Source LLC
Chambersburg PA
CBHW071742270326
41928CB00013B/2769